Spirit Summonings

Spirit Summonings

By the Editors of Time-Life Books

TIME-LIFE BOOKS, ALEXANDRIA, VIRGINIA

CONTENTS

Voices from Beyond

In ancient Greece, the gods spoke to mortals through oracles. In the Victorian period, spirits of the dead supposedly communed with the living by way of spiritualist mediums. Now, in the late twentieth century, certain gods and spirits seem to have forsaken both temple and séance room in favor of lecture halls, television talk shows, and videotapes. Their conduits are neither oracles nor mediums, but channelers.

Critics contend that channelers are charlatans, courting fame and amassing wealth by flimflamming the gullible. But to believers, channelers are among the heralds of the New Age, a dawning day of cosmic harmony and terrestrial peace. They purport to bring transcendental wisdom, wrung not only from the dead or deified but also from many strange and diverse entities—among them warriors and wizards, saints and sea mammals.

Some channelers claim to enter deep trances, allowing their invisible entities to take over their bodies and speak through them. Others retain their own identities, they say, while they relay information from realms beyond. Whatever the method, the messages tend to be similar. They speak of self-love, of eternal life, of etheric worlds beyond the world we know.

Are the entities real or illusory? Are their channelers prophets or frauds? In the absence of proof, skeptics answer one way and believers another, and the undecided observe and ponder. On the following ten pages appear some prominent New Age channelers, along with a sampling of the messages spoken by their entities.

7

"You Are Your Own Master"

Homemaker J. Z. Knight's life changed drastically in 1977, when, as she tells it, she was first visited by a 35,000-year-old warrior spirit called Ramtha. Supposedly, Ramtha hailed from the lost continent of Lemuria, and the legend of his deeds was so deathless that thousands of years after his demise, the Hindus used him as the pattern for Ram, an incarnation of their god Vishnu. Ramtha made J. Z. Knight the most famous, and probably the wealthiest, New Age channeler. She lives on a lavish horse ranch in Washington State.

Ramtha speaks: ''I am Ramtha, 'The Ram.' In the ancient language of my times it means 'the god.' I am the great Ram of the Hindu people. I conquered three-quarters of the known world. But my greatest conquest was of myself. When I learned to love myself and embrace the whole of life, I ascended with the wind into forever. I am now part of an unseen brotherhood who love mankind, greatly. We are your brothers who hear your prayers and your meditations and observe your movements to and fro. I have come to tell you that you are very important and precious to us, because the life that flows through you and the thought that is coming to every one of you—however you entertain it—is the intelligence and life force that you have termed God. I am a God who hath acclaimed himself by doing! And that which I teach you I will teach you by doing. To share with someone else may seem noble at first, but lo, I say to you, it is a most despairing and arduous job and has no rewards. Don't share with anyone; share with you. Don't share; love—you. Steadfast before you stands the greatest teacher of all time. You! You are your own savior; you are your own master. Know also that you are responsible for your life; take blame one else's at your own. of entities on this that you cannot and put it at any-kingdom, only The happiest plane are those who do pre-what they want to cisely do.''

"A Greater Cause"

California's Kevin Ryerson has the distinction of being the only channeler to play himself in a television movie. Ryerson re-enacted his first channeling session with actress Shirley MacLaine for the film version of her book, *Out on a Limb*. Moreover, two of his entities allegedly played themselves. One of these personalities was the Apostle John, a being of extremely strange syntax who purports to have been the follower of Jesus and author of the New Testament's fourth Gospel. Ryerson says that during his years as a channeler he has satisfied himself that his entities ''are who they claim to be.''

The Apostle John speaks: *''These are the days, indeed, as though old and young men shall have, as though, dreams and visions; and that, indeed, as though, the time has come to fulfill the element that, indeed, the people who may not have vision may be, indeed, as dead. But, indeed, the people who have vision are alive and filled, as though, with the vitality, as though, that is the spirit. It has come a time, as though, when, now, that, as though, ye have entered an age no longer of belief, but an age of knowledge and knowing—a greater exactitude, a greater maturity, as though, of the spirit. For it is indeed, as though, the times that faith is not, as though, only witnessed, as though, through signs; faith truly becomes the issue, not even any longer as evidence of things unseen, but is, indeed, as though, things seen, as though, within the self by, as though, a greater multitude. It is, as though, a time wherein, as though individually, individuals are harnessing, as though, their spiritual perspectives, and are bringing about, as though, a collective formulation of the manifestation of that which is called Christ Consciousness. The Christ Consciousness is, as though, the adherence to the alignment of the mind, the body and the spirit in service, as though, to a greater cause.''*

"The Wizard in Each of You"

Diana Hoerig asserts that anyone can consciously learn to channel, that the process is no more complex than learning to play a musical instrument. Hoerig says it was in 1980, while meditating, that she first encountered Merlin, King Arthur's fabled wizard. Merlin became her teacher, one of several so-called masters she channels.

Hoerig leads the Violet Flame Network, a Southern California group whose aim is "to concentrate energies toward creating truth and integrity in our social and governing institutions."

Merlin speaks: "*I shall step forward in what you might term the Merlin costume at this time. And I shall spread my light to each. I shall explain to you what Merlin might be termed is an Archetype, if you will. There have been many such embodiments throughout the time span of history on the planet Earth. In so doing, higher energy aspects have coagulated into a form and have incarnated into a physical manifestation. The purpose is to bring about in those whom they touch a remembrance of that same energy force within themselves. You see, what I represent is the wizard in each of you. And yet, it is true that I am what I am; a magical instrument of the light. The reason I have stepped forward to speak unto you is so that each of you shall align yourself with that which is the power of magic existing within you. We will create in unison so that each man, child and woman who views these sequences shall entertain within themselves the idea of their own wizardry. You see, it is true that man is growing up. Reaching his adulthood, so to speak. He shall have full cognizance of all the rays of his existence. To have a vision of Merlin is to have the vision of oneself. There are probably tens of millions of individual beings upon the planet who feel a specialized connection with myself. Believe me, it is not because we had past lives together. It is because of what I represent. I am simply a symbolic Archetype of a force, a power to manipulate nature.*"

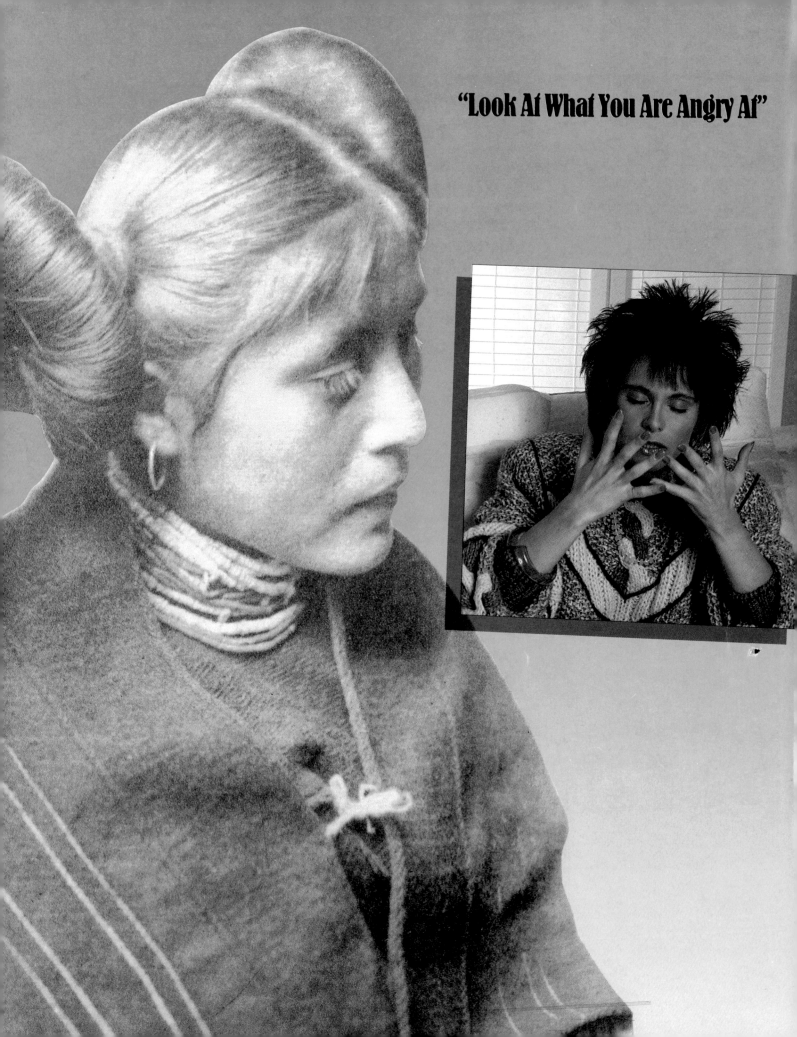

"Look At What You Are Angry At"

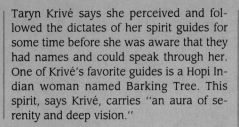

Taryn Krivé says she perceived and followed the dictates of her spirit guides for some time before she was aware that they had names and could speak through her. One of Krivé's favorite guides is a Hopi Indian woman named Barking Tree. This spirit, says Krivé, carries "an aura of serenity and deep vision."

Barking Tree speaks: *"When you feel resistance, when you feel a struggle, when you feel a pain inside of yourself, ask yourself, what am I doing, what is going on inside of me, what part of myself am I resisting? What is creating this reality that I don't want? First of all, look at those things that are part of your life that are not working the way you want. When you feel a judgment of somebody else, when you feel an anger at somebody else, look at what part of yourself you have judged, look at what you are angry at inside of yourself . . . and then come to peace with that, and look* to grow from that. Because it is possible to experience a life of peace, and of happiness and prosperity. Please remember that all you are seeking in your lives, all that you are searching for, this is also seeking you. All that you are seeking is inside of you already, waiting to emerge. And God is within you, and God is what you have come out of, and God is what you go back to. And each one of you has the ability within this life, within this moment, to discover that reality within you. Each one of you is a powerful and pure and divine being, created in the image of God.*

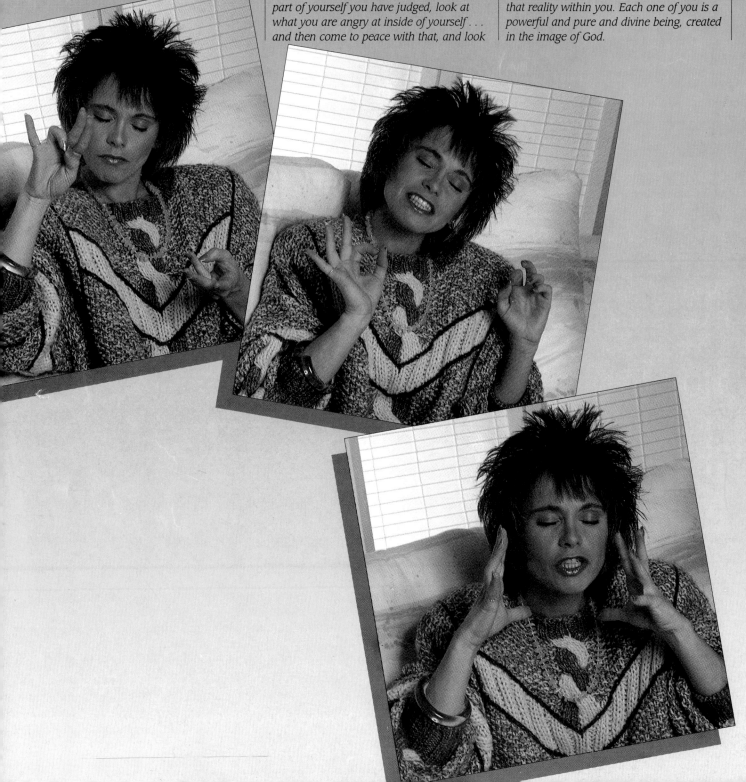

"Humans Are an Imbalancing Element"

The intelligent and appealing dolphin is for some a symbol of man's challenge to live in balance with other creatures. The cetaceans are especially important to channeler Neville Rowe, who claims to communicate with them. Rowe recalls first contacting the sea mammals at San Diego's Sea World. He communes, he says, with the group consciousness of six dolphins, known collectively as Cajuba.

The dolphins speak: *"I am Cajuba. Welcome to this interspecies communication between man and dolphin. We are sending communication as vibration from us to you. These vibrations are translated into English language words within the subconscious mind of this channel. We wish to assist you to understand more of your place, and ours, within this environment. You think you will always find* another intellectual or technological answer to any difficulties you bring forward. But understand that Mother Earth has a very different idea. Humans are an imbalancing element upon the earth's surface, and . . . you have greatly imbalanced nature and the vibration of the earth. Most of you do not understand your true spiritual nature. However, dolphinkind has much greater understanding of its spiritual

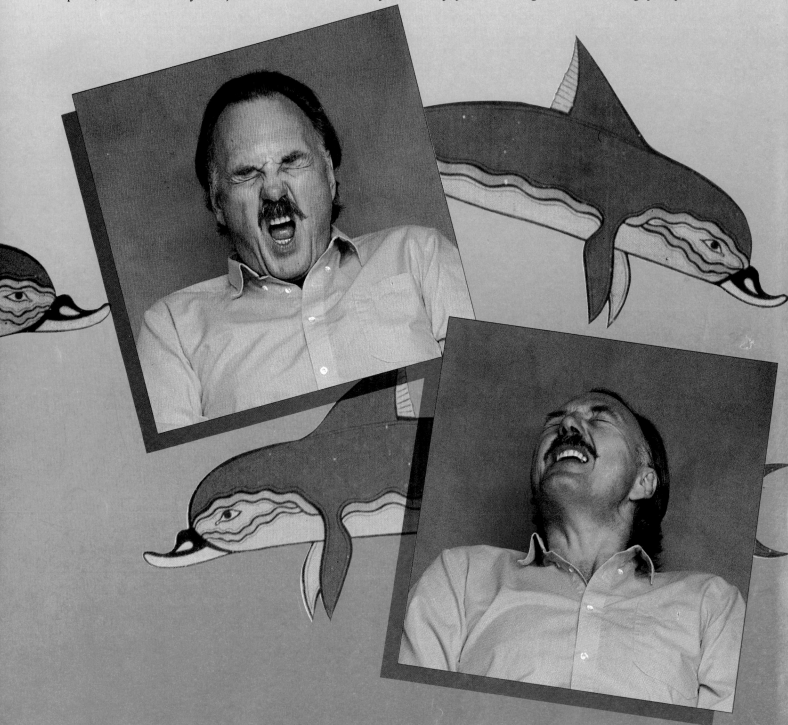

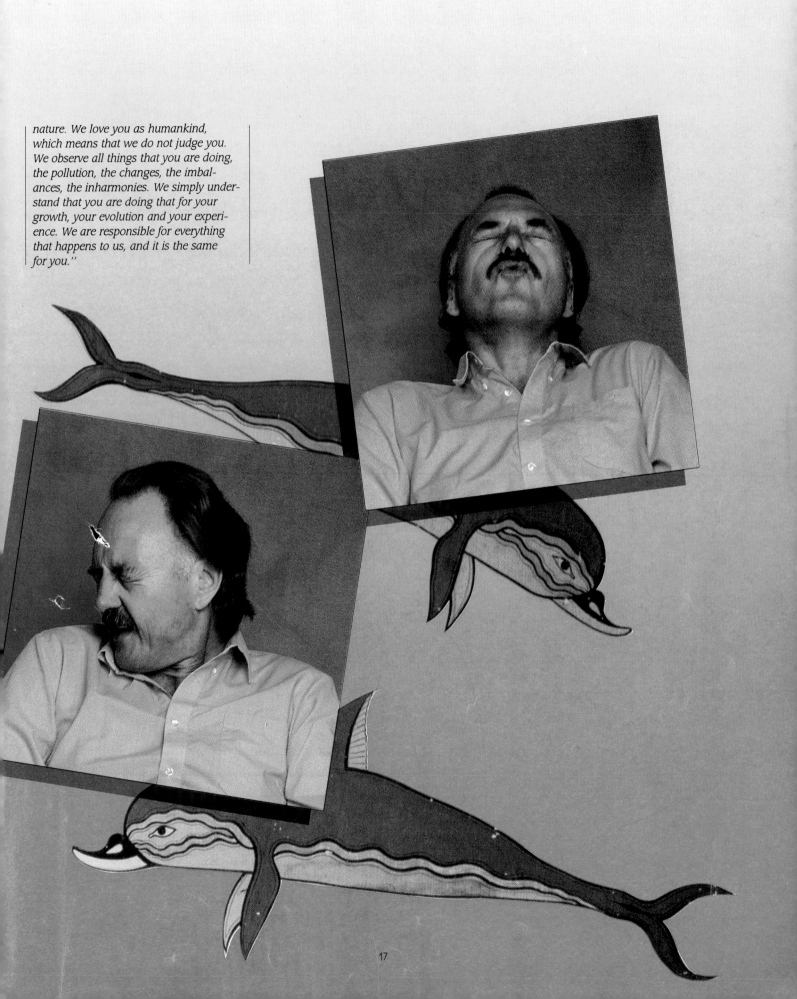

nature. We love you as humankind, which means that we do not judge you. We observe all things that you are doing, the pollution, the changes, the imbalances, the inharmonies. We simply understand that you are doing that for your growth, your evolution and your experience. We are responsible for everything that happens to us, and it is the same for you.''

CHAPTER 1

A Passion for Spirits

ne cold February night in the late 1980s, Saint Thomas Aquinas is speaking. He has been dead for more than seven hundred years.

"The one desire of the spirit world is to progress towards the truth," the saint says, *"that ultimate truth being the infinite mind of God itself. It is the one desire of the spirit that is within each and every one of you. The physical vessel carries that spirit which is you, and is unique to you, and individual to you. But it has that same desire, and that is to progress constantly, always, towards the highest truth, and in so doing to ultimately unite itself with God from which it was created."* Thomas pauses for a moment, then adds, *"Simple, isn't it?"*

Thomas Aquinas was not present in the flesh, of course. But purportedly he was there in spirit, briefly inhabiting the body of a living man and using his host as a vehicle for speech. The host was called a channel or channeler, indicating that he—like thousands of other practitioners around the world—claimed the ability to serve as a conduit for unseen spirits.

In the 1980s, channeling became the centerpiece for the metaphysical smorgasbord known as the New Age, a loose-knit movement that sees humankind as embarking on a time of exceptional enlightenment and spiritual progress. The New Age encompasses a great range of pursuits—psychic counseling, crystal gazing, past-life regression, holistic health, astrology, and the study of mystery religions, to name only a few. Although their paths are many and their dogma scant, New Agers have in common a desire to reach beyond the mundane world toward something transcendental, sublime. For many, channeling is the tool of choice. Returning spirits are armed with ancient and otherworldly wisdom, it is thought, and can therefore give unique comfort and counsel.

While millions ride this latest wave of metaphysics, comparatively few of them realize that the New Age in general, and channeling in particular, is not new at all. Spirits in legion have allegedly spoken through humans before. The hosts in the old days were called mediums, not channelers, but the meaning was the same. As for new ages, the last one dates back almost a century and a half.

It started in an ill-defined region of upstate New York known as the Burned-over District, so called for the fires of religious revivalism and social zeal that had swept over it. Odd sects and experimental movements seemed to flourish there, including Mormons and Shakers, come-outers, Christian Perfectionists, feminists, socialists, and communists. Some of these movements would mature into mainstream respectability, whereas others would fade past memory. But 140 years ago, they all seemed much the same to the eyes of detached observers. The Burned-over District was deemed generally a hotbed of radical goings-on. Common wisdom had it that with such an excess of exotic fervors, souls in the region had been charred past further combustibility. Common wisdom, however, was quite wrong.

Germinating in the district at midcentury was the most exotic foliage of all, a socioreligious movement that would touch millions—kings and commoners, rustics and intellectuals, reformers, conservatives, pious Christians, and devout atheists. Scientists would probe it, moralists abhor it, visionaries conjure with it, scoundrels profit from it. In its thirty-year heyday it would spread from the New York backwoods throughout America and much of Europe, mellowing past tawdry beginnings into long and multiform life. It would at once father the New Age and be reborn in it. It was called spiritualism.

The roots of spiritualism are traceable to two young girls, the Fox sisters, who probably had no idea what furor they were unleashing on the world. Kate and Maggie Fox were simple, unimaginative children, the daughters of simple, unimaginative parents. Stolid Methodists, John and Margaret Fox had no interest in the seething spirituality of the Burned-over District when they moved to its fringes from Canada. The only spirits John Fox knew were bottled, and those he had forsworn. He had at one time supported his wife and four children as a blacksmith, but fondness for alcohol had undermined his work, his finances, and his wife's patience, causing a lengthy rift in his marriage. Eventually, John renounced liquor and was reconciled with his

wife; although sobriety left him dour and taciturn, he was communicative enough to father two more children.

Daughters Margaretta and Catherine—known to the family as Maggie and Kate—were born when both their parents were well into middle age. They were thus the only offspring still living at home when the Foxes migrated to the tiny hamlet of Hydesville, New York, in search of a new life. In December of 1847, the family rented a ramshackle frame cottage, and as the cold winter gave way to the chill spring of 1848 Fox took up peppermint farming. He and Margaret were in their sixties by then. Maggie was thirteen and Kate not yet twelve.

It must have been a bleak existence for the two girls. Hydesville offered little diversion for the young, and for the most part Maggie and Kate were isolated in the shabby farmhouse with their reclusive father and their sweet but simpleminded mother. There were no intellectual resources

to fall back on, for neither girl was well schooled or immoderately bright. Brown-eyed Maggie was a spirited teenager, if heavy jawed and somewhat plain—"not decidedly a beauty," one observer would later put it. Kate, though less vivacious, was rather pretty. She had gray eyes and the pale delicacy that was admired in those days. But for all practical purposes, Maggie's charm and Kate's looks mattered little with no audience to appreciate them. No doubt the girls were bored and restless.

The boredom stopped abruptly one March evening after the family had retired for the night. Suddenly, strange noises began to shake the house. Some of the sounds suggested furniture being moved, but these were soon lost amid raps, booms, and crackings—pounding so loud, by some accounts, that the cottage actually shuddered. The Foxes sprang from their beds and scrambled in search of a source. They discovered nothing, but the next night the mysterious clamor returned—and the next, and the next, continuing for a week or more.

On March 31, unnerved and exhausted, the Foxes trudged to bed shortly after six p.m., hoping for a decent night's sleep. But the rapping recommenced, more insistent than ever. By this time the girls had moved their trundle bed into their parents' room, where young Kate was emboldened to confront the mystery. She snapped her fingers and asked the noise to answer. To her parents' utter amazement, it did. Recovering her composure, Mrs. Fox asked it to rap ten times. It obliged. She then asked it to tap out the ages, in succession, of her six children. It did. A miracle, concluded Mrs. Fox, who rushed out to tell the neighbors that very night.

Soon the questioning became more sophisticated, aided by a code the family worked out with the source: Silence signified a negative response; a rap meant yes. Speaking in this manner, the source identified itself as the spirit of a peddler who had been robbed and killed in the farmhouse by a previous tenant.

News of the rappings tore through the little community, and crowds eager to commune with the spirit packed into the cramped farmhouse day and night. In April, one E. E. Lewis of Canandaigua, New York, arrived on the scene, curious about tales he had heard of the unquiet dead. He interviewed family members and neighbors and hastily produced a pamphlet called *A Report of the Mysterious Noises Heard in the House of Mr. John D. Fox*. (Lewis could not have known it, but his little booklet would win a footnote in history as the first spiritualist publication.)

Even with this publicity, spiritualism might easily have remained a minor brush fire in the lore of the Burned-over District. But history had an ally in another member of the Fox family, Leah Fox Fish. News of the Hydesville Rappings, as they were now known, reached Mrs. Fish in mid-April of 1848. One of John and Margaret Fox's first four children, she was at that time in her midthirties, with a daughter Maggie's age. They lived alone in Rochester, New York, about thirty miles from Hydesville. Little is known of Mr. Fish save

that he had decamped, leaving Leah to fend for herself, and being a resourceful woman, she had managed. By teaching music, she succeeded in winning independence for herself and her daughter—no mean feat for an abandoned woman in Victorian times.

Leah got hold of Lewis's pamphlet, and as she read new vistas beckoned, for she had a keen mind, an ice-water temperament, and a shrewd eye for the main chance. If the other Foxes did not know a good thing when they saw it, Leah Fish did. She finished the pamphlet and promptly set off for Hydesville. In short order, she hustled her young sisters off to a private room and demanded to know how they were making the noises, for she had no doubt that they were. So they told her.

They had begun very simply by tying an apple to a string and, while lying in bed, bobbing it up and down to bump against the floor. The motive? Merely a wish to play a little joke on their gullible mother. The apple maneuver proved problematical once the so-called spirit started drawing crowds, however, so the girls improved their act. They found that by popping the joints of their toes, especially against a bedstead or the floor, they could surreptitiously make quite satisfactory raps. And the dead peddler was becoming ever more loquacious, thanks to a new code. By rapping at the appropriate point in a recitation of the alphabet, the spirit could spell out words, thus greatly expanding his vocabulary beyond a terse yes or no.

Posterity can never know what went through the fertile mind of Leah Fish at that moment. At the very least, she must have seen certain commercial possibilities. Perhaps she even glimpsed a world of wealth and power that few others in those wretched peppermint fields could envision or comprehend. As it happened, Leah would take her sisters far beyond the farm—to dim séance rooms and vast lecture halls, to homes of the great and famous, to a place in history. Leah would prosper and flourish. So would Maggie and Kate—for a time.

Following the Fox sisters, spiritualism spread like a

contagion. Five years after the Hydesville Rappings, there were, by one estimate, no fewer than thirty thousand mediums, professional and amateur, in America alone. The epidemic was observable even from abroad. "It came upon them like the smallpox," the noted English mathematician Augustus de Morgan wrote, "and the land was spotted with mediums before the wise and prudent had had time to lodge the first half-dozen in a madhouse." (Ironically, de Morgan's wife would become an early English convert to the faith, and he himself would study it with great interest.) By the end of the 1850s, millions of people had accepted spiritualism's central tenet: that the human spirit survives death and can communicate with the living.

A cheap, carnival air permeated the movement in its earliest days, and for the professional mediums, special effects could be counted on to draw a crowd. But spiritualism grew quieter and more serious as it matured, and its phenomena more mysterious. Some of the later mediums surpassed the Fox sisters in fame, and many produced far more sophisticated wonders. Today, only the truest believers hold that the Fox sisters, or most of their imitators, practiced anything finer than deceit. But some exploits by mediums have never been explained, and who is to say that these feats were not the work of an agency beyond the tangible and temporal?

Nevertheless, spiritualism's beginnings were marked by triviality. When it first spread to Europe in the early 1850s, its most popular manifestation was table turning, or table rapping. This oddity, perfected by the Fox sisters, involved a medium's presiding over a séance table that, sup-posedly untouched by human hands, would rotate or tip or sway, sometimes rapping out spirit answers to sitters' questions. Tables skittered for Queen Victoria and Prince Albert at their royal residence at Osborne. Tables rapped in Germany, where a prestigious newspaper pronounced the phenomenon "no cock-and-bull story, no American joke, no Yankee extravagance" but the real thing. Napoleon III and his beautiful empress, Eugénie, trifled with tables in Paris. In Vienna, ladies swooned and even writhed on the floor after watching a table spin unaided.

But if for some spiritualism was a raucous amusement or a modish toy, it was for others a passionate new religion capable of altering the path of human affairs. Spiritualists believed—some still believe—that a medium moved Czar Alexander II to free the Russian serfs and that Abraham Lincoln was similarly prompted to issue the Emancipation Proclamation. (This last contention is probably spurious, for Lincoln was not a spiritualist. But his wife, Mary Todd Lincoln, was a believer, and it is documented that the president attended séances in the White House and was fascinated by them. Queen Victoria, too, was intrigued with spiritualism far beyond the table-turning fad. When Prince Albert died, Victoria secluded herself in grief for years, causing great consternation in her troubled empire. It was rumored in those days—and not just by spiritualists—that she spent some of that time trying to contact Albert's spirit through the mediumship of a manservant.)

Beyond a doubt, spiritualism influenced the course of social history through its alliance with various reform movements. It was closely intertwined with abolitionism, for example. Harriet Beecher Stowe was a spiritualist, and in her day it was widely believed that spirits guided the writing of *Uncle Tom's Cabin,* the novel that helped to trigger the Civil War.

Indeed, spiritualism was sometimes meretricious and fraudulent. But that is not to say that it was limited to dilettantes and frauds. It was not. Neither was it the sole province of the credulous and ignorant. There were, certainly, thousands of those. At the same time, spiritualism listed in its ranks some of the finest minds of its day. Philosophical, political, and literary luminaries were among its converts, and renowned scientists gave it serious study.

How was it that a childish prank could burgeon to touch so many so profoundly? The answer is that spiritualism was a perfect child of its times—eccentric, perhaps, but in the nineteenth century there was a lot of eccentric behavior going around. It is doubtful that Leah Fish set out to found a social movement or a new religion, but it is quite possible that this canny woman sensed the time was right for some such result.

The year 1848—when the Fox girls learned to pop their toes—came amid turbulent times in the Western world. Old empires were being threatened in Europe. The Industrial Revolution was wreaking increasing misery on working-class lives, and socialism was on the rise in response. America was torn by the outrage of slavery. Even traditional religion was under siege, partly because it seemed so out of step with the century's social ferment. In England, reformers preached that Christianity had been historically indifferent to suffering at best and at worst had fostered it. In America, the rigid hierarchy of established religion was something of an affront to Jacksonian democracy. Dictating dogma and inserting intermediaries between God and man offended American individualists—as such practices had once offended Martin Luther—and the thrust of much of the century's rampant revivalism was to democratize religion. Spiritualism was, in a sense, a continuation of the Reformation.

Orthodox religion was also fending off attack from discoveries in such diverse fields as biblical criticism and geology. Textual studies of the Bible called into question its divine authorship, and new evidence about the earth's age and development threatened to undermine scriptural cosmogony. Charles Darwin's *Origin of Species,* published in 1859, would spark the final explosion, demolishing the most cherished notions of humanity's special and exalted place in creation.

Amid all this turmoil were the general hope and uneasiness that coalesced around the great passion of the age: science. The telegraph had been invented only four years before the Foxes first summoned the spirits, revolutionizing communications as surely as the telephone, television, and the computer would in their time. Railroads were just beginning to crisscross America. Most of all, electricity held an abiding fascination, fraught with promise and mystery. Everyone knew it existed and was immensely powerful, but no one was quite sure what it was or how it could be safely and effectively harnessed.

There were people who feared the encroaching materialism of science and industry. But for the most part, the nineteenth century was an optimistic era. Science offered

Spirits and the Shakers

A dozen years before the Fox sisters made spiritualism an international craze, a radical Christian sect known formally as the United Society of Believers in Christ's Second Coming routinely communed with spirits. In fact, the exuberant whirling and stamping dances performed by the congregation while in the presumed grip of spirits helped give the sect its more common name—the Shakers.

The Shakers were founded in eighteenth-century England as a splinter group of the Quakers. In America, the new sect flourished, and by 1826 there were some eighteen prosperous Shaker communities in the United States. They believed in equality of the sexes and practiced pacifism and celibacy. They also believed that they spoke face-to-face with their departed brethren as well as with dead notables such as Christopher Columbus.

August of 1837 marked the beginning of a decade of particularly abundant spirit activity among the Shakers. During a dance in the Watervliet community in upstate New York, a group of girls began to shake and whirl and speak in tongues. They claimed to be in contact with angels and spirits of the dead. The craze spread throughout Watervliet and to the other communes. One of its aspects was the presumed possession of community members by spirits of American Indians. Thus invaded, the Shakers would whoop and yell and speak in what were thought to be Indian dialects. Such episodes tapered off and ended about a year before the Fox girls began their career. Communion with the spirits became more circumspect, although the Shakers never renounced it altogether.

Still, the Shakers declined to ally themselves with the spiritualists. In the wake of the Hydesville furor, they sent emissaries to the Fox sisters, but some of the more bizarre aspects of physical mediumship offended the Shakers' religious sensibilities.

The Shakers' whirling dance, a centerpiece of their worship, became increasingly animated during

Shakers produced elaborate "gift draw-ings," usually parables for spiritual truths. The community at one time believed that spirits actually created the paintings, but subsequent interpretation made them the work of in-spired human artists. This 1857 ink and water-color is called A Tree of Love, a Tree of Life.

the time the Shakers thought themselves possessed by spirits. Outsiders flocked to watch the dancing, which was later closed to the public.

universal solution and salvation. The human mind had created, invented, imagined so much. Why should any barrier, even death, impede it? Given that outlook, spiritualism was peculiarly well suited to its time. In an age of wonders, contacting spirits did not seem especially strange. Miracles, while not commonplace, had become proximate, thinkable.

And in those unsettled days, spiritualism offered something for nearly everybody. It could accommodate almost any paradox. For those who wanted to bridge the gap between faith and reason, spirits were the span, promising—by their audibility, visibility, and even tangibility—to validate at last Christianity's promise of life after death. If they could be studied with the new tools of science, religion would be rid of stultifying myth and ritual. Thus spiritualism was useful for those who wanted to cling to old faiths as well as for those who wanted to modernize them.

It was just as serviceable to those who wanted to democratize or even destroy religion. Spiritualism cut across all social classes. Even in caste-ridden Europe, there was no reason why a housemaid might not be just as good a medium as a viscount—and with no help from a priest or minister and no weighty dogma to confuse or constrict the practitioner. As for those who wanted neither dogma nor God, spiritualism boded the existence of an afterlife without either one. This last advantage was particularly important to people grappling with the seeming inadequacy of old faiths to accommodate new facts.

When it came to social reform, spiritualism's uses were amazingly plastic. From their unique vantage point in another world, spirits could, and did, attest to the rectitude of causes in this one—of abolition or capitalism or socialism, of antivivisection or vegetarianism or temperance or free love. That spirit utterances often reflected the views of the medium or the sitters at a particular séance was of little concern. Doubtless, sincere and well-intentioned people truly heard from the spirits what they wanted and expected to hear, or at least they believed they heard it.

Finally, for masses of people not especially interested in causes or theology, spiritualism met needs not limited to the Victorian era or any other: It offered consolation and hope. For the bereaved, it gave assurance that their beloved dead were not really lost to them. And for those facing death, it made less dreadful that most imponderable of mysteries. It promised that death was a passage, not an end.

Just as spiritualism did not explode from a cultural vacuum, it did not erupt from a metaphysical one. Summoning spirits was nothing new. Arguably, prayer is a form of it, and thus spirit summoning could be traced back through all the world's great religions. Even before them, shamans called down gods to bless or curse, and presumably the first cave dweller who cringed before a lightning bolt or a woolly mammoth asked invisible powers for help. But by way of immediate forefathers, spiritualism owed much to three men: Franz Anton Mesmer, Emanuel Swedenborg, and Andrew Jackson Davis.

Franz Anton Mesmer was an eighteenth-century Austrian physician who theorized that everything exists within a "subtle fluid, which pervades the universe, and associates all things together in mutual intercourse and harmony." Early in his career, he believed that magnets could transmit healing power through this mysterious nexus. Later, he concluded that magnets were not needed: Humans could harbor and transmit the power. They could exert "animal magnetism." One magnetic function was to induce trance, and while entranced, some of Mesmer's subjects were said to display psychic powers, especially clairvoyance—the ability to see events outside the range of their senses. Those so gifted were called sensitives.

Mesmerism enjoyed great popularity in nineteenth-century America, where itinerant mesmerists entertained audiences with demonstrations of hypnotic legerdemain. When spiritualism arrived on the scene, the ground for belief in wonders had already been well plowed. Also, many of the new faith's adherents proposed animal magnetism as the spirits' possible conduit to the living. The idea had a certain quasi-scientific appeal about it. Almost overnight, erstwhile sensitives were transformed into trance mediums.

Where mesmerism contributed miracles, Swedenborgianism lent a basic philosophy. An important eighteenth-century Swedish scientist, Emanuel Swedenborg turned his considerable intellect to mysticism when, in midlife, he began having visions. He declared he was visited by God, Christ, and innumerable lesser beings—including spirits of the dead. He also had graphic visions of heaven and hell and of a hierarchical realm of six spiritual spheres surrounding the earth. Souls questing toward enlightenment proceeded from earth toward the outermost sphere.

Swedenborg wrote voluminously of his spiritual experiences. Some thought him deranged—brilliant, but a lunatic. Others, however, took his message so much to heart they founded a religion on its teachings. Its American incarnation was the Church of the New Jerusalem. By the 1840s, this small sect had prompted considerable interest in Swedenborg's writings. Most spiritualists eschewed Swedenborg's mysticism. They wanted, after all, to demystify religion, rid it of the occult. But they drew heavily from the Swedish seer in two areas—his testament to the soul's survival and his vision of spirit realms. The latter idea was especially useful

Mystic Emanuel Swedenborg described unearthly spirit realms, a concept adopted by spiritualists long after he died in 1772.

when critics carped that the spirits, even if they existed, could be dismissed as a dull and vulgar lot. (Ralph Waldo Emerson, for instance, called spiritualism a "rathole revelation," and Charles Dickens had this to say: "Although I shall be ready to receive enlightenment from any source, I must say I have very little hope of it from the spirits who express themselves through mediums, as I have never yet observed them to talk anything but nonsense.") Such spirits, came the reply, dwelt in a realm near earth and therefore could

not be expected to show a great deal of enlightenment.

Both Swedenborg and Mesmer influenced the man who came to be known variously as the Poughkeepsie Seer and the John the Baptist of spiritualism. Born in Orange County, New York, in 1826, Andrew Jackson Davis was a sickly and unhappy child. His mother was illiterate and rigidly religious; his father was a part-time cobbler and full-time drunk who abused the boy. Not surprisingly, perhaps, Davis began to hear disembodied voices when he was still a child. Some years later, after attending a lecture on animal magnetism, he found that he was easily mesmerized. He took to falling into trances in which he apparently became clairvoyant and had visions. In 1844, Davis said, he was visited by the spirits of Swedenborg and the Greek physician Galen. Galen gave him a magic staff and advised him to become a clairvoyant healer. There followed a successful career in which the entranced Davis diagnosed diseases and prescribed cures, much the same as a man named Edgar Cayce would do about a century later.

With hardly any schooling, Davis also became a ubiquitous lecturer and prolific writer. In 1847, when he was only twenty-one, his masterwork was published under the lengthy title *The Principles of Nature, Her Divine Revelations, and a Voice to Mankind, By and Through Andrew Jackson Davis, the 'Poughkeepsie Seer' and 'Clairvoyant.'* Davis claimed never to have read Swedenborg, but *Revelations* was replete with the Swedish mystic's concepts. The controversial book won a wide audience that included many spiritualists-to-be. Davis would largely fail in his efforts to give spiritualism a more philosophical cast and turn it away from a sole preoccupation with spirit communication. Nevertheless, what little dogma the movement did accrue—teachings about spirit spheres and the like—was largely his doing.

Davis's most memorable contribution to spiritualism, however, was his uncanny foretelling of its advent. In the 1840s, he declared: "It is a truth that spirits commune with one another while one is in the body and the other in the higher spheres." Davis went on to add, "This truth will ere long present itself in the form of a living demonstration." In notes dated March 31, 1848, Davis wrote, "About daylight this morning a warm breathing passed over my face and I heard a voice, tender and strong, saying: 'Brother, the good work has begun—behold a living demonstration is born.'"

March 31, 1848—the exact date on which little Kate Fox asked a mysterious rapper to answer some questions.

Called spiritualism's John the Baptist, Andrew Jackson Davis heralded the movement and helped shape its philosophy.

But perhaps the broader fulfillment of Davis's prophecy could be traced to the demonstrations that Leah Fox Fish was demanding of her sisters. At Leah's insistence, Kate and Maggie showed her how they produced rappings with their toes. Leah tried it herself, but her older, less pliable joints could not create the effect. She therefore needed the girls to facilitate her plans, and she brought forth some strange blandishments to win their cooperation. Despite what she herself had just seen and heard, Leah tried to persuade Kate and Maggie that the spirits were real. They had appeared to her personally, the older sister said, and revealed a great destiny for the girls. Maggie was doubtful for a time; even so, Leah was soon back in Rochester with the whole family in tow.

So began the whirlwind. Leah moved the household into a new home, hitherto unhaunted, and along with plentiful rappings there were such new and spooky effects as the supposed sound of blood splatting onto the floor. The spirits had multiplied from the original hapless peddler. A Methodist minister attempted to exorcise them, and other churchgoers took to dropping by to drive them out by speaking in tongues. In response, the spirits only boomed with heightened vigor. Word soon got around, and the famous Hydesville Rappings became the Rochester Knockings. Leah held séances at which the spirits would spell out advice for the sitters and perform other wonders as well. In darkness, a spirit face might appear. A spirit hand might grasp a sitter's wrist or pluck at a lady's dress. Many sitters discovered that they, too, could rap with the world beyond, and soon numerous households in Rochester and environs were cracking and popping apace.

For a year or so, the Rochester Knockings remained a provincial oddity, if a sensational one. Converts and the curious besieged the Fox home from morning to midnight, and it was about this time that Leah let herself be persuaded, as it were, to accept money for the séances. After all, with such furor precluding normal commerce, what else was the family to do? It was also about then that matters grew heated in Rochester, where community sentiment was not altogether favorable. Many people did not believe in spirits, and ominous mobs gathered occasionally in the front yard. Clearly it was time to seek wider pastures and higher peaks, but at this point the spirits seemed to rebel.

Maggie and Kate might have had second thoughts about the profound turn their lives had taken. What had started as a prank now threatened to chain them to a lie forever. There was still time to back out—but not much time. Leah, probably hoping to quiet doubters and gain new clients, wanted the girls to submit to investigation of the rappings. Most likely she was also toying with the idea of expanding operations beyond Rochester. Maggie and Kate must have balked, for in November of 1849 the spirits took

A drawing from Davis's book The Present Age and Inner Life illustrates his idea of a pipeline from a spirit world in the clouds to the earth below.

A New World for Women

The Victorian era was not a good one for women. In fact and often in law, Victorian females were chattel—property of fathers and husbands. Society was a patriarchy whose rigid morality enforced a double standard in all areas of life. In short, Victorian women were powerless—personally, politically, sexually, and financially.

It was little wonder, then, that spiritualism was a refuge for many of them. It offered at least a modicum of freedom, power, and equality. Even as an amateur medium, a woman who summoned spirits had power—an attractive aura of mystery and drama that offered escape from the drab routine that might have been her lot.

In a time when careers for women were few and women workers were drastically underpaid, mediumship offered equal opportunity. There were slightly more women mediums than men, and pay was the same—scant, for most. But the job still provided a livelihood and, for a few women, a vehicle to wealth, fame, and adventure.

Two such women were England's Emma Hardinge Britten and America's Cora L. V. Richmond, both successful "trance lecturers." Their performances entailed discoursing for an hour or more, under spirit guidance, on topics chosen by the audience. Both women won over hostile male audiences, who admired, if not the spirits, at least the ladies' talent for off-the-cuff oratory.

As for Cora Richmond, her speaking style was only one asset. She had a virginal prettiness—the Victorian ideal—that captivated men. Thus she was able to lecture on the male-threatening topic of women's rights without undue offense. One exception among the men who heard young Cora was writer Henry James. He turned her into Verena Tarrant, the heroine of *The Bostonians,* a book that linked spiritualism to feminism, condemning both.

James was one of many critics who saw spiritualism as a threat to the family and the natural order. In a sense, it was. It arose at a time when women in burdensome or abusive marriages had little recourse. Divorce was socially unthinkable, and adultery for women was regarded as nothing less than harlotry. Many spiritualists, however, believed in "spiritual affinities"—relationships decreed on a loftier plane than earth and therefore transcending

Three women who found spiritualism a path to fame—or notoriety—were, from left, Cora L. V. Richmond, Emma Hardinge Britten, and Victoria Woodhull.

marriage. Affinities justified divorce, among other things. Cora Richmond, for instance, was married and divorced at least three times. But affinities meant affairs to nonspiritualists, who decried mediums as home wreckers and worse. Their opinion was reinforced by the sexual dalliance that occasionally went on during séances under the pretext that spirits—not humans—were the dalliers.

Spiritualism also met opprobrium through linkage with women's rights, although the degree and direction of this alliance varied. Suffragists Elizabeth Cady Stanton and Susan B. Anthony, for instance, were interested in spiritualism but never committed to it. Nor did they care to upset the institution of marriage. But Victoria Claflin Woodhull, the one feminist leader who was also a practicing spiritualist, thought otherwise. If Stanton and Anthony made women's battleground the ballot box, Woodhull placed it squarely in the bedroom.

Woodhull was one of many children in a lower-class family that once ran a sort of traveling séance show. The star was Victoria's younger sister Tennessee, famed for her purported magnetic healing talents. The sisters settled in New York and became successful publishers and stockbrokers, largely with the help of the wealthy Cornelius Vanderbilt. (Tennessee was Vanderbilt's mistress for a time.)

In 1872 Victoria became the first woman to run for president. Her battle cry was free love, the concept that love alone—apart from any legal or religious contract—justified sex. Both she and Tennessee practiced what they preached, but in the end, Victoria opted for conventional respectability. She moved to England, married a banker, and denied that she had ever espoused free love. As for Tennessee, she, too, married: The one-time wonder child in a traveling spiritualist show ended her life as Lady Cook, viscountess of Monserrat.

Victoria Woodhull's advocacy of free love earned her the title "Mrs. Satan" from cartoonist Thomas Nast. In his 1872 cartoon, a burdened wife rebuffs a bat-winged Woodhull: "I'd rather travel the hardest path of matrimony than follow your footsteps."

a leave of absence. They rapped that they were departing because they could no longer abide the girls' disobedience to their wish for wider exposure. Fine, said the mediums. The spirits rapped out, "We will now bid you all farewell." And the house fell into eerie and unaccustomed silence.

It lasted twelve days. Who knows what threats and pleadings Leah Fish might have brought to bear during that time or what loss the girls themselves felt at a crashing anticlimax after almost a year's constant attention? If the risk of resummoning the spirits was great, the prospect of returning to their joyless prespirit existence must have been equally daunting. In any case, the spirits returned in veritable trills and arpeggios of raps.

A delighted Leah rushed to book Corinthian Hall, the largest public meeting house in Rochester, for a demonstration of the Fox sisters' mediumship. Young Kate would not perform, but Maggie and Leah would confront all critics, for while Leah had never mastered toe popping, she had learned some tricks of her own. Apparently, it was she who masterminded the séances, she who choreographed and cued the spirits' performances. In all probability, it was also she who expanded their repertoire to include new features—phantom tinkling of bells, sounds of sawing and hammering, and more ambitiously, martial music complete with bass drums and the reports of a distant cannon. Most novel of all, Leah's séance table was now motivated by spirit power. Even in well-lighted rooms, sitters saw it turn, tap, tilt, and scoot about the floor with no visible agency propelling it. The Corinthian Hall exhibition stretched from one evening to three days, and it was a circus from the start. A succession of committees devised various tests for Leah and Maggie. Most involved posing questions to the spirits, who while inconsistent gave enough right answers to make an impression. Another test required the women to stand on pillows with their skirts bound tight around their ankles. Even trussed up, the mediums produced shuddering raps (probably with the aid of a servant girl paid to stand beneath the stage and pound from below with a broomstick). There was a committee of women who checked the sisters' underwear for steel balls that might be used for rapping. The women found none.

Most members of the committees were hostile, and day and evening, at the Corinthian and at private homes, they probed and questioned. But on the third night they were constrained to tell a packed house that they had detected no fraud. Nonbelievers rioted, and there was general pandemonium, but the committees stood pat. The phenomena were genuine. Spirits of the dead were speaking through the Fox sisters, no doubt about it.

One night at the Corinthian, a clergyman named Potts got on the stage and proceeded to pop his own toes, assuring pleased onlookers that this trick explained the so-called spirits. Sometime later, a committee of doctors in Buffalo examined the sisters and concluded that at least some of the knocks were made by cracking knee joints. These critics may have been perspicacious, but they were also too late. The Fox sisters had come to the attention of the great and famous. The ship had sailed.

Horace Greeley, editor of the *New York Tribune,* heard of the Foxes and decided to conduct his own investigation. Greeley was grieving over the loss of a son, and the possibility that the dead might be accessible to the living was of immense interest to him. So it was that in the spring of 1850, he installed the three sisters and their mother in New York's Barnum Hotel. There the Fox sisters gave sittings every morning and afternoon for about two months, and they proved to be an enormous draw. The bejeweled elite crowded their rooms, and stylish carriages lined Broadway outside their hotel. Reliable reports said that the sisters were taking in more than a hundred dollars a day—an astonishing sum in those days.

Usually the spirits began the sessions by accommodating a sitter's request to commune with a dead loved one, often to great effect. Leah excelled at gleaning information from her subjects that helped the spirits toward correct answers. Then she would call in spirits of the famous dead, although they were not always impressive. When one sitter noted that Benjamin Franklin's spirit seemed surprisingly ungrammatical, one of the younger Foxes flounced away from the séance table with the injudicious pro-

A Scientist Turns the Tables

Michael Faraday was among the most brilliant of nineteenth century scientists. A chemist and physicist, he helped change electricity from a curiosity into a useful energy source. He also dampened the Victorian passion for table turning.

Faraday took an interest in the fad after other scientists proposed that some mysterious magnetic or electrical force was causing tables to turn on their own. Finding such ideas incredible, Faraday set out to disprove them. He theorized that the motive force for table turning was the involuntary and unconscious muscle contractions of séance sitters who wanted the tables to move. To demonstrate, he fashioned a table with two tops that were divided by a layer of ball bearings and joined by stout rubber bands. When séance sitters worked with the device, the upper tabletop moved first, showing that fingers were moving the table and not vice versa. Moreover, once the sitters knew the nature of the experiment, movement ceased. Apparently, the realization that they were the motive force removed the mystery from the experience— and with it the unconscious impulse causing the motion. For Faraday and most other scientists, the proof was ironclad. It even caused a small decline in table turning's popularity. Still, most believers scoffed at Faraday's finding, claiming tables not only turned but also lifted into the air and galloped about —behavior inexplicable in terms of fingers and wishful thinking.

Leah Fox Fish Underhill (left) profited handsomely from her sisters' medium-ship and her own. She added to her rich-es by marrying a wealthy banker, and her New York apartment (above) became the picture of Victorian elegance. Her less canny younger sisters died paupers.

test, "You know I never understood grammar!" The performances generally ended with Leah humming *Hail Columbia* while the spirits rapped along in rhythmic rapport.

Dubious though the séances were, they persuaded many of the Foxes' legitimacy. Business boomed, and soon Leah moved the family to New York permanently. She accepted Greeley's kind offer to see to Kate's education. As to Maggie's, however, Mrs. Fish declined. She would not give up her most bankable medium, who, when not rapping in New York, was packed off to other cities as yet bereft of the spiritualist message.

It was in Philadelphia that Maggie fell in love with Arctic explorer Elisha Kent Kane, the dashing scion of an aristocratic family. Kane's wealthy parents considered her quite unsuitable as a prospective daughter-in-law, and even the young man thought spiritualism was a humbug. Nevertheless, Maggie was married—more or less. Without benefit of judge or clergy, the couple exchanged vows and rings in the company of friends. The affair had a tragic ending when Kane, whose health had always been fragile, died in 1857. Maggie was left brokenhearted and virtually penniless. She had abandoned mediumship for love, but now financial need forced her to take it up again. She also took to drinking heavily, and her long decline began.

Kate, meanwhile, was faring somewhat better than Maggie. She performed for a time in England, where in 1872 she married a British barrister named H. D. Jencken. They had two sons. But after her husband's death in 1881, Kate quickly ran through the funds he left her. She had been drinking heavily even before the move to England, and the alcoholism grew steadily worse.

Eventually she returned to New York, and there, early in 1888, she was arrested for drunkenness and idleness. Welfare workers took custody of her sons. Maggie, who had remained close to Kate over the years, managed to get the boys to an uncle in England. But despair was gathering both sisters in. Snared by a joke that began innocently enough, they had spent lifetimes practicing deceit that probably ran against their natural grain. Now they were paying for it.

Maggie had actually considered suicide. Perhaps she rejected it because at the time she was thinking of converting to Catholicism. Or she may have hoped for a last chance at redemption: confession—a final effort to cleanse her soul or at least to free it.

Forty years distant from Hydesville, a sad and bloated Maggie tramped onto the stage at the New York Academy of Music. Before a packed house, she displayed her stockinged foot and demonstrated the physical peculiarity that had enabled her to summon the spirits. "I have seen so much miserable deception," she had told the press earlier in the day. "That is why I am willing to state that spiritualism is a fraud of the worst description." Sitting in a box overlooking the stage, Kate watched her sister's demonstration and silently affirmed the confession.

Maggie's oral confession was followed by a much-publicized written version. But spiritualists, now numbering in the millions, did not believe it. Having invested so much devotion to the cause and drawn such comfort from it, they dismissed the gesture as the rantings of a drunk. To their relief, Maggie recanted the confession later, and Kate dissociated herself from it as well. They were destitute. For both sisters, there was no livelihood without the spirits.

Nevertheless, some spiritualists still contend that the Fox sisters would never have renounced their mediumship at all save for their desire to spite Leah Fish, whom they hated. Indeed, Maggie and Kate did hate Leah, and with cause. By the end of the 1850s Leah, having legally jettisoned Mr. Fish, was remarried to a wealthy New York banker, Daniel Underhill. She had a fine house, social standing, and a reputation as a leading medium of her day. Invitations to her séances were coveted, and her regular sitters included Horace Greeley, writers James Fenimore Cooper and Washington Irving, poets Henry Wadsworth Longfellow and John Greenleaf Whittier. Leah Fox Fish Underhill, who had orchestrated it all, wound up rich, famous, sought-after, secure. When her younger sisters became a social embarrassment, she turned her back on them.

The Dazzling Davenports

William and Ira Davenport were still teenagers when they erupted from their hometown of Buffalo to begin one of the most successful stage careers in the history of spiritualism.

The brothers specialized in boisterous special effects produced from inside a medium's cabinet—an elaborate wooden prop of their own invention. It was seven feet high and six feet long, with three doors in front that opened to afford a full view of the interior. Inside the cabinet, the Davenports would sit on facing benches while volunteers from the audience bound them with ropes. The process could take as long as forty-five minutes. On a bench between the brothers lay musical instruments, seemingly out of their reach.

The binding completed, the cabinet's doors would be closed and the gaslights lowered. Almost at once, trumpets and strings and tambourines would blare and twang and jingle for amazed onlookers. Hands would appear in the diamond-shaped aperture on the cabinet's middle door.

Later, the doors would open to show the Davenports still securely bound.

The act was a sensation in America and Europe, and the brothers enjoyed nearly a quarter century of success before William died in 1877 while the brothers were touring Australia. A grieving Ira retired in New York. Years later, he was sought out and befriended by the magician Harry Houdini, who, although he loathed mediums, admired the Davenports as professional colleagues. Houdini learned some of his own impressive escape tricks from the masterful Ira.

Significantly, the Davenports never claimed to be mediums, despite the spiritualists who were quick to suggest they were. In fact, the brothers were among the earliest and best escape artists in the world.

The Davenport brothers, Ira and William, made a lasting contribution to spiritualism by inventing the medium's cabinet, which was featured on posters promoting their stage act (left).

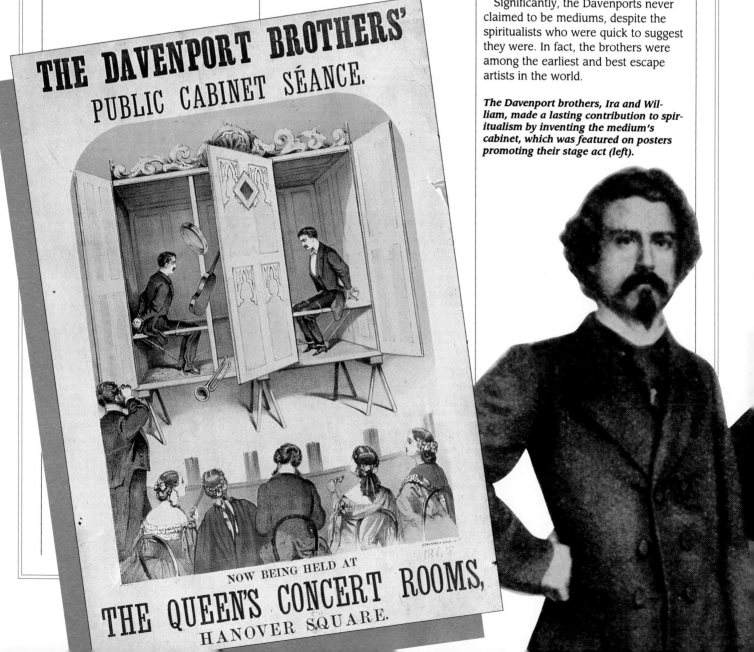

THE DAVENPORT BROTHERS'
PUBLIC CABINET SÉANCE.

1865

NOW BEING HELD AT
THE QUEEN'S CONCERT ROOMS,
HANOVER SQUARE.

Poor, hopeless, and sodden, Kate Fox died in 1892. Maggie died a few months later. Both women were buried in paupers' graves.

In the wake of the Hydesville Rappings, mediums—professional and amateur—multiplied almost exponentially. A few improved the Fox girls' routines. The most notable innovators were brothers Ira and William Davenport, who performed a successful theatrical act that was less a séance in style than a magic show. By the mid-1850s, the Davenports had invented the medium's cabinet *(page 36)*, an enclosure whose alleged function was to help harness the practitioners' psychic energies. Critics contended—usually with some accuracy—that the cabinet's true function was to help hide trickery. In one form or another, the cabinet was used by many mediums. The Davenports themselves used an elaborate wooden affair. Other mediums, however, made do with as little as a curtained-off alcove or corner.

The colorful Davenports notwithstanding, the early mediums were mostly an uninspired lot. They plied the standard wares—rappings, poppings, cumbersome ploddings through the alphabet, the occasional phantom hand or ghostly tune. They usually worked in darkness, relying on its cover—and on their patrons' need and willingness to believe—to present their chicanery as true marvels.

Waiting in the wings was a mammoth exception to the pedestrian norm. Two years after the Hydesville Rappings, mediumistic gifts would manifest themselves in a young Scottish immigrant living in the wilds of Connecticut. Before long, he would stun the world.

Much is known about Daniel Dunglas Home, and much is not. Although volumes have been written by and about him, he remains an elusive character, preserving the air of mystery appropriate to the uniquely gifted medium—or the consummate magician—he may have been. His detractors, and there were many, insisted he was an arrant fraud, an exceptionally magnetic conjurer who masterfully evaded detection. His followers, and there were many, maintained he was more than human. Impeccable witnesses declared that his mere presence could cause a whole room to tremble as though gripped by an earthquake. At his behest, 100-pound tables wafted weightlessly into the air. He could levitate, elongate his body, bathe his face harmlessly in live coals. Pentecostal flames were seen wreathing his head, and he could make spirits appear in full form. Or so his supporters said. Either he communed with a spirit world as he claimed, or he commanded a legerdemain unmatched before or since. In the world of mediums, D. D. Home was a colossus among pygmies.

Whatever his other talents, Home (he pronounced it "Hume") had a knack for reinventing his own persona. His name, for instance, may not have been his name. He was born in 1833 in the town of Currie, about six miles southeast of Edinburgh. According to British author Trevor H. Hall, who took the trouble to check Home's birth records, the medium was baptized Daniel Home—not Dunglas. He probably added the middle name later to support his fabrication of an aristocratic background. Dunglas figured among given names of the Scottish earls of Home, and Home maintained that his father was the bastard son of the tenth earl. The assertion was widely believed in Home's time and long afterward, but it had no basis in fact.

Home's father was actually a common laborer and an abusive drunk. (This family situation was something of a pattern among mediums.) In infancy Daniel was adopted by a childless aunt and her husband, who emigrated to America eight years later and settled in Connecticut. Home wrote that as an adolescent he began having premonitory visions, and by the time he was seventeen his presence evoked Fox-style raps and ambulant furniture. His aunt, a dogged Presbyterian, thought he was possessed by the devil and ushered him out of the family. Undismayed, Daniel took up the practice that would support him handsomely until he married into more stable solvency years later: He became a perpetual houseguest. He was most appealing in the role—attractive, attentive, charming. He had little formal education; nevertheless, he could play the piano, quote from popular books, and converse with wit on a variety of topics. Elderly ladies found him enchanting. Some men thought him a trifle effeminate, but he was personable and his séances were uncanny. Home quickly built a reputation based mostly on clairvoyance and healing. Then and later, he got along on hospitality and on his patrons' gifts, which often matched his kingly standing with the spirits. Never, in a twenty-year career, did he charge money for a séance.

Home soon gained attention from some early investigators of spiritualism, including Professor David Wells of Harvard, who tested the young medium and came up with astonishing results. In a well-lighted room, Wells and three other witnesses watched a table plunge in all directions, even though Home was nowhere near it. When two investigators tried to restrain it, they needed all their strength to hold it still. The table then rose off the floor and floated for several seconds. When it alighted, Wells sat down on it, but it continued to move. At one point, the table reared up on two legs and teetered on edge. Two more witnesses joined Wells atop the table, but still it rocked and trembled. The investigators eventually concluded that indeed some spiritual intelligence had to be at work.

By 1852 Home was, according to witnesses, levitating not just the furniture but himself. It was even said that sitters who tried to hold him down found themselves lifted up with him, dangling a foot or so above the floor while he floated. He also produced physical manifestations, including phantom hands that could be touched as well as seen and even head-to-toe apparitions.

If Home's manifestations were impressive, so was his personal presence. He was tall and thin, with curly auburn hair and compelling, deep-set gray eyes. He was handsome, in a poetically consumptive sort of way. In fact, he did suffer from tuberculosis, that most fashionable (if deadly) of

This Hamlet-like pose reflects medium D. D. Home's flair for drama. Some believe that his theatrics enabled him to repeatedly bamboozle suggestible sitters.

nineteenth-century ailments, and in 1855 the spirits purportedly suggested that he move to England for his health. One wonders why they deemed it salubrious for him to trade the dank chill of Connecticut for the dank chill of London, but perhaps they sought a more suitable climate for his talents. In America, spiritualism had a democratic flavor. In England, on the other hand, its greatest popularity resided with the aristocracy and the monied upper class.

So to England he went with high hopes, having altered his unsuitable origins. Home knew that among the rich, mediums were accorded a mixed reception. They might be welcomed into palatial homes, but if they were lowborn, class distinctions applied. However novel and entertaining the medium, he or she would still have only the status of an upper-echelon servant—a butler, perhaps, or a governess. Home aspired to better.

In London, Daniel once again depended on the kindness of strangers—rich ones—and they did not disappoint him. He was lodging at the home of a wealthy solicitor, John S. Rymer, when he held one of his most famous séances.

It was not particularly impressive technically, although

it included many of Home's staples. The heavy séance table rapped and tipped. Ghostly hands rang bells, and an accordion Home appeared to hold in only one hand played tunes. But the evening's real cachet lay with the clientele. Among the nine sitters were the illustrious poets Robert and Elizabeth Browning. In the climax of Home's performance, a spirit hand picked up a wreath of clematis from the table and placed it reverently on Mrs. Browning's head.

Elizabeth Browning, already intrigued by mesmerism and clairvoyance, was impressed. "To me it was wonderful and conclusive," she wrote to her sister. "We were touched by the invisible." The letter indicated sadly, however, that her husband was not persuaded.

Indeed he was not. At first, Robert Browning seemed little moved one way or the other, although he considered Home's manner with the Rymers rather smarmy. But only a day or two after the séance, when Rymer and Home called on the poets, Browning told the medium that if he were not out the door in half a minute, he, Browning, would personally throw him down the stairs. In print, Browning called Home's séance "most clumsy, and unworthy." Moreover, seizing on Home's chosen middle name, Browning took to calling him Dungball. A few years later, Browning wrote his famous poem "Mr. Sludge, the Medium," some two thousand lines of vituperation whose subject clearly was Home. If not the best of the poet's dramatic monologues, it was certainly the most hateful. It called the medium, among other unpleasant things, a cheat, a fraud, a leech, a toady, a braggart, and a sot.

Robert's attitude led Elizabeth to downplay her interest in spiritualism in favor of domestic tranquillity, but the fact remained that Home was the only sliver of contention ever publicized in the couple's legendarily idyllic marriage. Probably, Elizabeth herself never knew why her husband's loathing of Home seemed so disproportionate, nor will anyone ever know for sure. But reliable historians speculate that Browning had heard the rumor that would dog the medium throughout his career: that Home was homosexual. In 1855 the matter was far more scandalous than it is now,

and it is likely that Browning simply could not bear for such a person to have anything to do with his beloved wife. (Home did have profound influence over several young men during his career, but there is no evidence he ever acted on his homosexual inclinations, if indeed he had any.)

Browning's excoriation of Home was not a death blow; by now there were many adherents to counterbalance detractors, including literati just as luminous as Browning. Those favorably impressed by at least one séance each were author William Makepeace Thackeray, poet Dante Gabriel Rossetti, and Russian novelist Ivan Turgenev. Still, the Browning affair seemed to signal a brief dimming of Home's comet. In 1855 he set out for Italy, which presumably was better for both his lungs and his prospects. Armed with introductions to wealthy Britishers in Florence, he flourished for a time among them and their aristocratic Italian friends. On the whole, however, his stay was not happy. He was slightly injured in an assassination attempt perpetrated by superstitious Florentine peasants who believed he was a sorcerer raising evil spirits by feeding the Holy Sacrament to toads. Then his spirits informed him that his powers would forsake him for a year, and they did.

Nevertheless, 1857 found Home in Paris, in business, and hotter than ever. His clients theretofore had included a few British lords and an occasional Italian prince, but now he was summoned to the Tuileries for a séance with Napoleon III and Eugénie. It was a great success. The empress held a spirit hand that by a characteristic deformity of one finger she recognized as belonging to her dead father. Home allegedly enjoyed the full confidence of their imperial highnesses, although few details are known of their séances. No accurate records were kept. More shadowy still were the circumstances under which the medium hastily left France a year or so after he arrived. One story has it that enemies who resented his influence at court sabotaged a séance to make him look like a fraud. By another account, however, a charge of homosexuality was substantiated against Home, whereupon police spirited him off to prison. The gendarmes were soon aghast when he turned the tables, so to speak. Home supposedly told stories about dubious activities in high places, and he was prepared to back them up. There had been a homosexual scandal at court not long before, and the French wanted no more public exposure of crooked coronets. Home was ushered quietly out of the country.

Whatever the truth, Home proved again that not the least of his prestidigitation was a talent for landing on his feet. He went to Russia and in no time was hobnobbing with Czar Alexander II. So secure was the medium in his status, in fact, that he actually turned down two invitations from the czar in one week before meeting him for the first time. It was either a display of exquisite bravado or a near-genius tactic of whetting a prospective patron's appetite. And a patron Alexander became. In Italy, Home had met a rich and lovely young Russian aristocrat, Alexandrina De Kroll, whom he planned to marry. She was a member of the czar's inner circle and required royal permission to wed. Alexander gave enthusiastic blessings, not to mention valuable gifts. Obviously, Home's ersatz noble ancestry sold as well in Russia as it had elsewhere. Best man at the wedding was French novelist Alexandre Dumas *père,* of *Three Musketeers* fame, and groomsmen included Count Alexei Tolstoy, cousin of the great writer Leo Tolstoy.

The marriage was happy but short-lived. Madame Home contracted tuberculosis, and in 1862 she died. The widower, who had been amassing converts for free in England and on the Continent, suddenly found himself in financial difficulty. He toyed with alternative careers: In the Papal States in Italy, he tried to be a sculptor, but he was ejected after three days on grounds he was a sorcerer. There followed some successful stage performances in America as a dramatic reader, but they did not provide security. Although Home was by then one of the most famous men in the world, he could not seem to find the proper sinecure. Back in London in 1866, he was ill and down on his luck. On top of everything, his society friends were about to flee him in droves in the face of a very public scandal.

It started when Home was consulted by Jane Lyons, a seventy-five-year-old widow. Though lowborn herself, she had married the grandson of the eighth earl of Strathmore. Mrs. Lyons was generally shunned socially, being, as one historian put it, "hysterical, illegitimate, shabby." But she was very rich. Home summoned her husband's spirit, who assured the lady of his abiding postmortem affections. Pleased, she gave the medium a gift of thirty pounds. At the second séance, the dead Mr. Lyons informed his widow that Home was his spiritual son—and therefore her son—and said she should adopt him. She was still pondering that at the next séance, at which she doled out another fifty pounds. Mr. Lyons's spirit suggested that an annual retainer of seven hundred pounds might be more in order. This hint seemed to open the sluice gates of Mrs. Lyons's exchequer, and in following months she bestowed gifts to the princely tune of some sixty thousand pounds on the thirty-three-year-old man she now considered her son. The pair eventually had a falling out, however, and the widow sued Home for defrauding her. He was arrested and jailed.

The well-publicized trial reeked of farce. In court, Mrs. Lyons was by turns dotty and vulgar. She screamed invective when displeased by testimony. (When a housemaid gave evidence, for instance, the widow yelled that the girl was a "saucy, dirty, dangerous, story-telling slut.") The court eventually found in her favor, but not without noting that the plaintiff was "saturated with delusion" and that spiritualism was "a system of mischievous nonsense well calculated to delude the vain, the weak, the foolish, and the superstitious."

All things considered, the medium did not fare as badly as he might have in this debacle. He managed to maintain a becoming air of aggrieved dignity, and—as always seemed the case with Home—there were at least two interpretations of the Lyons affair. One was that Home had tried to fleece an old lady. The other was that she was using him—trying to buy her way indirectly into his social circle. In any event, at this low ebb Home engineered a miraculous comeback. It featured the most astonishing and controversial séance of his career.

eleven inches and watched him handle live coals without harm. But neither had seen anything quite so strange as the Ashley House séance.

Accounts differ—among the witnesses and among individual reports at different times—but the gist of the event was this: On December 13 or December 16, 1868, Home held a séance for Adare, Lindsay, and Wynne. The room was lampless but supposedly moonlit. After several spirits appeared and departed, Home began pacing the room. His body elongated, then lifted into the air. When he touched down again, he told his friends, "Do not be afraid, and on no account leave your places." Then he left the room. Lindsay heard a voice whisper in his ear, "He will go out one window and in at another." At this, the young peer cried out in alarm. The flat was on the third floor and was, by Lindsay's estimate, eighty-five feet above ground.

The sitters heard a window thrown up in an adjacent room. Shortly thereafter, they saw Home outside their own window, apparently floating in midair. He calmly opened the window from the outside, stepped into the room, sat down, and began laughing. Asked why he was amused, Home replied that had a passing policeman looked up to see "a man turning round and round along the wall in the air he would have been much astonished."

Accounts of the Ashley House levitation went a long way toward refurbishing Home's reputation, and his subsequent career, though short, was unblemished. Not long after the Lyons trial he married once more into the Russian nobility, to a woman who proved both devoted wife and adoring biographer. The pair settled at Auteuil, France. So-

The sitters were all young men beyond reproach: James Ludovic Lindsay, later Lord Crawford, a Scottish peer who would go on to a distinguished career in science and in Parliament; Windham Thomas Wyndham-Quin, Lord Adare, later Lord Dunraven, an Irish peer who would have careers in journalism and government; and Adare's cousin, Captain Charles Bradstreet Wynne, an officer stationed at the Tower of London and later a magistrate in his native Ireland. Home had cultivated friendships with both Lindsay and Adare. Indeed, Home and Adare shared the latter's flat at Ashley House in London. Adare kept diaries of Home's mediumistic feats, and both he and Lindsay had observed spectacular ones. They had seen Home levitate several times. They had seen him elongate his body by as much as

ciable as ever, Home enjoyed having friends in to admire his jewelry collection. His health was failing, however, and for the most part he lived quietly, working on his memoirs. Interestingly, much of the writing was devoted to decrying his fellow mediums as frauds. One exception was a lady he knew in London and worked with occasionally. She, he attested, was genuine. Her name was Kate Fox Jencken.

Home remains controversial. During his lifetime and long afterward, critics speculated endlessly on whether he was a fraud. Levitation can be faked, as any good magician knows *(page 125)*. So-called Fire kings who seemed able to handle live coals were performing in sideshows and theaters before Home ever came on the scene, and their tricks, while skilled, were not mystical. At least one vaudevillian, Clarence E. Willard, made a career on the illusion of elongating his body. It has also been noted that Home's practice of accepting hospitality instead of money for his work might have been a strategy of characteristic genius. An inquisitive paying customer might feel free to bait or test a medium in any number of ways, accusing him of trickery if so inclined. But if both medium and client were guests in someone's home, rules of courtesy applied. To insult the medium was to insult the host—unthinkable boorishness, especially in the circles Home cultivated.

Other detractors contend Home's greatness lay not with what he did but with what his clients *thought* he did. His charisma was renowned, his flair for drama superb. He could set a scene and create a mood like no other medium, and he had the habit of announcing an effect in advance. Thus his sitters were prepared to see it, expected to see it, and in most cases wanted to see it. Adare and Lindsay, for instance, had been carefully conditioned to believe in Home for months before the Ashley House séance.

It is not surprising that being of individual temperaments, witnesses did not always see the same thing. Reports of Home's séances are replete with accounts from honest, intelligent people who did not agree on details. The Ashley House séance is the most famous case in point. Some witnesses recalled a full moon that allowed them to see Home clearly. But according to Trevor Hall, who checked an almanac, there could have been little or no moonlight on either of the two nights variously given as the séance date. There was disagreement about who was in which room during the levitation. There was confusion over whether it took place on the third floor, the fourth, or even the first and over whether the windows where Home exited and entered were side by side or facing each other. There is even some question as to where the séance took place—at Ashley House or another London pied-à-terre of Adare's.

Enemies of spiritualism were particular enemies of Home. Charles Dickens called him "a ruffian and a scoundrel." The great magician Harry Houdini, who once offered to do the Ashley House levitation himself, said the medium was "a hypocrite of the deepest dye." But while many critics have offered explanations of how Home might have produced most of his marvels, not one has ever proved that he did perpetrate fraud. In two decades of mediumship, Home was never caught in trickery. That accomplishment alone made him singular among Victorian mediums.

Home died of tuberculosis in 1886 at the age of fifty-three. His widow petitioned the town council of Edinburgh to arrange for a memorial to honor him, and she offered to pay up to five hundred pounds for the project. The council was divided among members who thought Home was a scoundrel and those who were impressed by his status with royalty. The latter contingent won out, and in 1888 the monument was erected—a public water fountain that incorporated a bust of Home. Decades later, it fell into disrepair and was demolished.

In 1915, a devoted spiritualist bought the old Fox cottage—the movement's original shrine—and had it moved to the spiritualist colony of Lily Dale in western New York. The house burned down in 1955. For the Fox sisters and D. D. Home, monuments proved ephemeral. Their legacies, however, were quite another matter.

Invitation to a Séance

Snaring the famed medium Daniel Dunglas Home as a houseguest in the summer of 1855 was a coup for London solicitor John Rymer and his wife. True, the local vicar publicly preached against the devilish goings-on in their home in the suburb of Ealing, and stodgy neighbors doubtless sniffed disapproval behind the Rymers' backs. But Home gave the Rymers two irresistible gifts: the belief that they were communicating with their dead child and a link to London's smart set that the socially ambitious couple otherwise never would have had.

Newspaper reports of Home's séances inspired aristocrats, writers, and other prominent people to seek a welcome at Ealing Villa, the Rymer home. Among the celebrities was the poet Elizabeth Barrett Browning, who declared that Home was the most interesting person in England. Her husband, poet Robert Browning, disdained spiritualism, but she managed to wangle an invitation, which the Rymers were not at all reluctant to give. Thus, on July 23, 1855, the Brownings went to unfashionable Ealing for a séance that, while typical of the eerie experiences Home provided his sitters, would become famous because the poets were there.

Mr. & Mrs John Rymer request the pleasure of your company at a séance by Mr. D.D. Home on the twenty-third of July at nine o'clock Ealing Villa

Banished Guests and Tilting Tables

On arrival at Ealing Villa, Robert Browning took an instant dislike to the unctuous young medium. In a long letter describing the séance to a friend, the poet said Home displayed "unmanlinesses . . . in the worse taste"—affecting the manners of a child, "speaking of Mr. and Mrs. Rymer as his 'Papa and Mama,' and kissing the family abundantly." Browning added that "the family like the caresses, however, and reciprocate them."

The poet remained civil despite his distaste, and at 9 p.m. the fourteen people present sat down around a cloth-draped table. The table held a large oil lamp, which provided the room's only light, and several small ornaments. Host John Rymer offered "suggestions" for behavior, "which though polite were explicit enough," said Browning: "that we should put no questions, nor desire to see anything but what the spirit might please to show us."

The eagerly curious participants were not kept waiting. They soon heard rapping noises and felt the table assume a life of its own, vibrating and tilting this way and that. The raps, Browning said, were identified as "the utterance of the family's usual visitor, the spirit of their child 'Wat' who died three years ago, aged twelve." Then the proceedings came abruptly to a halt and five people—"pointed out by the spirit," Browning wrote to his friend—were asked to leave the room. Victorian mediums sometimes used this ploy to banish people who seemed too skeptical; in this case it also conveniently cleared space on either side of Home.

Again the table sprang to life, tilting and bumping. Suddenly it reared up at such a steep angle *(right)* that the astonished participants expected the lamp to crash to the floor. It remained fixed in place, however, as if glued to the table. Robert Browning—seen here from behind in the foreground, next to his wife, Elizabeth, and opposite Home, who is to the right of the lamp—said that "all hands were visible. I don't know at all how the thing was done."

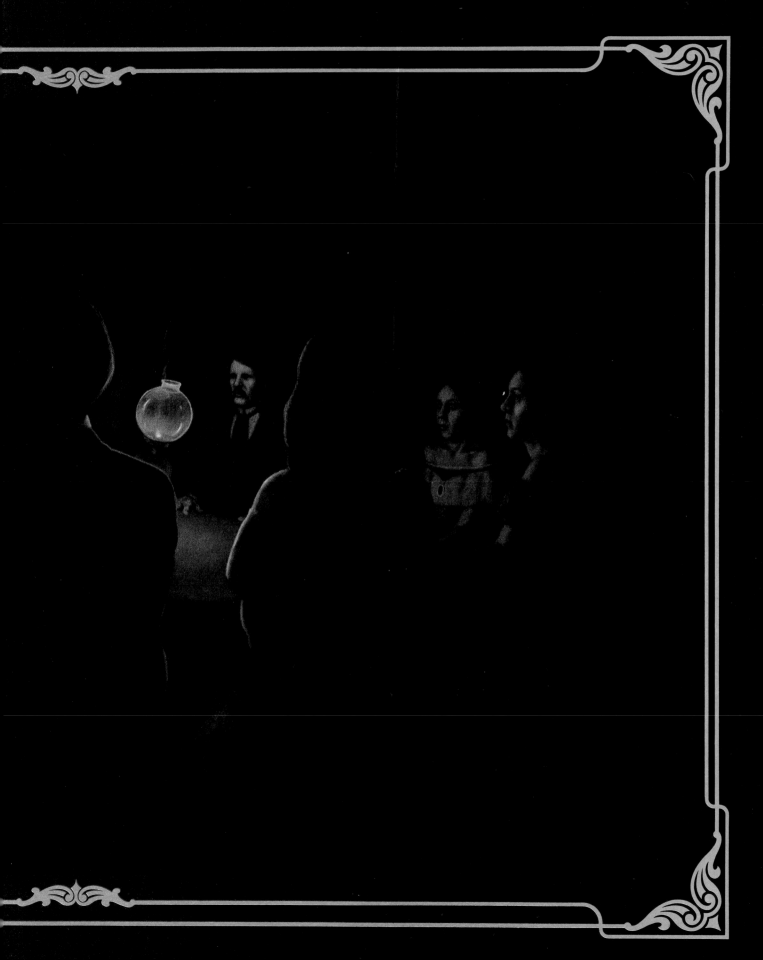

Tangible Signs from the Spirit World

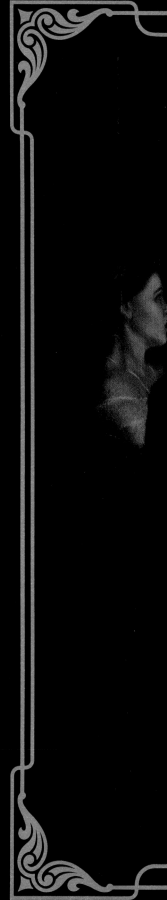

The table righted itself and the rapping continued, unnerving the novices among the sitters because they could not determine the source of the sounds. "All the raps seemed from or about the table," Robert Browning observed, "not the region outside us." But the participants' consternation was soon overshadowed by the emotional intensity of the séance's next stage, for the manifestations suddenly became more physical—and more personal.

Mrs. Rymer *(third from left)* was startled to feel someone or something touch her but saw no one. Sitting next to her, her husband, John—in this picture unseen behind the figure of Robert Browning—felt a similar touch. The couple believed that they recognized the entity that touched them as the spirit of their dead son, Wat.

Elizabeth Barrett Browning *(second from right)* was next to receive the attention of invisible forces. Her husband was baffled to see a part of her frock, near the waist, "slightly, but distinctly uplifted in a manner I cannot account for—as if by some object inside—which could hardly have been introduced there without her becoming aware of it." The unseen spiritual hand, if that is what it really was, repeated the act, tugging or pushing at the fabric of Mrs. Browning's dress a second time.

Then, by rapping in answer to questions, a spirit conveyed the message that it would play the accordion—and would let Robert Browning see its hand. Someone extinguished the lamp. The only light was that from a cloud-obscured moon, which barely penetrated the thin muslin curtains that hung on the French windows leading into the garden. The séance's ghostliest and most dramatic phase was about to begin.

A Strange Case of Moving Hands

The room was so dark, said Robert Browning, that "you could just distinguish" something if it was held up directly against the windows but "nothing of what was done *at the table.*" In this murky gloom, the guests saw a hand appear above the edge of the table opposite the Brownings. The hand, said Browning, "was withdrawn, reappeared and moved about, rose and sank—it was clothed in white loose folds, like muslin, down to the table's edge—from which it never was separated." More hands materialized. One picked up a small bell from the table and rang it. Another, "turning itself as if to be seen," flexed its fingers as it rotated.

Browning noted that the hands operated close to the table in the area around Home, "never in the open space of the room, tho' one hand crawled (as it were) up Mr. Home's shoulder." The poet was at first told by the spirits—through rapping, presumably—that he would be allowed to touch one of the hands, but when he pressed his request to do so, it was denied.

His wife put the apparitions to her own test. She held up her eyeglass to make sure the hands were "not a mere mental impression," she wrote later in a letter to her sister. Mrs. Browning was as convinced of the validity of the performance as her husband was doubtful. Noting that neither she nor Robert had touched the hands, she passed on to her sister as hard evidence a report from acquaintances who allegedly had done so at another séance: "The feel was warm and human—rather warmer in fact than is common with a man's hand."

At one point in the proceedings the room was lighted again and Home held an accordion—a two-handed instrument—beneath the table with one hand. Several tunes were then played. "The music was beautiful," said Mrs. Browning, and even her husband conceded that the airs were "played with expression enough."

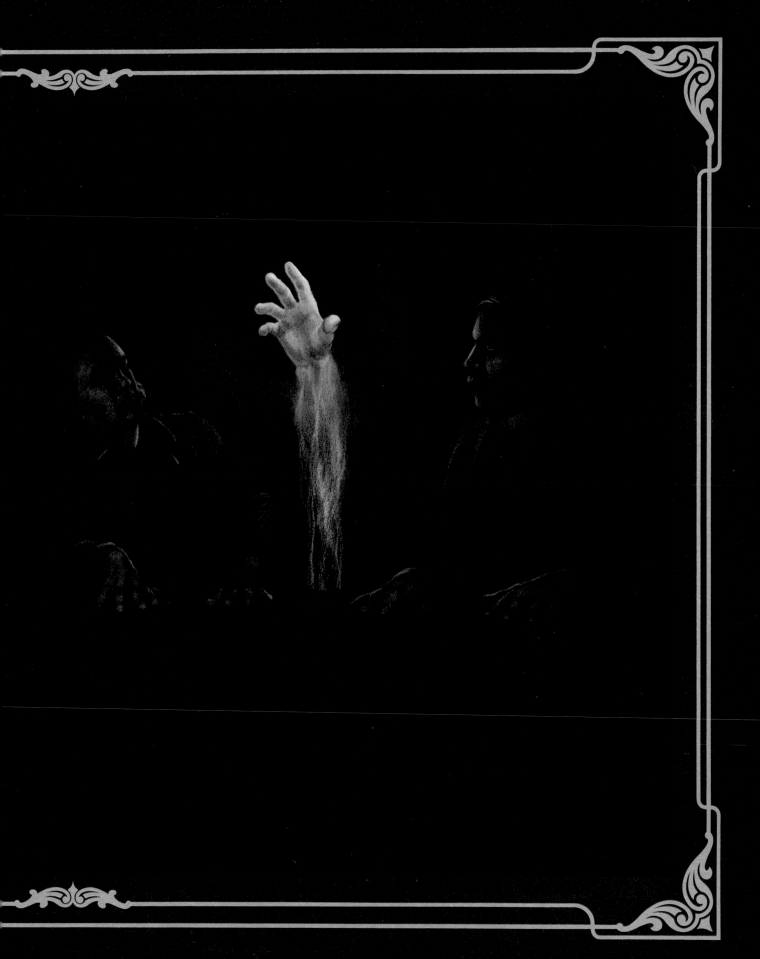

A Poet Crowned with a Flowery Wreath

While the room was still steeped in darkness, Home asked Elizabeth Barrett Browning to sit next to him. "The spiritual hands took from the table a garland which lay there," the poet later wrote to her sister, "and placed it upon my head." Her husband is seen here standing behind her as she is crowned with a wreath of clematis.

She described one of the hands that held the wreath as "of the largest human size, as white as snow and very beautiful. It was as near to me as this hand I write with and I saw it as distinctly. I was perfectly calm! not troubled in any way."

Although the spirits seemed partial to his wife, they did not entirely ignore Robert Browning. He felt himself touched several times—first on his knees and then on his hands—with what he described as "a kind of soft and fleshy pat."

The guests were asked to leave the Rymers alone with the medium for fifteen minutes. When they were called back, the room was lighted. Home said that the spirits would now lift the table off the floor so that Robert Browning could examine the phenomenon. "I looked under the table," Browning wrote, "and can aver that it was lifted from the ground, say a foot high, more than once—Mr. Home's hands being plainly above it." With that the séance ended.

Browning acknowledged that he could not explain "how the table was *uplifted altogether*—and how my wife's gown was agitated—nor how the accordion was played." Nonetheless, he later declared the manifestations to be an "impudent piece of imposture" and penned his long, scornful poem about Home, "Mr. Sludge, the Medium." Yet even in his conviction that Home was a charlatan, a belief his wife never shared, Browning could see that those who flocked to séances seeking sensational experiences were not blameless. In the words of his character, Mr. Sludge: "If such as came for wool, sir, went home shorn / Where is the wrong I did them? 'Twas their choice."

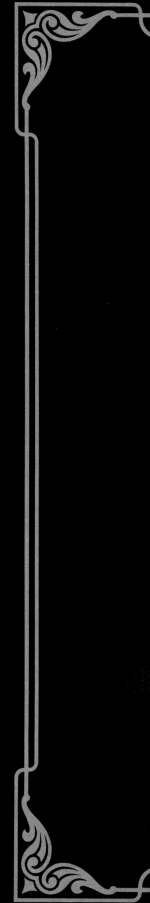

CHAPTER 2

Spirits in the Flesh

ll eyes strained through the gloom of the séance room toward the dark curtains of the medium's cabinet. Behind them lay a young woman named Florence Cook. She was securely bound, after the fashion of tying up mediums as a safeguard against fraud. And she was supposedly entranced, her spiritual energies coalescing. The curtains trembled, then parted slightly to reveal something white and diaphanous. It glided forward with ghostly grace, appearing to the dazzled sitters to grow, to acquire substance and form as the hangings fell away behind it. Now the audience could see it was the figure of a woman—barefoot, bare armed, draped crown to ankle in shimmering, opaque veils. She was lovely. Her name, she said, was Katie King, long-dead daughter of a long-dead pirate named John King. Florence had beckoned her from the spirit world, and she had come.

The spirit visitor (looking like a near-twin of the medium who summoned her) circulated among her earthbound guests, speaking with them, touching them, seeming as comfortably corporeal as they. She even allowed herself to be photographed. Spiritualists in the group were enchanted. This was not some disembodied rapping, some fleeting phantom hand or face, but a spirit in whole and indubitable flesh. What better proof could there possibly be of an afterlife? Spirits need not be limited to primitive communications nor be confined to insubstantial ether. They could assume the very bodies they had owned on earth, enjoying the same senses, breathing the same breath as the living.

But a keen observer was in the audience. William Crookes was a leading scientist of his day. Brilliant, original, and largely self-taught, he was a pioneer in both chemistry and physics. In 1861, when he was not yet thirty, he discovered the element thallium. Two years later he was elected to Britain's prestigious Royal Society, and he would go on to become its president. He would win most of science's highest accolades, earn knighthood, and receive the coveted Order of Merit. Here, surely, was the man to train a cold, appraising eye on the comely Katie King and to view Florence Cook with Olympian detachment.

Or so one might have thought. Soon after that séance, in London in

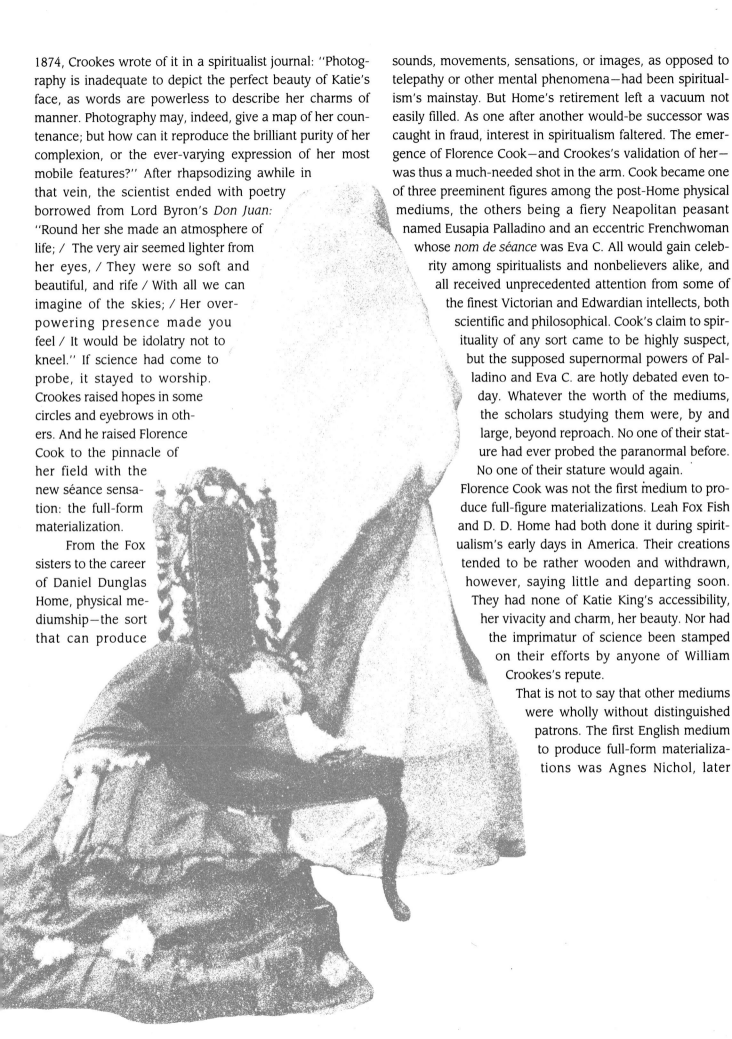

1874, Crookes wrote of it in a spiritualist journal: "Photography is inadequate to depict the perfect beauty of Katie's face, as words are powerless to describe her charms of manner. Photography may, indeed, give a map of her countenance; but how can it reproduce the brilliant purity of her complexion, or the ever-varying expression of her most mobile features?" After rhapsodizing awhile in that vein, the scientist ended with poetry borrowed from Lord Byron's *Don Juan:* "Round her she made an atmosphere of life; / The very air seemed lighter from her eyes, / They were so soft and beautiful, and rife / With all we can imagine of the skies; / Her overpowering presence made you feel / It would be idolatry not to kneel." If science had come to probe, it stayed to worship. Crookes raised hopes in some circles and eyebrows in others. And he raised Florence Cook to the pinnacle of her field with the new séance sensation: the full-form materialization.

From the Fox sisters to the career of Daniel Dunglas Home, physical mediumship—the sort that can produce sounds, movements, sensations, or images, as opposed to telepathy or other mental phenomena—had been spiritualism's mainstay. But Home's retirement left a vacuum not easily filled. As one after another would-be successor was caught in fraud, interest in spiritualism faltered. The emergence of Florence Cook—and Crookes's validation of her—was thus a much-needed shot in the arm. Cook became one of three preeminent figures among the post-Home physical mediums, the others being a fiery Neapolitan peasant named Eusapia Palladino and an eccentric Frenchwoman whose *nom de séance* was Eva C. All would gain celebrity among spiritualists and nonbelievers alike, and all received unprecedented attention from some of the finest Victorian and Edwardian intellects, both scientific and philosophical. Cook's claim to spirituality of any sort came to be highly suspect, but the supposed supernormal powers of Palladino and Eva C. are hotly debated even today. Whatever the worth of the mediums, the scholars studying them were, by and large, beyond reproach. No one of their stature had ever probed the paranormal before. No one of their stature would again.

Florence Cook was not the first medium to produce full-figure materializations. Leah Fox Fish and D. D. Home had both done it during spiritualism's early days in America. Their creations tended to be rather wooden and withdrawn, however, saying little and departing soon. They had none of Katie King's accessibility, her vivacity and charm, her beauty. Nor had the imprimatur of science been stamped on their efforts by anyone of William Crookes's repute.

That is not to say that other mediums were wholly without distinguished patrons. The first English medium to produce full-form materializations was Agnes Nichol, later

British medium Agnes Guppy (standing, right) links up with two friends in this so-called spirit photograph taken around 1872; the blur drifting toward her is purportedly a spirit caught on film. Spirit photography was a fairly short-lived fad—most investigators thought it woefully easy to fake. Many critics took a similarly dim view of Mrs. Guppy's activities.

Mrs. Samuel Guppy, whose wonders converted the great naturalist Alfred Russel Wallace. Independently of Charles Darwin, Wallace had worked out a theory of evolution based on natural selection. But he was disturbed by his own findings. Although convinced that the theory was generally correct, he felt that the human mind was exempt from it. The mind, the human spirit, was a unique act of creation. So believing, Wallace found comfort in spiritualism, which seemed to confirm humanity's spiritual singularity.

Wallace was first drawn to Mrs. Guppy not for her full-form spirits, which began appearing in 1872, but for her "apports" in the 1860s. Apports were physical objects said to materialize out of thin air at séances, supposedly dropped by spirits. Mrs. Guppy's apports were lavish, and she seemed able to produce special requests on cue. When a friend of Wallace's asked for a sunflower, for instance, a six-foot-tall specimen with clumps of earth clinging to its roots plunked down onto the séance table. When the duchess d'Arpino asked for sea sand, it arrived replete with live starfish. There were cacti, nettles, live eels and lobsters,

hothouse flowers in snow, fresh flowers wet with dew. But none of these rivaled the medium's most famous feat—her apport of herself.

Mrs. Guppy was a woman of positively elephantine proportions, which made her so-called transit all the more remarkable. The story goes that she was sitting at her London home doing household accounts. She had just inscribed the word *onions* when suddenly she was apported two miles away to a séance being held by two of her protégés, Frank Herne and Charles Williams. She appeared on their séance table holding her account book, her majestic bulk swathed only in a dressing gown.

For all her acumen at apports, Mrs. Guppy's full-form spirit manifestations were suspect. And her character, rancorous and spiteful, left much to be desired. Some investigators would have nothing to do with her. One was the Nobel Prize-winning physicist John William Strutt, Lord Rayleigh. His spiritualist leanings cleaved to his Christian faith, and he was at first favorably impressed by the medium. But her venomous nature changed his mind. "Mrs. Guppy I don't think I could stand," Rayleigh wrote in 1874, "even in the cause of science." She was, for a time, the reigning queen of London's spiritualists—but a jealous one. The grotesque Mrs. Guppy particularly loathed petite and pretty Florence Cook, whose "doll face" she conspired to ruin by having confederates throw acid in it. This revolting story circulated among horrified spiritualists and transited Mrs. Guppy from the heights she had once enjoyed.

As her star waned Florence Cook's ascended. Florence began her career giving séances at her family's home in the London suburb of Hackney. The early sittings were unremarkable, their highlight being the appearance of presumed spirit faces in the aperture of the medium's cabinet. But her skills soon improved under the tutelage of Messrs. Herne and Williams, both thoroughly tarred as frauds by several investigators some time thereafter. The ghost of the mysterious buccaneer John King was the staple of the Herne-Williams séances—theirs and innumerable others; for some reason, the dead pirate had been a frequent spirit visitor

Popular English medium Elizabeth Hope—who took the professional name Madame D'Esperance, French for "Lady of Hope"—was an expert at producing apports, objects supposedly materialized by spirits. One of them was this large golden lily, said to be a gift from the medium's spirit guide Yolande, who was described as a young Arab girl.

ever since 1850, when spiritualism began to take root. Suitably, Florence augmented her mentors' performances by materializing King's daughter, Katie. Soon the new spirit was all the rage, and Florence went into business on her own. She did not take money for séances, but she did enjoy financial backing from a wealthy spiritualist named Charles Blackburn. His stipend was crucial, since Florence and her family were not well-off. As time went on several sitters remarked on the distinct resemblance between Katie King and her medium. But in the main, Florence's career went well until late 1873, at which time her ghost got grabbed.

Touching a spirit was an egregious breach of séance etiquette. It was thought that the spirit took its form from essences of the medium's body and that touching this substance could injure or even kill its source. (Cynics noted that such reasoning also ruled out the easiest way to tell whether the spirit was legitimate or only the medium or a confederate decked out in ghostly garments.) In any case, during a December séance, one William Volckman grabbed Katie and refused to let go. The spirit managed to pull out some of Volckman's whiskers while, with the aid of other sitters, she freed herself. Later, curtains of the medium's cabinet were opened to show Florence—disheveled, but apparently still securely tied up. Nevertheless, Volckman declared to one and all that Katie King was none other than Florence Cook in white drapery.

Volckman's bad manners were castigated and his motives rightly impugned (he would later wed the conniving Mrs. Guppy after Mr. Guppy passed to the Other Side). Still, Florence's followers were shaken. Worse, one of the sitters at the disastrous séance was her patron, Charles Blackburn. It is likely that he threatened to withdraw his support, for Florence searched quickly for ways to salvage her reputation. Within days of the Volckman affair, she decided, as she put it, "to offer myself upon the altar of science." Crookes's particular altar seemed ideal. The positive judgment of so eminent a man would be well-nigh unassailable.

Florence claimed to be seventeen at the time. (She was probably two or three years older; many mediums lied about their age on the theory that the innocence of youth made fraud improbable.) In any event, she was young and fetching. And Crookes, if old enough at forty-two to be famous, was also young enough to be vulnerable. The two had met at least once before, and perhaps she sensed that he, though married to a woman then pregnant with their tenth child, was attracted to her. Besides, Crookes already had strong spiritualist leanings.

He was first drawn to the faith in 1867, when his youngest brother died of yellow fever. Crookes started attending séances about that time. Nevertheless, when he announced in 1870 that he was undertaking an investigation of spiritualism, Crookes sounded like a skeptic. "I have seen nothing to convince me of the truth of the 'spiritual' theory," he wrote, adding that he intended to introduce scientific reasoning to the subject in order to "drive the worthless residuum of spiritualism hence into the unknown limbo of magic and necromancy." He investigated several mediums, and predictably, the one who impressed him most was Daniel Dunglas Home.

Crookes devised some ingenious experiments. For example, he put Home's self-playing accordion in a cage, so Home could touch it with only one hand. (It did, indeed, still play, even though the part of the instrument bearing the keys was inside the cage and outside Home's reach.) But it appears that Home generally dictated the terms of the investigation. It was an old dodge, begun by Leah Fox Fish and persisting today: The medium, pleading aesthetic, emotional, or psychic requirements, manages to exert sufficient sway over the experiment to influence its outcome. After a series of sittings between 1871 and 1873, Crookes concluded that Home was above reproach and that his phenomena proved the existence of a "psychic force." The scientist and the medium became lifelong friends.

So it was that in 1873, after Home left for Russia, Crookes was already inclined to believe, and he was looking for a new experimental subject when winsome Florence presented herself on his vacant altar. The two began a series of séances that lasted five months.

For Crookes, the real test was observing Katie King and Florence Cook simultaneously, thereby proving that the medium and the message were not one and the same. The scientist claimed to have accomplished this feat on at least two separate occasions. Although he purportedly also photographed Katie and Florence together, the faces of the medium and the spirit were never visible at the same time. Supposedly, Florence had to cover her face because she was sensitive to the strong light that the camera required.

To bolster his case for Florence's legitimacy, Crookes chronicled differences between medium and spirit: Katie was taller than Florence; Katie had long, light hair, while Florence's was short and dark; Katie's ears were not pierced, and Florence's were; Florence had a blister on her neck, and Katie did not. Yet, for some reason, Crookes never asked the obvious question: Did Florence have a helper who posed as Katie on occasions when the medium herself was not playing the role?

Florence was unmasked before Crookes worked with her, and she would be again afterward. Moreover, Crookes himself had cause to doubt her, especially in 1875, when another young medium he studied, Mary Showers, confessed to him her own fraud. Mary and Florence sometimes held joint sittings for Crookes, and it seems almost impossible that he could accept one medium as genuine when he knew the other was a fake. Disillusioned by Mary's confession, Crookes abandoned his psychic research and returned to his laboratory. But he never retracted his endorsement of Florence.

Maybe chivalry forbade it: The gentleman's code outweighed the scientist's ethics. Or perhaps vanity—a common affliction among scientists in those days of certitude—prevented his admitting that he had been gulled. But another explanation, advanced by several scholars, is that Crookes dared not expose Florence because the two had been lovers. Had she publicly revealed the affair, Crookes would have lost all pretense of scientific objectivity, as well as of personal honor.

Florence may not have been totally reticent, however. She reportedly told two subsequent lovers that she had been both a fake medium and Crookes's mistress. Still, she was not the soul of honesty on any front, and her confession must be viewed accordingly. The theory that she and Crookes were intimate remains plausible but not proven.

Crookes's investigations of the paranormal lasted only five years, yet he never lost hope in the possibility of an afterlife. Finally, bereavement—which had ignited his spiritualist belief as a younger man—restored him to it in old age. Whatever his eye for a pretty face, Crookes deeply loved his wife. When she died in 1916 after sixty years of marriage, he was desolate. Comfort came in the dubious form of "spirit photography," a spiritualist fad in which souls of the dead were supposed to appear in photographs. Almost all scrupulous psychical researchers were skeptical of the phenomenon, so easily could it be faked by double exposures and other methods. But Crookes was convinced his dead wife appeared to him through it. He began attending séances again and apparently died a believer in 1919.

As for Florence, her halcyon days as Crookes's protégée were short-lived. Her career grew ever shabbier, and she died in poverty in 1904.

Arguably, Crookes—and several investigators who came after him—were handicapped by their own integrity. Honest men and women themselves, they could not conceive of deceit as a way of life, which it was for a good many mediums. By the same token, the investigators were often ill-equipped to separate possible psychic wheat from fraudu-

The chemist and physicist Sir William Crookes was one of the most respected scientists of his day, despite the controversy surrounding his interest in spiritualism. The rumor that he and Florence Cook were lovers clouded his investigation of the pretty medium. Many séances that figured in this inquiry occurred at Crookes's London apartment building (background).

Looking remarkably like her medium, Florence Cook, the alleged spirit Katie King stands primly at the side of William Crookes. Crookes often photographed Katie during his investigation of her, but he did not want any pictures of the two of them together to be made public; this rare example was taken in about 1873.

lent chaff. Moral absolutists, they believed that to practice fraud was to be a fraud. There was no room for the possibility that somewhere in trickery lay a germ of truth.

That very possibility plagues modern scholars looking back at the career of Eusapia Palladino. Eusapia cheated, she cheated often, she even admitted cheating. But after her fraudulent phenomena were explained away, a residue remained, inexplicable happenings that raised the nagging question: *Did she cheat all the time?* And if she did not, how could the nonfraudulent wonders be explained?

With those questions alone rests Eusapia's abiding mystique, for she had none of the Fox sisters' novelty, Home's polish, or Florence Cook's allure. She was short, buxom, and unkempt; her only claims to beauty were her luxuriant black hair and expressive dark eyes. She was a child of the Neapolitan streets, coarse, earthy, and illiterate. Yet she sometimes reduced her presumed social and intellectual betters (for whom she often harbored sublime contempt) to awe. "E una Palladino!" she often said. "There is but one Palladino!" She was right; she was special.

Eusapia was born in southern Italy in 1854. Her mother died shortly thereafter, and her father was killed by bandits when the girl was twelve. It is said that even at that young age, she was already experiencing the poltergeist-like phenomena that often heralded mediumship: rapping furniture, invisible hands that tore away her bedcovers at night. The orphaned Eusapia went to Naples, already too fiercely independent to accept the kindness of adults who tried to befriend and nurture her. In her early teens she worked sometimes as a nursemaid, sometimes as a laundress, before finding her true calling.

It happened in an odd way. Living in Naples were a couple known to history only as Mr. and Mrs. G. Damiani, both ardent spiritualists. One day at a séance Mrs. Damiani encountered the ubiquitous ghost of John King, who said that a powerful medium named Eusapia had come to Naples and that he intended to produce wonderful phenomena through her. King even supplied Eusapia's address, and Mrs. Damiani sought her out and commissioned a sitting. No sooner had it started than John King made a spiritual appearance. From then on, he remained Eusapia's chief "control," or spirit guide.

Eusapia slowly caught on, though from the outset her séances were bizarre even by mediumship's broad standards. There were, for instance, her curious apports. At a séance where clients sat anticipating flowers, perhaps, Palladino produced instead a dead rat. And she had a disagreeable habit of apporting in reverse, as it were. Rather than materializing valuables, she made them disappear. More than one sitter was parted from a watch, or a hat or cloak, only to return home and find the missing object there—sometimes. On other occasions, the items simply "dematerialized" for good.

Then, too, there was the peculiar *style* of her séances. Eric J. Dingwall, the twentieth-century British anthropologist and psychical researcher, described with genteel restraint the "hysterical paroxysms" to which Eusapia was subject, her look of "voluptuous ecstasy," and the "brilliance of eye and smile of contentment which must have been singularly disconcerting to diffident sitters." After sittings, Dingwall wrote, Eusapia would "sometimes, in a half-dreamy state, throw herself into the arms of men attending the séance and signify her desire for more intimate contacts in ways which could hardly be misinterpreted except by the most innocent." This decidedly un-Victorian behavior led some of Palladino's earliest investigators to conclude that her psychic powers were a form of redirected sexual energy.

Eusapia remained a local oddity throughout her youth, but in 1890 she came to the attention of the noted psychiatrist Cesare Lombroso, best known for his pioneer work in criminology. Lombroso was a die-hard skeptic; nevertheless, he was intrigued by reports of Eusapia and agreed to hold two sittings with her. At the end of the second, a remarkable thing happened. The séance was over—it had not been especially impressive—and lights in the room were turned up. Lombroso stood with some colleagues discussing the evening's events. Eusapia was still bound with linen strips to a chair, which was situated about a foot and a half in front of a curtained-off alcove that served as her medium's cabinet. Suddenly, there were scraping noises inside the alcove. The curtains began billowing, and a small table poked through and inched toward the medium. Lombroso and his associates leaped for the alcove, sure it sheltered a confederate who was pushing the table. No one was there. Nor, apparently, was anything attached to the table that could be either pushing or pulling it. Still it glided, coming to rest only when it reached Eusapia.

Lombroso was confounded. He was unable to explain what he had seen or to deny having seen it—not that he necessarily accepted any spiritual agency. Following his own discipline, the psychiatrist posited that Eusapia suffered from some mental disorder, especially considering her bizarre sexual behavior. But the issue of the moving table remained. Whatever the cause, the medium seemed to have produced a legitimate paranormal event. Lombroso was convinced, and the legend of Eusapia, Queen of the Cabinet, was launched.

With rare exceptions, such as Wallace and Crookes, scientists had shied away from what they saw as spiritualist hocus-pocus. But Lombroso's conversion encouraged wider pursuit of the movement's elusive phenomena. In 1892, he and a handful of other eminent thinkers summoned Eusapia to Milan for a series of sittings. Always temperamental, she balked at certain conditions the investigators sought to impose. No, she said, she would not stand during the levitation of her séance table—one of her regular feats. The psychic effort of raising it made her knees tremble. She preferred to sit, she would sit, and she did sit, most likely using her knees and feet to lift the table.

In theory, one researcher or another was always touching both her hands and feet. But rarely could anyone swear he was in contact at all times. Eusapia did indeed tremble. She twitched and fidgeted. All the nervous movement enabled her detractors to claim that she was able to free one or more limbs during a sitting and that observers who thought themselves each holding a hand were actually holding two sides of the same hand. Those monitoring both feet were feeling opposite sides of a single foot.

Fraud? Probably. The lady herself held that when she was in a trance, she was apt to behave as her spectators expected. If they were looking for fraud, they got it, and it was their own fault. But even with a free hand or foot, could Eusapia have managed all the oddities they reportedly observed? Objects that were nowhere near her moved. Chairs—empty ones—gathered themselves around the séance table. Sometimes they ended up atop it, and twice Eusapia herself, still bound to her chair, rose from the floor and landed on the table. Sitters felt breezes from no discernible source and touches from invisible hands. Knots were tied and untied in pieces of string beyond the medium's reach. One investigator had his glasses pulled off his nose by an unseen agent. On another occasion, researchers turned up the lights to find Eusapia, still tied to her chair, wearing a coat belonging to one of them. When all was said and done, the Milan Commission, with only one dissent, endorsed her phenomena as genuine.

The lone dissenter was Dr. Charles Richet of France, a professor of physiology who some years later would win a Nobel Prize. An avid researcher of mediums, Richet was not at first convinced by Eusapia. But he was interested. In 1894 he invited her to the Île Roubaud, an island he owned off the south coast of France. He also gathered other prominent psychical sleuths, including Frederic W. H. Myers and Oliver Lodge, two leading lights of the Society for Psychical Research. The SPR, formed around a nucleus of intellectuals

The Durable Buccaneer

It seemed in Victorian séance circles that although various mediums came and went, the spirit of pirate John King endured forever. Believed to be the spirit form of Welsh buccaneer Henry Morgan, a dashing swashbuckler who died in 1688, King made his debut in 1852, only four years after the spiritualist movement began. From that point on, he was a staple of some of its greatest exponents, including the Davenport brothers and Eusapia Palladino. The secret of his ubiquity is unknown; perhaps the image of a virile and rakish pirate was titillating to the ladies who frequented séances. In a spirit photograph from a London séance (above, right), his burly head seems to materialize.

Morgan/King made his first alleged spirit appearance at the home of Jonathan Koons, in Athens County, Ohio. Koons and his family, who charged admission to their frequent séances, hosted not only John King but also some fifty of his relatives, including daughter Katie. The Koonses, whose dubious séances also featured raucous spirit concerts, soon faded from the scene, but John and Katie King moved on to further renown, in America and abroad. (In the lithograph shown above, Katie pays a spectral visit to an 1874 séance in Philadelphia.) Katie King gained her greatest fame in her three-year association with English medium Florence Cook.

Although John seemed an unchanging spirit, Katie evolved. In her early American materializations, she made small talk in a voice described as shrill and common. By the time she caught up with Florence, however, she had apparently mastered the art of genteel conversation.

A photograph of Eusapia Palladino, taken early in her career, captures something of the famed medium's appeal. She was at once earthy and imperious—the child of the street who rose to become Queen of the Cabinet.

from Trinity College, Cambridge, England, had been organized in 1882 to probe the paranormal *(pages 71-79)*. Polish investigator Dr. Julien Ochorowicz was there as well. All four men were widely experienced in arts of the séance; all had uncovered their share of fraud.

Eusapia could be hostile and unproductive when she disliked her investigators or her surroundings, but the relaxed informality of the little island, where four men danced constant attendance, suited her fine. She treated them to a broad cross section of marvels—most of what she had done in Milan, along with an array of mysterious luminous objects, phantom aromas, and apparently self-playing musical instruments. Most wondrous of all, she seemed to extrude from her body some sort of pseudopod, a third limb that could grasp and push much like a hand. For this protuberance, Richet coined the term *ectoplasm.*

There were times, to be sure, when Eusapia appeared to cheat, trying to free a hand or foot from the control of her investigators. If confronted, she took refuge in rage. "Here am I taking all this trouble to show you these phenomena," she ranted, her eyes flashing, "and you don't even hold my hands, so that I cannot do them normally; it is too bad!"

Despite the trickery, Myers and Lodge were much impressed. They asked SPR president Henry Sidgwick, a Cambridge professor, and his perceptive wife, Eleanor, to join their researches. The Sidgwicks agreed—reluctantly. They were highly skeptical of physical mediums. Nonetheless, in August of 1894 they set off for Richet's château near Toulon, where Eusapia was then holding court. In the ensuing séances, Mr. Sidgwick con-

Facing the camera, Eusapia seems to levitate a small table with an accordion on it, just to her left. At her right is German baron Albert von Schrenck-Notzing, who followed her mediumship for more than twenty years. This sitting took place in Munich in 1903.

at Frederic Myers's home in Cambridge. The venture proved disastrous for Palladino.

The affair at Myers's home was as much a study in culture shock as in spirit power. Into the ordered and refined world of the British intelligentsia dropped Eusapia, a walking vortex of chaotic vitality, blatant passions, and dubious appetites. She was crude, primitive, noisy, naughty, and woefully unconcerned with personal hygiene. Her hosts, if rattled, were unfailingly polite. They took her shopping at their expense. They played croquet with her. (She cheated constantly.) The venerable Henry Sidgwick, a paradigm of sober dignity, did his awkward best to flirt with her, knowing her fondness for male attention.

Still, Eusapia was sadly off her form. She was probably uncomfortable, and her insecurity was apt to manifest itself as imperiousness. She was the great Palladino. She would cheat simply out of scorn, to show she could get away with it, to show up this dull lot of snobs. To make matters worse, Hodgson all but invited her to cheat. Pretending credulity bordering on imbecility, the archskeptic relaxed controls on the séances to give Eusapia every opportunity to free a hand or foot. And, predictably, she took full advantage. Everyone saw her cheat. She left Cambridge in mid-September, not yet aware of how thoroughly she had failed. Myers and Lodge never quite gave up on her, but the Sidgwicks, who were the heart and conscience of the SPR, were purists. Eusapia had been caught cheating; therefore she was a cheat. In April of 1896 the SPR declared its findings to that effect and closed the book on her.

The SPR was influential. For a lesser medium, its denunciation might have spelled doom. Not so, however, for the Queen of the Cabinet. Eusapia had loyal supporters on the Continent, Richet among them, who defended her and denounced the SPR for shabby entrapment. Of course she cheated, they argued. When her powers were low, she often cheated as an easier alternative to expending the energy required for genuine phenomena. Investigators had already discovered this weakness in Milan, in Rome, in Warsaw. But was the SPR so blind as to assume that a free hand or

trolled Eusapia's right hand, Mrs. Sidgwick her left. Another observer lay beneath the table and held her feet. The room was always light enough for investigators to see the medium's every move. Still, Eusapia reportedly produced some wonders. One time, a large melon and a wicker table lifted up from behind her and alighted on the séance table. Also, a piano apparently beyond her reach sounded occasional notes. Even the Sidgwicks concluded that some of the phenomena were supernormal.

Another important member of the Cambridge group was unpersuaded, however. Dr. Richard Hodgson, an Australian-born lawyer, had not attended the sittings, but he felt sure his colleagues had been hoodwinked. It was thus decided that more séances would be held in the late summer of 1895 so Hodgson could see for himself, this time

Arms outstretched, Eusapia Palladino appears to levitate a table during a séance for members of the Society for Psychical Research. Ever watchful, the British society photographed the proceedings from two angles; here, the cameraman taking the picture has caught his colleague in the background.

foot could account for all the things she did? Did they not see that the very clumsiness of her cheating belied her being an accomplished fraud?

Eusapia went on to greater glories. In Paris she was investigated by a group of academicians that included Marie and Pierre Curie, who had just won the Nobel Prize in physics. The Curies helped devise elaborate monitoring systems to detect deception. But in a series of bravura performances that went on intermittently from 1905 to 1908, the fraud detected was outweighed by marvels. At one séance, a monitoring device moved at Eusapia's bidding before soaring over Pierre Curie's shoulder and landing on the séance table. ("It made a pretty curve," he noted.)

As the nineteenth century gave way to the early years of the twentieth, Eusapia was at the height of her fame. She easily held the record for the number of investigations she had undergone at the hands of savants all over Europe. Along with those already mentioned, there were, for example, astronomers Camille Flammarion of France and Franco Porro of Italy; Germany's Baron Albert von Schrenck-Notzing, a physician with an interest in abnormal psychology; and the eminent Italian psychiatrist Enrico Morselli. More like subjects than scientists, they sought her favors, begged for sittings. And, for a price, she obliged them all.

Finally, she even avenged herself on her Cambridge tormentors. Against continuing raves from the Continent,

the SPR could go on ignoring Eusapia only at the risk of appearing hopelessly closed-minded. Thus in 1908, three SPR investigators were dispatched to Naples. The SPR hoped to save face, however, by besting Eusapia at her own game. The men they sent were not philosophers or scientists, but experts on fraudulent mediums. Everard Feilding, son of the earl of Denbigh, was a self-described skeptic with an impressive record of debunking. Hereward Carrington had written the most detailed analysis then extant on sham mediums. Wortley Baggally was a practiced magician who claimed to have investigated almost every post-Home medium in Europe and found all to be frauds.

Feilding compiled a minute-by-minute account of the eleven séances he and the others attended. It described a panoply of Eusapia's psychokinetic feats and other wonders besides—the appearance of disembodied hands, of faces that seemed to be made of cobwebs, of sparkling blue-green lights that played about the medium, and of her strange pseudopods, which Feilding described as "curious black long knobbly things with cauliflowers at the end of them." The SPR trio was satisfied. Eusapia had waylaid her would-be ambushers.

But it was her last great coup. The Queen of the Cabinet was getting old. She had grown fat and awkward, and the incredible force of personality that had cowed and captivated so many was deserting her. A year after the Naples sittings, she set off to tour America—a venture that would prove her undoing. Breathless newspaper accounts of shipboard séances heralded her arrival, and blaring publicity accompanied her every move. In Europe she was the Queen, but America treated her more like a sideshow freak. Detecting her cheating was not a scientific pursuit but a challenging game: If Europeans could not dethrone her, Americans would show them how. Tired, dispirited, disgusted with sensation seekers who, as she put it, lacked "weight in the front of their foreheads," Eusapia was at her worst. She was caught in fraud again and again. She returned to Europe after a seven-month stay, and news of her failures preceded her. No longer sought after, she faded into obscurity.

The great Palladino died in 1918, her riddle intact. Was she merely a cheat, or was she uniquely gifted, a true medium who happened to be temperamentally inclined to cheat when it was expected or when it was easy? The great minds of Europe had not solved the puzzle.

If ectoplasm was born with Eusapia, it came of age with Eva C. Eva was as perverse and neurotic as Palladino was obvious and direct. But the women had much in common. Both, for instance, displayed vocal and visible signs of sexual excitement during their séances, though Eva's seemed less occasioned by males in her audience than by her female assistants. Also, Eusapia and Eva shared two well-known investigators who helped immortalize them: Charles Richet and the baron von Schrenck-Notzing.

In 1905, Richet was drawn to Algiers by reports that

Working independently, Baron Albert von Schrenck-Notzing of Germany (left) and Nobel laureate Charles Richet (right) of France investigated most of the major mediums of their day. Although more matter-of-fact than some of their British counterparts, these Continental investigators were, ironically, also more credulous. Both men endorsed Eusapia Palladino and Eva C. as genuine, while England's Society for Psychical Research had profound doubts about them.

In this 1913 photograph taken by Schrenck-Notzing, a Polish medium known as Stanislava P. extrudes ectoplasm through veils attached to her hands and face in order to minimize trickery. During a French investigation in 1930, Stanislava was caught in flagrant fraud.

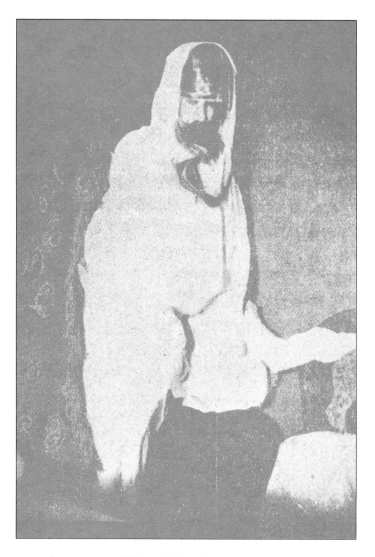

the daughter of an officer in the French garrison was a medium worth studying. In those days she went by the name she was born with, Marthe Béraud. Eva C., an alias, would come later. The nineteen-year-old Marthe was living with a French general and his wife, the Noels, at their home, the Villa Carmen. She had been engaged to their son, who had been killed in the Congo a year before. Now indispensable to the family as a medium, Marthe's specialty was summoning a full-form spirit named Bien Boa, supposedly an Indian Brahman some 300 years dead. But Richet also found she could produce "a kind of liquid paste or jelly," as he described it, that "emerges from the mouth or the breast of Marthe, which organises itself by degrees, acquiring the shape of a face or a limb." Ectoplasm, in short.

By that definition, Bien Boa himself was made of ectoplasm, in that he supposedly emanated from the medium's body. His appearances occurred this way: Mme. Noel would "magnetize" (hypnotize) Marthe. About half an hour later, with Marthe inside the medium's cabinet, a luminous white ball would appear outside its curtain. The ball would float a moment, then soar upward, and there—"as though issuing from a trapdoor," Richet observed—would stand Bien Boa. The spirit was sartorially strange. He wore a metal helmet with a dangling chin piece and long white robes with a cowl that pulled up over the helmet. His black beard had a distinctly glued-on look. He was more than six feet tall. At the end of a séance, his entire length would seem to sink to the ground and disappear under the curtains and into the cabinet, making a clunking noise as it went.

Richet photographed the spirit. Clearly, it was not the medium in masquerade; the two were sometimes simultaneously and wholly visible. Bien Boa would generally begin and end his appearances while the curtains of the medium's cabinet were closed. But in the intervening time, while the supposed spirit exchanged pleasantries with guests, the curtains were sometimes drawn open, and the entranced Marthe could be seen. Richet examined the séance room, its furniture, the medium's cabinet. He convinced himself that no confederate could enter the room or the cabinet unob-

served. He assured himself there was no trapdoor. Next, he concocted an experiment to show that the ectoplasmic manifestation had human attributes; for instance, it exhaled in the ordinary way. The scientist had Bien Boa breathe through a tube into a bottle of baryta water. The liquid turned white, showing the presence of carbon dioxide. The several sitters at the séance were so enthused by this turn of events that they applauded and shouted "Bravo! Bravo!" prompting Bien Boa, who had withdrawn into the medium's cabinet, to return for three curtain calls.

Richet found Bien Boa persuasive, all the more because fraud on behalf of the medium and her intimates was unthinkable. Marthe was an officer's daughter, after all, and surely General and Mme. Noel were above suspicion.

Be that as it may, fraud was heavily indicated soon after Richet published accounts of his work at the Villa Carmen. In February of 1906, a physician whose name survives only as Dr. Z. gave a lecture in Algiers on the subject of Bien Boa. The doctor said the dead Brahman was really an Arab named Areski, whom the Noels had fired as their coachman. Marthe had confessed to the hoax, according to Dr. Z., saying that indeed there was a trapdoor in the séance room, and through it the so-called Bien Boa came and went. Richet's response was profound outrage at being contradicted. Areski had never been in his presence in the séance room, the scientist declared, and to suggest otherwise was "so impossible that I have difficulty in believing that any person of common sense could be found capable of crediting it." He denied that Marthe had confessed, denied there was any trapdoor—denied, in fine, that he could possibly have been wrong. Even so, Bien Boa quit the precincts of the mortified Noels, never to return, and Marthe Béraud disappeared from the spiritualist scene—for the time being.

A short time after the Bien Boa debacle, the now-notorious Marthe moved to Paris and changed her name to Eva Carrière, or, as she was called in accounts of her mediumistic thaumaturgy, Eva C. Eusapia Palladino had always worked alone, but Eva preferred duos. She seemed to work best with a second party to serve as a sort of commentator and impresario. In Algiers, the role had been played by Mme. Noel (a lady who seems to have had no suspicion that she was being bamboozled). In Paris, the part went to Juliette Bisson, a sculptress and the wife of playwright André Bisson. Mme. Bisson induced Eva's trances

Amorphous masses of ectoplasm oozed from the mouth and other orifices of Marthe Béraud, who took the name Eva C. in Paris; eventually, the emissions featured faces, such as the one in this 1912 photograph. Critics thought some of the faces resembled magazine cutouts.

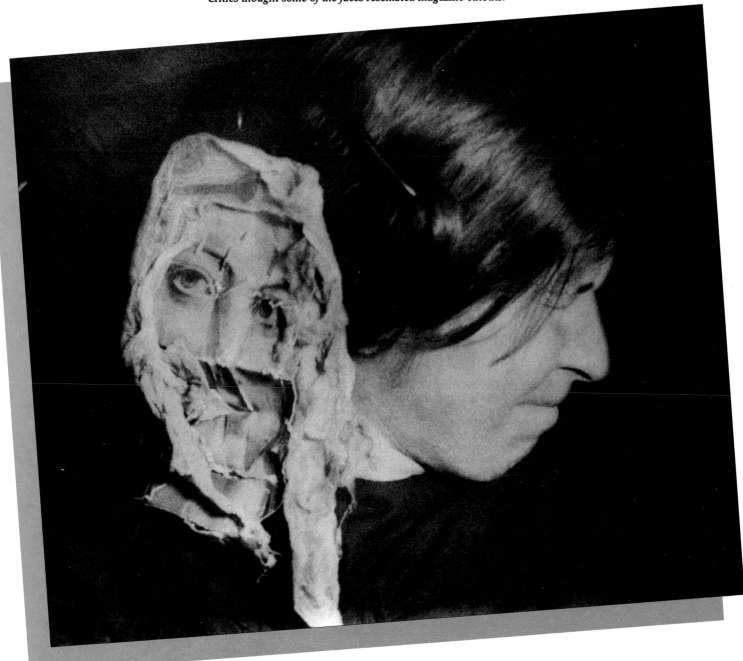

Clutching the curtains of her medium's cabinet, Eva C. (right) extrudes an ectoplasmic face. It was photographed in 1912 during a sitting with Schrenck-Notzing, who believed the faces, suspiciously artificial to many observers, were so-called ideoplasts—images conjured from Eva's mind. A 1920 SPR analysis showed the ectoplasm to be chewed-up paper. Whatever it was, it appeared even when Eva was strip-searched before séances and forced to wear a tight leotard.

and did running commentaries on her performances. She also wrote a book about them. The two were close, and by 1912, following the death of M. Bisson, Eva was living in the older woman's apartment. Mme. Bisson wrote of séances that took place there, with only the two of them present, in which Eva performed miracles that none of her investigators would ever see. With the possibility of concealed trickery all but eliminated—Eva was nude—she produced such curious phenomena as ectoplasmic pseudobirths.

Schrenck-Notzing began investigating Eva in 1909 and would write a book called *Phenomena of Materialization* detailing his research. (Curiously, though both Schrenck-Notzing and Mme. Bisson knew that Eva and Marthe Béraud were one and the same, neither wrote of the fact.) For most British investigators, spiritualist phenomena were inextricably tangled with religion. But Schrenck-Notzing, Richet, and other Continental researchers cared nothing for theology. They were concerned not with spiritual origins of physical manifestations, but with their existence and their nature. In Eva's case, strange excrescences of some sort obviously existed. They were widely observed and often photographed. What they were remains problematical.

In the earliest Paris séances, Eva produced a white-robed figure that seemed to be a replay of Bien Boa minus the beard. He soon departed, however, making way for emanations of a wholly different kind. Amorphous masses of white or gray material would appear to issue from various parts of Eva's body, most often from her mouth, and hover around her. It was an indeterminate substance, sometimes resembling smoke, sometimes sheer fabric. On some occasions it appeared light and airy, on others sticky.

Juliette Bisson, a close friend of Eva C., conducted the medium's popular séances in Bisson's Paris home from 1909 to 1913.

It seemed possible, of course, that Eva was hiding some material either inside her cabinet or inside her person, to be produced during the séance as ectoplasm. Later mediums were commonly found to have swallowed chiffon or some other substance for regurgitation during séances, and even more bizarre extrusions were also performed. But Schrenck-Notzing was careful about such contingencies. He closely examined the premises before every séance. He also (as Richet had before him) participated in a thorough and matter-of-fact search of Eva—the kind of search the British would probably have found unthinkable. She was then dressed in a tight leotard, over which went a coverall that was sewn to the leotard at the waist.

By 1911, Eva's ectoplasm was beginning to assume forms. Hands, feet, whole limbs were appearing, soon followed by faces, which usually took shape on the back of the medium's head. Later, they also appeared on the outside of the séance curtain, looking more or less attached to it. In some respects, the faces were considerably less eerie than the ectoplasm itself. Photographs show them looking two-dimensional and thoroughly static. Some are creased, as though they had been folded—which, quite possibly, was the case. Several of the supposedly ectoplasmic faces closely resembled those of living people whose photographs appeared in the magazines of the day. One critic noted that a materialized female head produced by Eva bore the letters *LE MIRO*. Might the head have come not from the medium's essence, but from the popular publication *Le Miroir?* Indeed, the phantom head and the published one were identical.

Schrenck-Notzing, in no way discomfited by this suggestion, had an ingenious explanation. He postulated that

Eva had a condition called hypermnesia—very acute memory—that was common among hysterics (which he and others considered Eva clearly to be). This condition was coupled, he said, with cryptomnesia, the ability to recall a mental image that had never impinged on her consciousness. Together, the conditions generated phenomena he called ideoplasts. Eva, Schrenck-Notzing explained, *was* producing images from her own essence. Quite naturally, they took the form of her own memories. Thus, if a spirit face resembled a photograph in *Le Miroir,* it was merely because Eva had seen the picture, did not realize that she had seen it, but reproduced it from memory while in a trance. Manifested in ectoplasm, the memory became an ideoplast. Eva's detractors opted for the more straightforward assumption that the medium was smuggling cutouts from periodicals into the séance room. They could not, however, explain how she was doing it.

Just as Schrenck-Notzing determined that no skullduggery was going on and that Eva's ectoplasm was genuine, Gustave Geley reached the same conclusion a few years later. Director of the Institut de Metapsychique in Paris, he took over from Schrenck-Notzing in 1914 after the outbreak of World War I limited Germans' access to France. Geley's work was interrupted in 1920, when Eva and Mme. Bisson received a request—tantamount to a summons—to visit London for sittings with the SPR. Given the group's aversion to physical mediums, the invitation itself was something of a coup. But the outcome was disappointing. Nothing happened in half the forty sittings, and very little in the other half. The SPR did, however, obtain a sample of Eva's ectoplasm. Analysis showed it to be chewed-up paper. The regurgitation theory was advanced. The SPR was not impressed by Eva.

Neither were investigators at the Sorbonne two years later, when a series of séances also proved unproductive. Soon afterward, Eva married and went into retirement. She was never the medium the Great Palladino was, but unlike her unfortunate Italian colleague, Eva knew when to quit.

Though less impressive than Home or Palladino, Eva has her supporters even today. The respected British scholar Brian Inglis, for instance, rebuts the regurgitation theory. He points out that Eva was often made to drink bilberry juice or coffee and eat cake before a séance. Clearly, these substances would stain anything anywhere in her alimentary canal. Nevertheless, her ectoplasm was almost invariably white. He also disputes the contention that cutouts accounted for all the figures Eva produced, noting descriptions from Richet and others of shapes forming gradually, slowly materializing into a final design. And, of course, the fact remains that in her day Eva was endorsed by one good scientist (Schrenck-Notzing) and one great one (Richet).

Sadly, the case can be made that scientists, however adept in their own fields, were not necessarily the best-qualified medium watchers. They were hampered not just by their own good character but by their faults as well. A bit smug in their particular disciplines, perhaps, they brought arrogance to their probes of the paranormal: If they, in their wisdom, could find no fraud, then obviously there was no fraud. (And even if there was, did a venerated master of science care to admit it in public?) In fact, there very often was fraud, and as later investigations would suggest, magicians versed in tricks of the trade were far better at explaining the workings of the séance than scientists were. Scientists were people who lived by logic, but logic is a doubtful tool for studying the essentially illogical—just as methods of proof may ultimately fail to unravel questions that are, ultimately, matters of faith.

And faith persisted, though the heyday of the physical mediums was over, by and large, by the 1920s. Eusapia and Eva had stood near its apex; they had also helped speed its decline. Some of their phenomena may have been genuine, but there had been too many fakes for most people to care what nuggets might gleam in the rubble. Besides, there were mediums of another sort to be studied, who seemed much more promising. For some time, more philosophically inclined spiritualists had been turning inward, looking not for physical wonders but for marvels of the mind.

Explorers of Unknown Worlds

On January 5, 1882, a curious gathering took place in an elegant London home. Sir William Barrett, a physics professor, had summoned some university intellectuals known as the Cambridge Group to discuss how to redeem psychical research from what one observer had called the clutches of "cranks and knaves."

The meeting led to the founding about a month later of the Society for Psychical Research—conceived to examine objectively matters that seemed inexplicable.

Barrett knew when he proposed the society that its founders would endow it with an intellectual and social cachet, fortifying it against the rebukes of a skeptical public. What Barrett probably did not know, however, was that each of the four who would form the SPR's core philosophy—professor Henry Sidgwick; his wife, Eleanor; Frederic W. H. Myers; and Edmund Gurney—had suffered, or would suffer, a personal crisis *(pages 73-78)* that would lend urgency to the quest into the unknown. For each of them, the issue of the soul's survival after death was nearly as important as life itself.

No one present that night in 1882 could have foreseen the strange directions the society would take or that its membership would soon include bishops, prime ministers, and renowned scientists. Yet each shared, as Frederic Myers would recall, "the consciousness that the hour at last had come; that the world-old secret was opening out to mortal view; that the first carrier pigeon had swooped into this fastness of beleaguered men."

Henry Sidgwick: A Crisis of Faith

The son of an Anglican minister, Henry Sidgwick seemed a most unlikely pioneer of psychical research. A shy young man with a stammer, Sidgwick entered Trinity College, Cambridge, in 1855, intending to follow his father into the church. Over the course of a sterling academic career, however, Sidgwick found his beliefs shaken by new philosophical and scientific ideas. He was particularly dazzled by the theory of organic evolution, as propounded in Charles Darwin's *Origin of Species.*

Gradually turning away from his clerical ambitions, Sidgwick studied history, theology, and philosophy in an effort to resolve his misgivings—all to no avail. Eventually, he began to explore psychical research as a means of reconciling religion and science. In this pursuit, as in all things, he proceeded cautiously. Said to possess "the most incorrigibly and exasperatingly critical and skeptical mind in England," Sidgwick became a lecturer in moral science at Cambridge on the strength of his outstanding scholarship and balanced opinions. His pupils, it was said, felt themselves to be like "companions of Socrates."

Slight acquaintances who mistook his shyness for aloofness sometimes found Sidgwick dauntingly cool and prim. But he invariably won the love, devotion, and unstinting admiration of those who knew him well. He was to many a tactful and patient mentor and to others an affectionate, good-natured, and unfailingly loyal friend. Above all, the earnestness of his struggle for faith was beyond doubt, his integrity beyond question. Myers and Gurney, who had studied under him, regarded him so highly that they agreed to become involved in the SPR only if he served as the society's president.

Sidgwick devoted forty years to psychical investigation. But it never brought him the religious certainty he sought, and he was far too honest to pretend that it had. Twenty years before his death, he summed up his dilemma: "I sometimes say to myself 'I believe in God,' " he wrote to a friend, "while sometimes again I can say no more than 'I hope this belief is true, and I must and will act as if it was.' " He passed away in 1900, convinced that his tireless exploration of the paranormal had been a failure.

Sidgwick probably would have smiled in sad agreement with the wry observation once made of him by the great Cambridge economist John Maynard Keynes: "He never did anything but wonder whether Christianity was true and prove that it wasn't and hope that it was."

Eleanor Sidgwick: A Brother's Death

Eleanor Sidgwick's efforts on behalf of psychical research were perhaps even more remarkable than her husband's; her interest began well before their marriage in 1876 and continued for thirty-six years beyond his death. Eleanor was the eldest of eight children of the renowned Balfour family. Two of her brothers—Arthur, a future prime minister of England, and Gerald, an outstanding philosopher—were students of Professor Sidgwick's at Cambridge, and it was in that connection that Eleanor met her husband. The two became the center of the Cambridge group, their home a gathering place for young intellectuals debating the ideas of the day. (A dinner guest once described conversation at the Sidgwick table as "a mountain stream, full and sparkling," but added that the talk had to be scintillating "to distract attention from the food." Apparently, the domestic arts were of little interest to Eleanor.)

She did, however, share bountifully in the genius that seemed to run in her family. She was a gifted mathematician and, along with her husband, a crusader for women's education. In fact, she and Henry campaigned for the founding of Newnham College, Cambridge's first college for women, and in 1892 Eleanor became its principal.

After her marriage she enthusiastically joined in her husband's investigations. But her interest in the subject had a deeper root than mere wifely devotion. In July of 1882—only six months after the founding of the SPR—her beloved younger brother, Francis Maitland Balfour, perished at the age of thirty-one while mountain climbing in the French Alps. The loss gave a personal impetus to her lifelong commitment to finding proof of life after death.

Young Balfour's untimely death grieved Mrs. Sidgwick, but there is no evidence it affected her judgment. Like her husband, she was cautious, a skeptic, a tireless worker who sought to amass voluminous facts before venturing opinions. Unlike him, after many years she came to believe in the human spirit's survival and in the possibility of communication between the living and the dead. Even so, her certainty appeared to do little to ease her sorrow. "Mine has been a grey life," she remarked in her old age. But she added hopefully, "I think grey is a beautiful color, and it has many colors in it."

Frederic Myers: A Tragic Love

Easily the most flamboyant of the Cambridge group, Frederic Myers had few friends and several enemies while at the university. Tall and plump, with a silky beard framing his handsome face, Myers struck one acquaintance as "medieval and lordly," with a manner resembling that of "a Venetian merchant-prince." He was rather humorless and pompous in his early days—a brilliant speaker, but with the irritating habit of maintaining his florid rhetoric even in casual conversation. A student of the SPR once said that among its founders, Myers's voice "rang, perhaps, the most sonorously of all, but to me he always rang a little false."

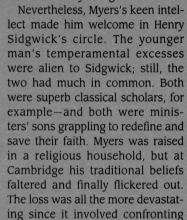

Nevertheless, Myers's keen intellect made him welcome in Henry Sidgwick's circle. The younger man's temperamental excesses were alien to Sidgwick; still, the two had much in common. Both were superb classical scholars, for example—and both were ministers' sons grappling to redefine and save their faith. Myers was raised in a religious household, but at Cambridge his traditional beliefs faltered and finally flickered out. The loss was all the more devastating since it involved confronting the possible finality of death, a topic that had preoccupied Myers since boyhood.

Even so, he might not have given himself so wholly to psychical research had it not been for the sorrow that touched his life in 1876. Walter Marshall, Myers's first cousin, had long been prone to depression and nervous fatigue, which visits to resorts and health spas did little to ease. Myers, who often visited Marshall, found himself drawn to his cousin's long-suffering wife, Annie. In time, the two fell in love.

The affair, probably a platonic union rooted in mutual sympathy, ended tragically. Marshall had to be committed to an asylum; Annie, burdened by years of living with her husband's erratic behavior, was despondent at realizing there was no hope for his improvement. On September 2, 1876, at the Ullswater home of her father-in-law, she slashed her throat with a pair of scissors and waded into Lake Ullswater to die. It was a crushing blow to Myers, who spent the next two decades and more seeking her through mediums.

The young Myers had been something of a mystic, though he grew more cautious and skeptical with age—less prone to romantic effusions and more passionate in his search for truth. He came in the end to a certainty, based more on faith than on proof, that there was a realm beyond the grave and that Annie Marshall was waiting for him there. Eager to join her, he rejoiced at the advent of his own death. As he was dying of Bright's disease, he wrote to William James that even the suffering was welcome, since it helped wean him from earth.

Edmund Gurney: Death on the Nile

The youngest of the SPR's founders, Edmund Gurney had much in common with his companions at Trinity College. He, too, was the son of a minister, and he, too, was beset by religious doubt. He was perhaps the most sensitive of the group and therefore the most emotionally vulnerable.

Gurney was popular at Cambridge. He was intelligent, handsome, witty, spirited, and most of all extremely sympathetic and responsive to the troubles of others. Nevertheless, there was a melancholy strain to his nature that became more pronounced over the years. When he was able to elude it, he was

capable of great enthusiasm and prodigious bursts of energy. But the happy and productive times were always followed by periods of depression and lethargy. Once during his undergraduate days, he suffered a nervous breakdown.

Gurney seemed to have every academic gift, but his great love was music rather than scholarship. Unfortunately, that was the one discipline in which his talent fell short of affording him a promising career. Abandoning the hope of becoming a musician or a composer left him even more depressed.

The greatest tragedy of Gurney's life, however, came in 1875; three of his sisters, touring Egypt, drowned when their barge overturned in the Nile River. He was close to all three, especially the youngest, and after their deaths Gurney was unrelentingly somber. He remarked once that "the mystery of the Universe and the indefensibility of human suffering" were never far from his thoughts. Human suffering, in fact, was what drew him to psychical research. His extreme sensitivity to the pain of others—undeserved and unremedied suffering that he seemed to see all around him—made him almost desperate to find some larger meaning to life and death. Eschewing any outside career, Gurney devoted himself exclusively to tireless work for the SPR. Among other achievements, he was the chief author of *Phantasms of the Living*, the society's massive study of apparitions.

Sadly, Gurney's labors did not resolve his perplexity and despair. He died in 1889, at the age of forty-three, in a hotel room in Brighton, with a sponge bag of chloroform pressed over his nose and mouth. He often used chloroform to relieve severe headaches, and an inquest determined that the overdose was accidental. But his colleague Henry Sidgwick confessed a "painful doubt" about possible suicide, and he was not alone in the thought. Whatever the cause, Gurney's death was a grievous loss to his friends, one of whom fondly recalled him as "the most lovable and beautiful human being I ever met."

CHAPTER 3

Messages from the Other Side

Philosopher-statesman Arthur Balfour, once prime minister of England, was old and ill. Death was near, and as he lay on the sitting room couch in his brother's country house one cool October day in 1929, he seemed to know it. He had the look of a man mindful of mortality's yoke and bearing it heavily, uneasily, as though after more than eighty years there was yet something in his long and productive life that was unresolved, incomplete.

A woman, a medium, sat near the couch, her eyes closed as she entered her trance. Lord Balfour's eyes were closed, too. He seemed to be listening reflectively to the Bach air playing in the background, but his still-handsome, patrician face betrayed a hint of mixed pain and longing.

The medium began to speak, so softly at first that Balfour had to strain to hear. She spoke of people she saw beyond death's curtain—a "dark young man," apparently Balfour's brother Francis, a brilliant Cambridge professor killed years before in a mountain-climbing accident. There was also a "beautiful lady," the medium said. "She's all bright and light, and she says to me, 'How long I have been waiting to send this message!' You know, she's trembling because she's so eager, and the dark young man explains to her that if the message is to be sent she must control her feelings. And you know she's so full of passionate tenderness that she can't and she keeps on saying 'Oh, my dear, oh, my dear, oh, my dear!' "

The words were coming now in torrents. "She wants you to sleep much more than you do, because when you are asleep you see them and are happy; and always when you wake, you forget," the entranced woman said. "But it doesn't matter, and she knows that you know all about her; and she's not troubling about evidence now—that's done with—it's just companionship. Deep calling unto deep. Such a longing to comfort and help, but under all the absolute certainty of joy.

"She's leaning down and stroking, like that," the medium said, taking Balfour's hand and stroking it. "And saying—and suddenly she tells me the most important thing she has to say, 'Tell him he gives me joy.' "

Throwing off a lifetime's aloofness and polite reserve, the old man suddenly seized the medium's hands with a fierceness belying his age and infirmity. His eyes glittered. He had always believed in the Christian notion of an afterlife, but now he did not merely believe that souls survive, he *knew.* He knew without question, and now death would be welcome when it came for him. Waiting for him beyond it was the woman he loved and had loved all his life—a woman who had been dead for more than fifty years.

The climactic Balfour séance was but a thread in a great psychic tapestry that came to be known as the SPR Cross-Correspondences. It involved as many as a dozen trance mediums and spanned some thirty years. Working independently and sometimes separated by vast distances, the mediums received cryptic messages—odd symbols, snatches of poetry, classical allusions—that often made no sense individually. But taken together, they acquired portentous form. They appeared to have been delivered piecemeal by seven discarnate intelligences, three of whom purportedly were, in life, Henry Sidgwick, Edmund Gurney, and Frederic W. H. Myers, founders of the SPR. Some of the messages were personal ones, as in the Balfour love story. In total, they also constituted a grand design for a new, peaceful world order. So compelling were the Cross-Correspondences that they convinced many one-time doubters of life—and perhaps even love—after death.

Remarkable as they were, the Cross-Correspondences were not the only works of trance mediumship making believers of skeptics as the Victorian age gave way to modern times. Even as the antics of physical mediums led cynics to dismiss spiritualism out of hand, a new kind of mediumship emerged. It relied almost solely on presumed mental contact between the living and the dead, and it produced phenomena that could not be explained away as fraud. Great mental mediums such as Leo-

nora Piper in America and Gladys Osborne Leonard in England were enigmas in their own time, and their riddles persist today. For decades, they proved again and again their capacity to know information not available to them through any normal sensory channel. And in so doing, they brought spiritualism to a fork in the road, with one branch continuing toward religion and the other going toward psychology and parapsychology.

Leonora Piper was in the vanguard of the new breed. She provided no pyrotechnics. In her sedate presence, furniture politely kept its place; no sheet-draped ghosts materialized; no ectoplasm extruded. The very decorum of her séances was a pleasant relief to the great Harvard psychologist and philosopher William James, who began sittings with her in 1885, when she was only in her midtwenties. By that time James, a founder of the American branch of the Society for Psychical Research (ASPR), had had his fill of what he called the "rat-hole type" of séance, which featured "holding a tricky peasant woman's feet." Indeed, willowy and attractive Mrs. Piper could scarcely have been more different from crude and lusty Eusapia Palladino, to whom James snidely referred. Mrs. Piper was very much a lady, her voice soft, her manner demure. She was born and bred in Boston, wife of a white-collar store employee, mother of two children. Her education was ordinary, and her mental attainments, to all outward appearances, were mediocre. But in her quiet way, she was even more extraordinary than the Great Palladino. No fraud was ever proved against her, and her investigators—the best in the field—invariably concluded that either she was communicating with spirits or she possessed extraordinary psychic abilities.

At a particular séance with James, for instance, she informed him that an aunt living in New York had died that very morning at 12:30. He knew of no such event, but on returning home he found a telegram that read, "Aunt Kate passed away a few minutes after midnight."

James was so impressed with Mrs. Piper during sittings in 1885 and 1886 that he wrote his colleagues at the SPR about her. Intrigued, the British group dispatched the wily skeptic Richard Hodgson to investigate—the very same Hodgson who had decisively debunked Palladino, among others. Hodgson arrived in Boston in 1887, confident of adding Mrs. Piper to his list of charlatans. Instead, he spent the remaining eighteen years of his life studying her, and because of her he died a believer, certain that human personality survives death.

James was never persuaded of survival. Nevertheless, he did believe that Mrs. Piper alone was enough to establish the existence of supernormal powers, even if *all* other mediums were frauds. Some years after meeting her, he wrote: "If you wish to upset the law that all crows are black, you must not seek to show that no crows are: it is enough if you prove one single crow to be white. My own white crow is Mrs. Piper. In the trances of this medium, I cannot resist the conviction that knowledge appears which she has never gained by the ordinary waking use of her eyes and ears and wits. What the source of this knowledge may be I know not, and have not the glimmer of an explanatory suggestion to make; but from admitting the rest of such knowledge I can see no escape."

Traumatic childhoods often figure in the making of mediums, but the life of young Leonora Simonds was unremarkable up until her eighth year. While playing outdoors one day, the child felt a blow on her right ear, followed by a hissing sound that resolved into the letter *s*. Then, the story goes, she heard a voice say, "Aunt Sara, not dead, but with you still." The odd event reportedly coincided with the aunt's death. Leonora was also troubled by occasional visions of lights with faces in them, but the phenomena had apparently ceased by the time she reached adulthood. At age twenty-two she married William Piper of Boston and settled down to normal housewifely duties.

Boston medium Leonora Piper was untainted by fraud, in part because she avoided dubious feats such as table tipping. Her one physical performance was a demonstration with flowers: She reportedly extracted their scent and made them wilt.

After participating in séances with Leonora Piper, the great Harvard psychologist William James declared that the medium possessed "supernormal powers" and encouraged his colleagues to study trance phenomena. Although James did not believe Mrs. Piper could communicate with spirits, he did credit her with telepathy and clairvoyance.

Her life changed suddenly about three years later, when after suffering minor injuries in an accident, she consulted a clairvoyant healer. Sitting with him, she apparently entered a spontaneous trance herself and was prompted to write a message for another sitter, a Judge Frost of Boston. The message purported to be from his dead son, and it impressed the judge more than anything else in his extensive spiritualist pursuits. He spread the word, and Mrs. Piper was soon besieged with requests for sittings. Bewildered by the sudden attention, she at first would accommodate only friends and relatives. She did, however, accede to a request to sit with Elizabeth Webb Gibbens. Thus did she reach the attention of one of America's greatest minds, for Mrs. Gibbens was William James's mother-in-law.

James was interested in psychical research, but then, he was interested in almost everything. As a young man, he dabbled in mathematics, logic, and art before taking up chemistry at Harvard University. Two years later he switched to physiology and eventually became a doctor and a physiology instructor at his alma mater. His special interest was neurology, and he became the foremost psychologist of his time. After doing landmark work in the field, he dismissed psychology as "a nasty little subject" and went on to other things. He had an abiding interest in metaphysics and philosophy, and his writings explored the human will, immortality, the nature of reality. He refined and made popular the philosophical method known as pragmatism, which held that the truth or error of any idea is determined by its consequences. There was a certain liberalizing innocence in pragmatism, since it called for a completely open mind and excluded no possibility from study; hence, James was quite at home with the psychical research that so appalled some of his fellow intellectuals. Spiritualism interested him little. But he was fascinated by the possibility of unexplored realms within the human mind. James's restless intellect was lionized both in America and abroad. So it was that when he discovered Mrs. Piper, her place in history was assured.

After his own visits, James sent some twenty-five other sitters to the medium, all under assumed names to reduce the possibility of her researching them ahead of time or connecting them with any information she might already know. Results were sufficiently impressive for him to write, "I am persuaded of the medium's honesty, and the genuineness of her trance," and "I now believe her to be in possession of a power as yet unexplained." The trances must have been genuine to some extent: While in them, Mrs. Piper could be cut or blistered or made to sniff ammonia without displaying any reaction.

James doubted that Mrs. Piper's spirit guides—a shifting procession over the years--were really the returning dead, however. He believed that the medium's powers were psychic, not spiritual. The first of the guides purported to be an American Indian girl with the improbable name Chlorine. She was soon joined by composer J. S. Bach, poet Hen-

Great mediums of the last 100 years have inevitably attracted the interest of psychologists eager to demystify their apparent communications with spirits of the dead. Undeniably, some mediums share similarities with people suffering from a pathological condition called dissociative, or multiple, personality.

First described scientifically in 1815, the condition was made famous by Robert Louis Stevenson in his tale of the normal Dr. Jekyll and his monstrous alter ego, Mr. Hyde. Its hallmark is the displacement of a person's principal identity by another personality with completely different characteristics. The alternation of personalities is beyond conscious control, and the victim has no memory of what the secondary personality says or does. The disease arises when in the wake of a severe emotional shock—often the loss of a parent or a tragic love affair—the victim represses certain memories and feelings. Symptoms such as headaches, amnesia, and insomnia hint that something is awry before the new personality appears.

The first medium studied in depth by a psychologist was Hélène Smith, who joined a circle of Geneva spiritualists in 1891, when she was thirty. Within months, companions at séances attributed a range of powers to her: In her presence tables moved, and she predicted the future and gleaned facts by telepathy. More riveting was the deep voice of a supposed spirit named Leopold who spoke through Smith during trances. He said that in an earlier life he had been Count Alessandro Cagliostro, eighteenth-century medium, alchemist, healer, courtier, and admirer of Marie Antoinette. Later, Smith said in a trance that she was the reincarnation of the French queen.

Before enthralled audiences at her séances, the beautiful medium acted out

Eileen Garrett (left) subjected her supposed psychic powers to scientific scrutiny to learn more about the mind. Versed in psychology, she suspected that what seemed to be spirit controls were products of her unconscious.

The Mental State of Mediums

dramatic scenes peopled with players visible to her alone. Smith sometimes became Simandini, alternately a sixth-century Arab princess or the fifteenth-century bride of a Hindu prince. Smith also spoke in a language she claimed to have learned on Mars.

A frequent witness of Smith's trances was Theodore Flournoy, a professor of psychology at the University of Geneva. Looking for signs of dissociative personality, he pointed to a childhood event he believed underlay her condition. One day she had been attacked by a dog but was rescued by a man who left the scene before she could learn his name. Leopold asserted that he was the rescuer and that he had been her guardian ever since. Flournoy also learned that throughout childhood Smith had experienced daydreams that verged on hallucination.

Flournoy's further probing revealed that Leopold could not understand Italian and knew little of eighteenth-century history. But the psychologist was stumped by Simandini. In that role, Smith spoke Hindustani and displayed a knowledge of Indian history and customs that nothing in her past seemed to account for.

In his 1899 study *From India to the Planet Mars*, Flournoy granted reality to some of Smith's psychic powers, including telekinesis and telepathy, but declared her spirit controls the products of her unconscious. Hurt and angered, she banished him permanently from her séances.

Hélène Smith had seemed destined from childhood for an extraordinary psychic life, but psychologists were hard-pressed to find anything unusual about Pearl Curran of St. Louis. She was apparently a thoroughly ordinary woman until July 8, 1913, when she, her mother, and a friend were amusing themselves with a Ouija board that spelled out a message: "Many months ago I lived. Again I come—Patience Worth is my name." It soon became clear that Patience, who claimed that she was a Quaker born in seventeenth-century England, sent messages through Curran only. Soon Curran was dictating Patience's lengthy communi-

nications as rapidly as her husband could get them down on paper. Over the years the poems, novels, and plays that poured from Curran's lips found an eager readership throughout the United States.

Professor Charles Edward Cory of Washington University, who had treated a patient suffering from dissociative personality, was intrigued by Curran and frequently attended her séances. In his view, Patience was the secondary personality of an intelligent, sensitive woman who had repressed her creative gift until she finally found an acceptable outlet. Cory, who never doubted Curran's honesty, knew that her education was sketchy at best. But he asserted that she could still have unconsciously absorbed the knowledge required for works set in periods as diverse as first-century Palestine and medieval England.

Cory's diagnosis was challenged by Walter Franklin Prince of the American Society for Psychical Research. He argued that before 1913 Pearl Curran had never shown symptoms, such as amnesia, indicating a nascent secondary. Nor could he unearth a trauma likely to have triggered mental instability. Prince also doubted

French-speaking Hélène Smith wrote descriptions of Mars in a mysterious language and script (above) during trances. Psychologist Theodore Flournoy claimed these "Martian" words were a product of her unconscious modeled on French.

that a person so ill educated and uninterested in history and literature could have possibly learned so much by unconscious processes. Although he thought there was "respectable evidence" for the survival of spirits, Walter Prince stopped short of declaring Patience a discarnate being. Curran herself apparently never wavered in her belief that the Quaker was a genuine spirit control.

Irish-born Eileen Garrett, Pearl Curran's fellow medium, did raise the possibility that the four voices speaking through her during trances might be unconscious aspects of her psyche. Two were personalities similar to Leopold and Patience Worth—Uvani, who claimed to be a medieval Arab soldier, and Abdul Latif, who identified himself as a seventeenth-century Persian physician. The other voices were not personages in the usual sense: Tehotah symbolized the divine word and Rama the life force.

Garrett did not doubt her other psychic abilities, demonstrating apparent feats of ESP and psychokinesis for such observers as psychologists William McDougall and J. B. Rhine. Nor had she questioned the survival of spirits since her girlhood, when the uncle who had raised her appeared to her weeks after his death.

Nevertheless, the uncertainty about her trance voices plagued her, and in 1957 she consulted psychotherapist Ira Pogroff. He learned of two devastating shocks—first the suicides of her parents in 1893, when she was an infant, and then the death of her surrogate father. After many conversations with her four voices while Garrett was hypnotized, Pogroff surmised that they were, as Garrett had thought, creatures of her unconscious. They allowed her to air ideas she would otherwise have suppressed.

A famous, respected medium, Eileen Garrett remained the skeptic until her death in 1971. Two years before, she wrote, "I prefer to think of the controls as principals of the subconscious. I have never been able wholly to accept them as spiritual dwellers on the threshold, which they seem to believe they are."

ry Wadsworth Longfellow, financier Cornelius Vanderbilt, and actress Sarah Siddons. But after a year or so, all of these supposed spirits were supplanted by a raucous, profane personality who said he was a French physician named Dr. Phinuit. He was implausible in several ways. If a real Phinuit ever existed, there were no records to prove it. His French was execrable and his knowledge of medicine scant. Nevertheless, he was at least a qualified success. Phinuit would usually come on the scene shortly after Mrs. Piper entered her trance. Her voice would become harsh and masculine, and there would issue forth slang and swearing utterly atypical of the prim medium in her conscious state. Phinuit's revelations about the dead were not always on target, by any means. But on a good day he could reel off information that sitters certified was accurate down to the tiniest detail, even mimicking inflections and gestures characteristic of the lost loved ones. Skeptics posed the possibility that Mrs. Piper was merely reading reactions of her sitters and elaborating on these clues to produce correct information. But such a method, most assuredly used by a number of mental mediums, could never be laid firmly at her door and could scarcely have accounted for all the detailed data Phinuit produced.

When Richard Hodgson arrived from England, his first order of business was to make sure Mrs. Piper was not using confederates or otherwise gleaning information about her sitters fraudulently. He had her and her family followed for several weeks, but bored detectives found only that her life was bland. (In an unkind moment, Frederic Myers of the SPR once called her the "insipid prophetess.")

Hodgson arranged some fifty sittings, taking care that all the sitters were strangers to Mrs. Piper and used either false names or no names at all. With some of them, the medium failed to enter a trance. At other times, the facts she gave were wrong. By and large, however, she delivered enough veridical or evidential information—data that could be checked and verified—to impress even Hodgson. And she had veridical messages for the investigator himself. She discussed his family in Australia, describing such intimate minutiae as his cousin Fred's childhood ability at leapfrog and the boy's untimely death from convulsions. It pained his self-esteem to admit it, Hodgson said, but he was convinced that the medium had supernormal powers.

Under Hodgson's auspices, Mrs. Piper visited England twice for testing by the SPR, which during the first trip in 1889 paid her thirty shillings a day. The niggardly sum suggested that, whatever her motives, she was not a medium for the money. In any case, it was little recompense for certain indignities she endured. When she visited Sir Oliver Lodge in Liverpool, for instance, that pillar of the SPR searched her luggage and examined all her mail. She did not object; indeed, she seemed anxious to cooperate in every possible way. The medium, who never insisted on a spiritualist explanation for her work, told Lodge she feared she might have some aberrant mental condition, which she hoped the investigators could diagnose.

No such disability was found. Instead, the SPR tentatively concluded that Mrs. Piper's psychic powers were genuine. Moreover, the investigators were satisfied with the medium's integrity, even though they thought Phinuit was a rather shady character. He was not above inane babbling and blatant fishing for information. The SPR concluded that Phinuit was not a spirit, but a secondary personality emerging from Mrs. Piper's unconscious mind. Whoever he was and whatever his faults, the SPR said, Phinuit when in good form could be uncannily accurate.

Lodge heartily concurred in validating the medium's extraordinary powers, having himself been the sitter at a notable exhibition of them. But he was not so quick to rule out spirit communications as a viable explanation. During a séance at his home in Liverpool, Lodge handed the entranced medium a gold watch borrowed from an uncle for the occasion. It had once belonged to the uncle's twin brother, who had died twenty years before. As Mrs. Piper handled the watch, Phinuit reported that its owner was a Lodge uncle who "had been very fond of Uncle Robert." After some fumbling, the medium produced the name Jerry, thereby correctly naming both uncles. "This is my watch, and Robert is my brother, and I am here," the control relayed. "Uncle Jerry" went on to recall some of the twins' boyhood adventures—swimming in a creek, playing in a field belonging to someone named Smith, owning a peculiar snakeskin. Lodge checked the information. His uncle Robert remembered the creek and the snakeskin but could not remember Smith's field. A third brother still living remembered the place well, however, and confirmed that he and the twins often played there.

These were not earthshaking revelations; nevertheless, they astonished Lodge. They suggested that if Mrs. Piper's chief gift was telepathy, it was telepathy of a high order. In the Uncle Jerry case, she could not have read Lodge's mind because he knew nothing of the particulars she described. For telepathy to be the answer, she would have had to scan the minds of two men living far from Liverpool.

In 1890, Mrs. Piper began a fifteen-year association with Hodgson, giving him almost exclusive control over her sittings. The result was a detailed record of séances spanning her most productive years. Early in the collaboration, something happened that caused Hodgson to scrap the telepathy hypothesis for that of spirit communication.

At a séance in March of 1892, a new control appeared. His name was George Pellew, or GP, a philosophically inclined young man who had been killed in a riding accident a few weeks earlier. A casual friend of Hodgson, Pellew had been to one sitting with Mrs. Piper, but he had attended anonymously, and there was no reason to believe she knew anything of consequence about him. Hodgson attested that the discarnate GP very much resembled Pellew in life. GP knew intimate details of Pellew's affairs and invariably recognized objects the living Pellew had owned. When 150 sitters were introduced to the entranced medium, GP recognized the thirty—and only the thirty—that Pellew had known in life. Moreover, GP adjusted the style and content of his conversation with each of them in ways appropriate to the individual's particular concerns. Unlike the odd Dr. Phinuit, whom he replaced, GP seemed real—real enough to

convince Hodgson that this was indeed a surviving spirit.

With GP at the helm, Mrs. Piper's mediumship took a new course. Along with relaying messages from the dead, the new control seemed adept at allowing them to speak directly through the medium—something Phinuit seldom did. Moreover, Mrs. Piper added to her repertoire automatic writing, in which purported spirits controlled her hand to inscribe their messages. At times, she even seemed able to transmit simultaneous messages from two spirits, one spoken and one in script.

GP held sway as Mrs. Piper's main control until 1897, when he was edged out by a group of controls known only by sobriquets—Rector, Doctor, Imperator, and the like. These presumed spirits were more concerned with solemn moral teachings than veridical information. James thought they showed a spiritual acuity beyond Mrs. Piper's normal range; still, the Imperator Band, as it was called, was less interesting from an evidential standpoint than earlier Piper controls. The Imperator group began fading away after 1905, when rather predictably, a new control appeared—none other than Richard Hodgson, felled by a heart attack in 1905 while playing racquetball.

Mrs. Piper died in 1950 at the age of ninety-one. By that time she had been fairly inactive as a medium for many years, although earlier on she had been one of the famous Cross-Correspondents.

One of Mrs. Piper's uncanny abilities, especially in her Cross-Correspondence phase, took the form of automatic writing containing classical allusions far beyond her educational level. In August of 1915, she reported such an alleged communication from the deceased Myers, who in life had been an outstanding classical scholar. The message was intended for Oliver Lodge, and it said, "Myers says, you take the part of the poet and he will act as Faunus." Mrs. Piper almost certainly did not know it, but the reference was to a work by the Roman poet Horace. In it, Horace thanks the god Faunus for protecting him from being badly injured by a falling tree. Lodge took the message to mean that some blow

Sir Oliver Lodge, shown here with his wife, risked his reputation when he launched an inquiry into spiritualism. Other scientists, ignoring his credentials as a world-renowned physicist and fellow of the Royal Society, denounced Lodge as a humbug.

The "Raymond photograph," one of spiritualism's prime documents, sealed Sir Oliver and Lady Lodge's belief that they were in touch with their late son, shown circled at right. Medium Gladys Leonard (far right), with no apparent access to a copy of the photograph, described it to Lady Lodge so accurately that it seemed as if the discarnate Raymond had to be Leonard's source.

was about to befall him but that Myers would come to his aid. On September 14, the prophecy seemed to prove out. Lodge got word that his much-loved son Raymond had been killed in the Battle of Ypres in Flanders.

Eleven days later, Lady Lodge accompanied a friend, a Frenchwoman living in London, to a séance with a medium the Lodges did not know. The medium transmitted several communications in French before suddenly breaking into English to say she had a message from someone named Raymond. The message was, "Tell father I have met some friends of his." Lady Lodge asked if he could name any of them. "Yes," the purported spirit replied. "Myers."

This message and subsequent related ones would convince Lodge once and for all of human survival, and he would write a book about the experience, entitled *Raymond*. The book made an instant celebrity of the medium who delivered Raymond's initial message, a woman who came to be known as the British Mrs. Piper. She was a former actress named Gladys Osborne Leonard.

About the time Leonora Piper was discovering her mediumship in Boston, Gladys Osborne was starting life at Lytham on the coast of Lancashire, England. As a child she had beautiful visions of landscapes she called her Happy Valleys, but she suppressed them when they incurred the disapproval of her wealthy, conventional family. The family suffered financial reverses just as Gladys was entering her teens, and she went on the stage, singing and dancing with touring theatricals. She grew into a handsome woman—tall, fair, and stately, with intense blue eyes. After marrying an actor named Frederick Leonard, she continued with her own career, and theater backstages were the birthplace of her mediumship.

It started in the old way of the physical mediums, with table tipping. Mrs. Leonard and two other actresses played at this diversion for some time with no results, by her account; but finally one day the table began to move. It rapped out purported messages from Mrs. Leonard's dead mother, among other spirits, before spelling a long and unpronounceable name beginning with the letter *F*. The presumed spirit gave assent to a shortened version—Feda—and thus Mrs. Leonard met the spirit guide who would see her through five decades of mediumship. Feda claimed to be a Hindu by birth; she also identified herself as Mrs. Leonard's great-great-grandmother, reporting that she had married young and died in childbirth at the age of fourteen.

Feda had a high, piping voice and childish mannerisms that were at once endearing and exasperating. Nevertheless, she avowed a serious mission. As the First World War neared, the control foretold the coming catastrophe and informed Mrs. Leonard that it was her duty to help people who would be left bereaved. Sittings were to be only with such individuals and only in private. Mrs. Leonard took heed and labored in obscurity in this manner for a time—until her encounter with Oliver Lodge.

About the time Lady Lodge first visited Mrs. Leonard, messages purporting to be from Raymond began coming through a number of mediums. One medium told Lady Lodge that her son was in a group photograph taken shortly before his death. The Lodges could find no record of the picture, but two months later, the mother of one of Raymond's fellow officers wrote to say that she had such a photograph and would send a copy. Before it arrived, Oliver Lodge had a sitting with Mrs. Leonard in which "Raymond," speaking through Feda, recalled the picture. He said that in it he was sitting down while other men sat or stood behind him. One officer, he said, was leaning on him. Feda added that the photograph was taken out-of-doors and showed a black background with vertical lines. When the picture arrived four days later, it confirmed the séance account in nearly every detail. Particularly striking was the fact that another officer was leaning on Raymond's shoulder. Raymond, Lodge noted, looked "rather annoyed" by the presumption. There appeared to have been no way Mrs. Leonard could have seen the photograph before relaying an accurate description of it.

Lodge published his account of the Raymond episode in 1916, and thereafter Mrs. Leonard was accorded much the same status and recognition that Mrs. Piper enjoyed. Like Mrs. Piper, Mrs. Leonard willingly submitted to SPR investigations, which began with Lodge in 1916 and lasted until the late 1940s. There were other similarities as well. Both women were deemed unimpeachably honest by most investigators. Both worked mainly by speaking while in a trance, using a so-called control as an intermediary to bring presumed messages from the dead. Yet with both it was difficult to separate supposed spirit communications from telepathic and clairvoyant feats. Both reported having out-of-body experiences in which their spiritual essences separated from their physical selves—a phenomenon that sometimes figures in apparent clairvoyance. But in some ways Mrs. Leonard was unique.

There was, for instance, the curious "direct voice" that appeared from time to time in her later séances. Feda, transmitting ostensible messages from beyond the grave, would be interrupted by a whisper that seemed to come from empty space a foot or two in front of Mrs. Leonard. The voice would amend or embellish Feda's statements. Acoustical tests could never determine whether the mysterious voice came from the medium or some other source.

Two other striking anomalies of the Leonard mediumship came to be called the book tests and the proxy sittings, both designed to segregate possible spirit messages from psychic phenomena. Legend has it that the book tests were first proposed by Feda herself. In such a test, Mrs. Leonard described a house she had never entered, then specified a bookcase in the house, a shelf in the bookcase, the location of a particular book, and a page number in the book. In a successful test, the designated text would reveal a message pertinent to a particular sitter. One of the most famous book tests was recorded by Lady Pamela Glenconner, whose son Edward Wyndham Tennant, known to his family as Bim, was killed in 1916 in the battle of the Somme. A great family joke among the Glenconners had to do with Lord Glenconner's passion for forestry. He was said to manage the woods of his estate with punctilious care, and he even visited Germany to study government-supervised forestry. The

Edward Wyndham Tennant apparently reestablished contact with his family through Gladys Leonard after his death in World War I. Following the medium's directions, relatives located book passages that seemed to allude to a joke known only to them, an example of the so-called book tests for which Mrs. Leonard was famous.

bête noir of Glenconner's near obsession was a beetle that preyed on trees. "You see all those quirks—those sudden bends in the new growths?" the lord was apt to say. "Those show the beetle has got them." The rest of the family regarded his preoccupation with beetles as an endearing eccentricity, and Bim was known to mutter to his mother, "See if we get through this wood without hearing about the beetle." If His Lordship was in a dour mood, his son would joke, "All the woods have got the beetle."

As Lord Glenconner sat with Mrs. Leonard in December of 1917, Feda delivered the following message: "Bim now wants to send a message to his father. This book is particularly for his father. Underline that, he says. It is the ninth book on the third shelf, counting from the left to right, in the bookcase on the right of the door in the drawing-room as you enter; take the title and look at page 37." The title of the designated book was *Trees*. On pages 36 and 37 were the words, "Sometimes you will see curious marks in the wood; these are caused by a tunneling beetle, very injurious to the trees."

Lady Glenconner, who firmly believed her son communicated through Mrs. Leonard, declared that the medium knew nothing of the family joke or the book's existence. According to investigators, this and other book tests indicated that to rule out spirit communication was to credit Leonard with telepathy and clairvoyance of the most extraordinary kind.

The proxy sittings carried similar import. In these tests, a stand-in would attend a séance on behalf of a third party, about whom both sitter and medium knew as little as possible. The arrangement seemed to forestall the medium's getting information by reading the sitter's mind. One proxy case, involving a ten-year-old boy who died of diphtheria, extended over eleven sittings. In this, the Bobbie Newlove case, Feda delivered a wealth of accurate data. She described a dog-shaped saltcellar the boy had owned, a masquerade costume he had once worn, exercise equipment in his room, visits to a chemical laboratory with his grandfather, a little girl the boy had been fond of, a nose

injury he had suffered. The control even described Bobbie's hometown, complete with place names. Strangest of all, Bobbie's spirit—if such it was—said repeatedly that some weeks before his death, contact with poisonous pipes undermined his resistance to the diphtheria that killed him. In connection with the pipes, he described cattle, a barn, running water. His family did not recognize the references, but an investigation turned up pipes in the setting specified—a locality where the boy had played. It appeared possible that Bobbie had drunk contaminated water from them.

Mrs. Leonard died in 1968 at the age of eighty-six. Among the many investigators who had monitored her work was Eleanor Sidgwick, who, like her husband, Henry Sidgwick, and her brothers, Prime Minister Arthur Balfour and Gerald Balfour, had served as president of the SPR. Mrs. Sidgwick paid special attention to the book tests. In 1921 she concluded that of 532 tests, "only" 192 were whole or partial successes. The one-in-three ratio, she noted, left open the possible objection that similar results might be had by chance. When that possibility was tested with nearly two thousand trials, however, the success rate was only one in twenty. "On the whole," concluded the ever-cautious Mrs. Sidgwick in 1923, "I think that the evidence before us does constitute a reasonable prima facie case for belief." By that she meant belief in clairvoyance—not survival. Only in light of the Cross-Correspondences would Mrs. Sidgwick come to believe in communing spirits.

A cross-correspondence occurs when a purported spirit communication through one medium corresponds in some inexplicable way to a communication through another who is working independently. For example, Raymond Lodge's ostensible messages delivered through several mediums constituted a cross-correspondence. But the SPR Cross-Correspondences were by far the most lengthy and complex interlinking communications in the history of psychical research. They were studied minutely by expert SPR investigators, who sifted through thousands of pages of complicated scripts. Eventually, the researchers concluded that the scripts were evidence not only of survival, but also of the ability of discarnate intelligences to show protracted design.

Three SPR founders who dedicated much of their lives to the question of survival did not live to see the turns such studies took in the twentieth century. Edmund Gurney died in 1888, Henry Sidgwick in 1900, and Frederic W. H. Myers in 1901. Shortly after Myers's death, messages said to be from him or from Gurney or Sidgwick began appearing in the automatic writing (and occasionally in the trance speech) of five women connected with the SPR: Margaret Verrall, a classical scholar and the wife of a Cambridge classics professor; Mrs. Verrall's daughter Helen, also a classical scholar, who later married psychical researcher W. H. Salter; Alice Kipling Fleming, sister of writer Rudyard Kipling and wife of a British officer living in India; Winifred Coombe-Tennant, who was well-known in British public life and was once a representative to the League of Nations; and Leonora Piper, the only professional medium of the group. Some of the women knew each other; some never met. Similarly, some knew Myers, Gurney, and Sidgwick in the men's lifetime, and others did not.

The Cross-Correspondences proceeded until 1932. Over the years, as many as seven lesser mediums joined the five main contributors. And four more purported discarnate entities appeared to complete the group of communicators from the so-called Other Side. One of them was Annie Marshall, the woman Frederic Myers loved in life and lost to suicide. It seemed the two were united in the afterlife. Another communicator was Mary Catherine Lyttelton, known to her family as May, who was Arthur Balfour's lost love.

Scripts allegedly dictated by these communicators through the various automatists (mediums using automatic writing) were fragmentary and extremely abstruse, often referring to obscure works in Latin and Greek—languages known to only two of the participating mediums. They were most often signed "Myers" or "Gurney." Taken individually, they seemed meaningless, and they went on for some time before anyone noticed that they seemed to be parts of some large and elaborate verbal puzzle. Once investigators began

looking into them, the scripts showed every evidence of having been designed by some person or persons intimately acquainted with the classics—as Myers, Sidgwick, and Gurney had been. The evidence was all the more tantalizing because Myers had once written that a good test of survival after death would be the combined action of a group, rather than an individual.

There even seemed to be forethought in matters extrinsic to the messages' actual content. For instance, Mrs. Fleming in India was producing scripts from "Myers" for quite some time before she was aware that mediums elsewhere were doing the same thing. One script instructed her to send it to 5 Selwyn Gardens, Cambridge, England. She had never visited the city and did not recognize the indicated address—which turned out to be that of Margaret Verrall. Mrs. Verrall was the first medium to try automatic writing in hopes of summoning Myers's spirit.

Eventually, all the Cross-Correspondences were funneled through the SPR, where investigators such as Eleanor Sidgwick and her brother Gerald Balfour painstakingly pieced them together. It was hard work. The scripts were disjointed, freighted with symbolism. It was as though the dead were in no hurry for the living to solve the puzzle but were being deliberately obscure in order to force a continuing accumulation of evidence. The communicators also suggested that they were taking care to be cryptic lest some easily accessible phrase trigger a medium's own associations, causing her to inject misleading matter into the scripts. Perhaps, too, the difficulty of bridging two worlds was sufficient in itself to cloud communications. The discarnate Myers likened the process to "standing behind a sheet of frosted glass—which blurs sight and deadens sound—dictating feebly—to a reluctant and somewhat obtuse secretary." And "Gurney" spoke of "the passionate desire to drive into incarnate minds the conviction of one's own identity, the partial successes and the blank failures."

Some skeptics have said that the SPR investigators of the Cross-Correspondences unconsciously read sense and

A Ghostly Jigsaw Puzzle

Working through medium Leonora Piper, an SPR researcher asked the presumed spirit of Frederic Myers to inscribe a triangle within a circle to manifest his presence in cross-correspondence scripts. Shortly thereafter, the Myers spirit ended a script by a different medium with the two drawings that are shown above.

As a prober of the paranormal, Frederic W. H. Myers was a pioneering spirit—perhaps literally. Myers did landmark labor for the Society for Psychical Research before his death in 1901. Afterward, a supposedly discarnate Myers seemed bent on keeping up the work, this time as ringleader of a band of disembodied intelligences who were thought to communicate through the automatic writing *(pages 92-99)* of several mediums. The eerie messages, called scripts, became known as the SPR Cross-Correspondences.

The name referred to the apparent fact that related information turned up in the scripts of mediums working independently, each unaware of the content of her colleagues' writings. Some correspondences seemed to deal with weighty themes. Others involved no meaning other than the one implied by the mere fact of their existence: that human intelligence not only survives death but also is capable of elaborate communication with the living.

Between 1901 and 1930, the SPR accumulated some 3,000 scripts. Some contained private information about various people and were buried in the SPR archives, marked for public release in 1996. But the remaining scripts, comprising thousands of pages, were the subject of years of collection, collation, annotation, and study by diligent SPR scholars.

Certainly, scholarship was required to decipher the scripts, whose import usually hinged on obscure literary references and complicated symbols. The spirit "Myers" puckishly called them "a tangle for your unravelling." The tangle's staggering complexity has defied the best academic efforts to simplify or summarize it. But some notion of its nature can be discovered from examining the high points of a comparatively simple correspondence known as the Hope, Star, and Browning Case.

It began on December 3, 1906, when medium Alice Kipling Fleming, living in India, inscribed a purported message from Myers that contained the words, "Ah Starry hope that didst arise / But to be overcast." The lines were from Edgar Allan Poe's poem "To One in Paradise." Investigators would later find significance in the references to stars and hope and in the allusion to a moon—the light that overshadows the starry hope in Poe's work. On December 4, Mrs. Fleming wrote another script, this one containing quotations in which the word "hope" appeared twice.

On January 16, 1907, thousands of miles away, the American medium Leonora Piper was in England conducting a séance for the SPR. While she was in an apparent trance state during the session,

SPR researcher J. G. Piddington addressed Myers through her, asking him to give some sign when a cross-correspondence was being attempted. Piddington suggested a triangle within a circle. A week later, Myers's supposed answer came in a script by Margaret Verrall, a Cambridge medium. "An anagram would be better," Mrs. Verrall's Myers decreed. "Tell him that—rats, star, tars and so on . . ." (In life, Myers had been extremely fond of anagrams.) He suggested two more anagrams, "tears" and "stare," and went on to say, "but the letters you should give tonight are not so many—only three . . . a s t."

In a script written by Mrs. Verrall on January 28, Myers appeared to take up where he had left off. He wrote "Aster" (Greek for "star") and anagrammed it "Teras" (Greek for "wonder"). The two words seemed to set off a free association on the themes "wonder" and "star." Myers went on at some length, stitching together poetic lines in both Greek and English about wonder, hope, love, and desire. In addition, the script made special mention of the Robert Browning poem "Abt Vogler." The subject of the poem was Abt, or Abbe, Georg Joseph Vogler, an eighteenth-century German musician. In the complex work, Browning makes music a kind of spiritual metaphor for the cosmic scheme—"the music of the spheres," as it were. The poem mentions stars, moons, and hope. It also contains the line, "On the earth the broken arcs; in the heaven, a perfect round."

The poetic arc image may have figured in the conclusion to the next Myers message through Mrs. Verrall. Significantly, it was signed with two drawings—one of a triangle within a circle, just as Piddington had suggested through Mrs. Piper, and another of a triangle within an arc. Myers seemed to be accommodating

the request that he signal when a cross-correspondence was in progress.

On February 3, the Myers spirit appeared to turn up in the script of a fourth medium, Mrs. Verrall's daughter, Helen. This script contained a number of drawings, including a star and a crescent moon, which were accompanied by the admonition, "The crescent moon, remember that, and the star."

On February 11, the spirit communicator was back with Mrs. Piper. He seemed to want to make clear his own certain knowledge—and therefore his authorship—of previous messages through other mediums. Through Mrs. Piper, he discussed the January 28 script of Margaret Verrall: "I referred to Hope and Browning," the Piper script asserted. "I also said star . . . look out for Hope, Star, and Browning."

On February 17, the Browning theme resurfaced in a script by Helen Verrall. The spirit Myers drew a star, then wrote: "That was the sign she [Margaret Verrall] will understand when she sees it . . . No arts avail . . . and a star above it all *rats* everywhere in Hamelin town . . ." The spirit seemed to be returning to his game of anagrams with "arts," "star," and "rats." The "Hamelin town" referred to a Browning poem about the Pied Piper of Hamelin. This reference, in turn, was most probably also a pun on the medium Leonora Piper's name. (The living Myers had loved puns almost as much as he did anagrams; the Cross-Correspondences are full of them.)

The Hope, Star, and Browning Case ended with three scripts from Mrs. Piper's Myers. The first, on March 6, noted that he had included the triangle and circle in Margaret Verrall's previous script. A week later, the communicator mentioned the emblem again and added that it "suggested a poem to my mind, hence BHS"

(that is, Browning, Hope, Star).

In this last remark, according to investigators, Myers may have been giving the key to the case, outlining the postmortem thought processes responsible for it all: Judging from the earliest script, the one written by Mrs. Fleming in India, the notions of stars and hope were already present in Myers's mind. Piddington's subsequent suggestion that cross-correspondences be indicated by a circle and triangle triggered new associations—passages from Browning, along with related anagrams, such as "star" and "rats." Myers went on to develop these particular themes, among others, in the scripts of two more mediums, Margaret and Helen Verrall, before returning to Mrs. Piper with an explanation of what he had done.

The case's final communication came through Mrs. Piper on April 8, 1907, when the supposed Myers, as though wanting to make certain that no one was missing the point, stressed again that in a previous script he had drawn a star and a crescent moon.

Whether the dead Frederic Myers was the true source of these and other cross-correspondences remains an unanswered question to most people who have studied the case. And if he was, they ask, did the pioneering spirit intend to hint at some meaning in "Hope, Star, and Browning" beyond the considerable mystery inherent in the mere fact of the scripts themselves?

Perhaps there is a clue to be found in "Abt Vogler," in which the poet reflects on the afterlife—the existence of which Myers, in this world or the next, seemed so eager to prove. Browning speaks of "the wonderful Dead who have passed through the body and gone, / But were back once more to breathe in an old world worth their new."

	Alice Fleming	Margaret Verrall	Helen Verrall	Leonora Piper
STAR	Dec. 3, 1906 Dec. 19, 1906 Mar. 20, 1907	Dec. 17, 1906 Jan. 23, 1907 Jan. 28, 1907	Feb. 3, 1907 Feb. 17, 1907	Feb. 11, 1907 Feb. 27, 1907 Mar. 6, 1907 Mar. 13, 1907 Mar. 20, 1907 Apr. 8, 1907
HOPE	Dec. 3, 1906 Dec. 4, 1906 Dec. 19, 1906	Jan. 28, 1907		Feb. 11, 1907 Feb. 27, 1907 Mar. 6, 1907 Mar. 13, 1907 Mar. 20, 1907
BROWNING	Dec. 4, 1906 Dec. 19, 1906 Mar. 20, 1907	Jan. 28, 1907	Feb. 3, 1907 Feb. 17, 1907	Feb. 11, 1907 Feb. 27, 1907 Mar. 6, 1907 Mar. 13, 1907 Mar. 20, 1907
LOVE	Dec. 4, 1906 Dec. 19, 1906 Mar. 20, 1907	Jan. 28, 1907		
BIRD		Jan. 28, 1907	Feb. 3, 1907	Mar. 6, 1907
MOON	Dec. 3, 1906 Mar. 20, 1907	Feb. 3, 1907	Apr. 8, 1907	
PARADISE OR SKY	Dec. 3, 1906 Mar. 20, 1907	Jan. 28, 1907		Mar. 6, 1907
MUSIC OF THE SPHERES	Dec. 19, 1906 Mar. 20, 1907	Dec. 17, 1906 Jan. 28, 1907	Feb. 17, 1907	

The SPR made intricate tables to keep track of seeming concordances in the Cross-Correspondences. This variation on an SPR chart shows how themes and subthemes of the Hope, Star, and Browning Case were tracked. It notes the dates on which recurrent topics appeared in the scripts of the various mediums.

order into them. Wishfulness would be understandable, given the years they had expended in the study of survival after death. But there is reason to discount this explanation. The integrity of Eleanor Sidgwick and the others was unassailable. And although the correspondences were cryptic and fragmentary, their ultimate import was an amazingly cohesive and complete one. They set forth a plan for a harmonious world order for which the Roman Empire's Pax Romana served as an imperfect model.

In life, Myers had been a great student and admirer of Rome. At the end of his book *Human Personality,* he compared the "nascent race of Rome" to "the whole nascent race of man." It seemed that the postmortem Myers was thinking in much the same vein when, on March 2, 1906, he supposedly dictated a script to Mrs. Verrall in Cambridge containing a line of Latin verse from Vergil's *Aeneid.* The line was part of a narrative of the fall of Troy. (The *Aeneid* recounts how Aeneas, a royal Trojan fleeing his city's fall, goes on to found Rome.) In that script and two more written on March 4 and 5, there are references to several Roman emperors, to the Roman persecution of the Christians, and to certain Roman Catholic popes who were important to the history of Christianized Rome. In short, the three scripts seemed to present a thumbnail history of Rome.

Two days after the last Verrall script in this series, Mrs. Fleming, thousands of miles away in India, produced a script that seemed to take up the theme. It included the words: *"Ave Roma immortalis.* [Hail, immortal Rome.] How could I make it any clearer without giving her the clue?"

The *Ave Roma immortalis* case, as this came to be called, was one small hint in the pervading theme of a new world order that would reflect the old. The new order was to be promoted by a great number of disembodied intellects, of which Myers, Gurney, and the other five communicators were members and prophets. Their minions among the living would be a new race, the "children of the spirit," they said, who would suffer through world wars and other catastrophes to bring about the prophesied utopia.

Interwoven in the grand design of the Cross-Correspondences were smaller, intimate themes, among them the eerily lovely Palm Sunday love story—a tale involving two privileged, distinguished British families, the Balfours and the Lytteltons. Arthur Balfour was one of eight children, Mary Catherine Lyttelton one of twelve. The young people of both families moved in the same social circles and were linked by friendship and sometimes by marriage. It was as though the outgoing, fun-loving Lytteltons held some special attraction for the Balfours, who tended to be somewhat shy, serious, and reserved.

Arthur met Mary in 1871 at a Christmas ball at the home of her uncle, Prime Minister William Gladstone, and fell in love with her at once. She was not beautiful, aside from her abundant, gold-streaked hair. But her gaiety, wit, and ardent nature attracted many beaux. For her part, Mary thought young Balfour brilliant, good-hearted, and charming, if a trifle cautious and withdrawn for her taste. It seems she was not in love, at least at first, but the two shared a deepening friendship. Matters went on that way for some four years, for Arthur was indeed cautious. No doubt he felt there was plenty of time to woo Mary and wed her. There was not. He finally spoke to her of his love in 1875, and apparently the two shared an understanding, if not yet a

formal engagement. But Mary contracted typhoid fever. The illness went on for several withering weeks. In delirium, she spoke of Arthur in ways that showed she had come to reciprocate his love—too late. On Palm Sunday of 1875, she died.

Although Balfour kept his grief to himself, Mary's death turned his bright world to ashes. He gave her sister Lavinia an emerald ring that had belonged to his mother, asking that Mary be buried with it. Mary's glorious hair had been shorn during her illness, and he commissioned a silver casket, lined with purple and engraved with periwinkle and other spring flowers, to hold a lock. The casket was inscribed with two verses taken from I Corinthians: "For this corruptible must put on incorruption and this mortal must put on immortality. But when this corruptible shall have put on incorruption and this mortal shall have put on immortality, then shall come to pass the saying that is written, Death is swallowed up in victory."

Balfour wrote to Lavinia's husband, "I think—I am nearly sure—that she must have grasped my feelings towards her . . . now, perhaps, when she watches the course of those she loved who are still struggling on earth, I may not be forgotten." He went on to a long, illustrious career of public service. But he never married. And every year until his death, unless affairs of state intruded, he spent Palm Sunday in seclusion with Mary's sister.

The Cross-Correspondences are replete with suggestions that Mary's spirit survived and tried over many years to communicate to Balfour her enduring love. The clues came in scripts from four automatists—Helen and Margaret Verrall, Mrs. Fleming, and Mrs. Coombe-Tennant. There is no evidence that any of them knew of the old love affair. In fact, hardly anyone outside the Balfour and Lyttelton families knew of it, and many family members were ignorant of details. However much the public man, Balfour was almost obsessively private about his personal feelings. The Balfour family honored his privacy. The Palm Sunday scripts were kept secret for many years. They were eventually bequeathed to Balfour's niece by marriage, Jean,

Various telling details persuaded Arthur Balfour (right) that Mary Lyttelton was sending him messages through the Palm Sunday scripts. He linked repeated references to candles and candlesticks, for instance, with a photograph showing Mary holding a candle (below).

Countess Balfour, who decided to have them published through the SPR in 1960.

Assuming that the Cross-Correspondences were exactly what they purported to be—messages from the dead—it appears that Mary had tried to make herself known almost from the time the scripts began. But for some ten years, her messages were lost in obscurity or swallowed up in larger themes, as though her voice were not yet strong enough to reach the living. In 1912, however, the scripts of Mrs. Coombe-Tennant began insisting that Gerald Balfour, Arthur's brother, sit with the medium. He did, and—on Palm Sunday—the scripts began to fill with Mary's presence. In July came what seemed to be a poignant cry from Mary through the medium: "Oh, look back, she says . . . Far back I came—years ago I have been beating at this door. Shall I ever reach him?"

Had the SPR researchers then heeded the call to look back, they would have found many allusions to Mary in earlier scripts from the various mediums. There were, for example, mentions of the Palm Maiden, May Blossom, the Blessed Damozel, and Berenice. (Palm was for the day of her death; May was her family's affectionate name for her; the Blessed Damozel in Dante Gabriel Rossetti's poem was a dead maiden who waits in heaven for her lover; the Berenice of legend was famous for sacrificing her beautiful hair.) There had also been references to a candle and a candlestick (a haunting photograph of Mary showed her with a candlestick), to a metal box, and to purple, periwinkle, and a lock of hair (Balfour's silver casket and its contents). After Gerald Balfour joined the sittings, the allusions continued and expanded. Mentioned were Palm Sunday, a sister's death, old graves, emeralds. There were phrases such as "She was carrying a candle, Madonna della Candela" and references to the Arthur in Alfred Lord Tennyson's *Idylls of the King* and *Ode on the Death of the Duke of Wellington.* (Arthur Balfour was sometimes jokingly called King Arthur by his friends. He had been named for the Duke of Wellington, who was his

godfather.) Clues continued to mount over the next four years. But it was not until 1916 that the disparate parts of Mary's message began to take form for the investigators. After passionate pleas in Mrs. Coombe-Tennant's scripts, Arthur Balfour himself agreed to sit with her.

The séances were, of course, emotional for Balfour. He immediately recognized clues unreadable to anyone else, for hardly anyone else knew their significance. (Only then, for example, did he tell his brother Gerald about the silver casket and the lock of hair.) And he could not have failed to be moved by such passionate communications as Mary's quoting from *Sonnets from the Portuguese* by Elizabeth Barrett Browning: "And if God will I shall but love thee better after death."

But in all the long years, Balfour had not lost his caution. Like his sister Eleanor, he had the habit of skepticism. Nevertheless, as time passed and evidence amassed he edged ever closer to acceptance. Finally, that October day in 1929, belief came.

There is no way of knowing all that transpired between Arthur Balfour and Mary Lyttelton when both were young and life burgeoned with promise. Perhaps his love at first outstripped hers because she did not sense beneath his cool surface a nature as passionate as her own. Perhaps she taxed him with it, asking where in all his rational brilliance lay the joy that so suffused her life. Whatever the case, the phrase "Tell him he gives me joy" must have meant something to him alone, breaching some final wall of doubt. A few months later, Balfour had a stroke, and after lingering a few days, he died. His niece Jean, who was with him during his last illness, knew nothing of the Palm Sunday case at the time. Still, she had the sense that he met death joyfully.

Arthur Balfour once wrote in sympathy to a friend who had lost a loved one. "The pain is indeed hard to bear," the letter said, "too hard it sometimes seems for human strength. Yet, measured on the true scale of things it is but brief; death cannot long cheat us of love."

A silver box containing a lock of Mary Lyttelton's hair was Arthur Balfour's secret for forty years.

CHAPTER 4

The Witch of Lime Street

ir Arthur Conan Doyle was in Nottingham and about to give a lecture. Based on experience, he knew that his words would reap as much derision as praise. With all the passion of his conviction, he would speak of spirits and of the life they promised after death. He hoped that some receptive minds in his audience would be convinced. Some would at least listen. Others, he knew, would scoff.

There was the balm of warm applause as he mounted the lecture platform in the October sunshine. Then came a tug at his sleeve, and a telegram was thrust into his hand. Sir Arthur read that his eldest son, Kingsley, wounded in the battle of the Somme, had died. For the briefest instant, the author's tired, old eyes moistened. He had loved his son beyond all telling. Then, squaring his massive shoulders, Doyle crumpled the telegram into his pocket and took the stage. He gave his lecture, dry-eyed and composed. His strength betokened not a lack of grief, but a surfeit of faith, for in the deepest well of his soul he knew that his son was not, in any final sense, dead.

That was in 1918, when Sir Arthur was fifty-nine years old. In 1930, as he neared the end of his life, he sketched a melancholy caricature of himself as a flea-bitten old workhorse hauling a cart full of bricks. Each brick bore the label of a different aspect of his life and work. His famous fictional detective, Sherlock Holmes, was but one small brick in the pile, of no greater weight than those marked Poems or Historical Novels or Medical Practice. But the heaviest brick to carry must have been the one marked Psychic Research, for it was to this pursuit that Doyle devoted forty years of study, along with much of his personal fortune. As early as 1902, as he waited at Buckingham Palace to receive his knighthood, he could not resist drawing his fellow honoree, physicist Oliver Lodge, into a discussion of mediums and séances. After his conversion to spiritualism in 1916, Sir Arthur's early enthusiasm for psychic research grew into an all-consuming passion. During the next three years, he undertook several lecture tours, became active in the Society for Psychical Research, and authored two books on spiritualism. The carnage of World War I only deepened his sense of urgency. In such dark days, he believed, his message could comfort thousands, for he had learned that "the change in vibration which we call death did not destroy our personality and that communication was still possible. . . . I KNOW it to be true."

That knowledge sustained him after Kingsley's death. For the rest of his life, Doyle remained convinced that he was in contact with his son through physical mediums. His greatest frustration was that the general public stayed willfully blind to the source of his solace. At one séance where Kingsley supposedly appeared, Sir Arthur wept openly and cried out, "My God, if only people knew—if only they could know!"

None could fault the strength of the scholar-knight's conviction, but championing the spiritualist cause laid him open to frequent and often unjust ridicule. Doyle was wont to speak of the ways and habits of spirits, whose lives, he asserted, were not unlike our own. A reporter once asked whether spirits had amusements on the Other Side. The author affirmed they probably did. Did they play golf, perhaps? the reporter pressed. "I never heard them say it," Doyle replied. Nevertheless, the next day's headlines read, "Doyle Says They Play Golf in Heaven."

The strain of the crusade took its toll. In middle life Doyle retained the powerful athlete's physique of his youth; but his shoulders sagged and his step slowed, and fatigue pulled at the corners of his eyes. He maintained his rigorous schedule, how-

ever—writing, visiting mediums, and lecturing at every opportunity.

Although he created Sherlock Holmes, that paragon of cold rationality, Sir Arthur was often shockingly credulous himself in the matter of spiritualism. Nevertheless, his prestige was so great that it gave weight to psychic investigation at a time when such research might otherwise have foundered. With the passing of its guiding lights, Britain's Society for Psychical Research lost prominence in the years before World War I. But Doyle, who joined the SPR in 1893, just three weeks after the death of his father, helped ensure that psychic matters remained in the public eye. He had been much impressed by the distinguished individuals who supported the cause before him, notably Arthur Balfour. Indeed, the character of Lord Holdhurst in the Holmes short story "The Naval Treaty" was modeled on the brilliant statesman.

With the coming of the war, spiritualism's course changed dramatically. Death touched tens of thousands of households on both sides of the Atlantic, as it had touched Sir Arthur, and there arose a greater need and willingness to believe. As a result, physical mediumship, in decline for decades, enjoyed a resurgence. Friends and relatives of fallen soldiers flocked to séances, desperate for word from dead loved ones. Many mediums who set up shop during this period were shameless frauds, callously exploiting the bereaved.

Predictably, this bumper crop of pseudopsychic vultures prompted outcries from skeptics bent on discrediting them. Foremost among the skeptics were professional magicians, including Harry Kellar and John Maskelyne, who were convinced that the learned psychical researchers were singularly ill-equipped to discover even the most elementary fraud among the mediums preying on the innocent. For many magicians, it became a point of honor to expose these sham mediums, who they believed were no more than magicians themselves—and very poor ones at that.

Easily the most vocal antispiritualist crusader of them all was Harry Houdini, the legendary master of escape. The son of an immigrant rabbi, Houdini had spent long years struggling in the obscurity of dime museums and variety halls before achieving world renown. It galled him to see the public bilked by unscrupulous mediums whose talents, he thought, were so inferior to those of honest practitioners of magic. In addition, he had a more personal reason to despise these fake mediums.

Throughout his life, Houdini was devoted to his mother. Her death in 1913 was such a crushing blow that the magician fainted at the news, and it was months before Houdini appeared on stage again. Even the passing of time could not reconcile him to the loss: He was determined to find a way to contact his beloved mother in the world beyond.

Over the years that followed, Houdini attended hundreds of séances around the world, but his desperate need to reach his mother was always thwarted. Although he wanted to believe, he knew the stratagems of mediumship so well that faith eluded him. Early in his career, penniless and starving, Houdini himself had served a brief turn as a medium to earn a few extra dollars. He had been a fraud, and he found that the mediums he sought out after his mother's death were no better. Eventually, his disappointment turned to rage, and he dedicated himself to exposing fakery. As

Doyle became the champion of the spiritualist cause, Houdini became the scourge.

As such, the magician never leashed his dramatic flair. He often attended séances wearing a false beard and mustache, the better to observe anonymously. When he had gathered enough evidence to make an exposure, he would leap up and tear off his disguise. "My name is Houdini," he would proclaim to the medium. "You are a fraud!"

It is difficult to imagine two men more different than Arthur Conan Doyle and Harry Houdini. Even physically, the contrasts were striking—Doyle, the gentle, patrician British gi-

Standing on a curb in Rochester, New York, Harry Houdini gives his mother, Cecilia Weiss, a tender kiss. After Mrs. Weiss's death in 1913, her grief-stricken son became obsessed with spiritualism. But the escape artist easily saw through the trickery of the many mediums he visited, denouncing them as creators of "the most monstrous fiction."

ant whose sleepy expression and droopy mustache called to mind a friendly walrus; and Houdini, the short, muscular American noted for his quick temper and restless energy. Yet the two men forged a curious friendship, based, ironically, on sharply disparate but shared interests in the subject of spiritualism.

They first met in 1920, when Sir Arthur brought his family to see Houdini perform in Portsmouth, England. The two began a lively correspondence, and Houdini visited Sir Arthur's home in Sussex, where he delighted the Doyle children with magic tricks. While lecturing in America, Doyle paid a reciprocal visit to Houdini's home on West 113th Street in New York City. He admired the magician's extensive collection of books on magic but chided him for a collection on spiritualism authored solely by skeptics.

Doyle greatly revered Houdini's talent, but there was a subtext to the fascination the conjurer held for him. Incredibly, Sir Arthur believed that Houdini, the vituperative anti-spiritualist, was himself a powerful medium. Prominent among Houdini's many psychic powers, according to Doyle, was the ability to reduce his body to ectoplasm in order to achieve his fantastic escapes from handcuffs and packing crates. Thus attenuated, the writer reasoned, Houdini simply oozed free of his bonds. "My reason tells me that you have this wonderful power," Doyle wrote to the magician, "for there is no alternative." Later, Doyle put the matter even more pointedly. "Who was the greatest medium-baiter of modern times?" he wrote in one of his spiritualist tomes. "Undoubtedly Houdini. Who was the greatest physical medium of modern times? There are some who would be inclined to give the same answer."

For his part, Houdini was alternately flattered and bemused by his British friend's beliefs. Writing to his colleague Harry Kellar, Houdini noted that when Sir Arthur saw a stage performance, he "was so much impressed that there is little wonder in him believing in spiritualism so implicitly." Houdini repeatedly denied having supernatural powers. Of course, he could have settled the question quickly enough by revealing his true methods to Doyle, but professional pride would not permit this.

Perhaps it was inevitable that the strong passions of the two men would reach a crisis at opposite ends of a séance table. It happened in June of 1922, as Houdini and his wife, Bess, visited the Doyles in Atlantic City during the first of Sir Arthur's two postwar American lecture tours. With her husband's enthusiastic encouragement, Lady Doyle had begun trying to contact the spirits through automatic writing. Approaching the Houdinis on the beach one day, Sir Arthur hinted that, should Houdini agree, Lady Doyle would hold a special séance in his honor. There was every reason to hope, Doyle said, that a very significant message might come across from "the other side." Houdini knew at once this could mean only one thing: Lady Doyle proposed to contact the spirit of his mother.

On the evening of June 17, Houdini, Sir Arthur, and Lady Doyle gathered in the Doyles' hotel suite to begin the séance. Mrs. Houdini had been excluded in the hope that conditions would prove more favorable with fewer people present. Although Houdini had attended hundreds of similar affairs by this time, he resolved to suspend doubt. The Doyles, he knew, were wholly sincere in their beliefs. If ever he was to experience a genuine spirit phenomenon, it would be now. "I excluded all earthly thoughts and gave my whole soul to the séance," the magician wrote. "I was *willing* to believe, even *wanted* to believe." In the darkened hotel room, the sitters joined hands and waited, a pad of paper on the table before them. Soon, Lady Doyle's body stiffened as, it seemed, she was seized by a spirit presence. Her right hand, holding a pencil, shook violently. In a trembling voice she enjoined the spirits to give her a message.

Her pencil moved falteringly toward the paper. She marked the sign of the cross. Sir Arthur asked aloud if the spirit present was that of Houdini's mother. In response, Lady Doyle's hand, apparently guided by another's will, rapped the table three times. Sir Arthur fixed the magician with a knowing gaze. Tonight Harry Houdini would find the proof he sought.

All at once, Lady Doyle's pencil began racing across the paper. The message came so furiously that her scrawl could barely contain it. "Oh, my darling," it began, "at last I'm through—I've tried, oh so often—now I am happy." The message continued at length, until Sir Arthur broke in to suggest that Houdini ask his mother a specific question. Under other conditions, the magician would have posed one of his "fraud-breaking" questions, asking for some bit of information that only his mother could know, such as the pet name she once called him. This time, however, Houdini was at a loss. Sir Arthur suggested that he ask, "Can my mother read my mind?" Houdini agreed. At once the spirit message continued: "I always read my beloved son's mind. There is so much I want to say to him. . . . If only the world knew this great truth." After several pages had been written in this vein, the pencil fell from Lady Doyle's hand. The séance was at an end.

The three sat in silence for a while. Lady Doyle struggled to collect herself after the draining experience, while Sir Arthur pondered with satisfaction the conversion of spiritualism's greatest skeptic. But Houdini was far from converted. The entire experience had left him uneasy. Why had his Jewish mother made the sign of the cross at the start of her message? How had his Hungarian-born mother managed to communicate in flawless English, a language she had never mastered in life? By a strange coincidence, the séance had been held on his mother's birthday. Why had the spirit message made no mention of it?

Sir Arthur broke the uncomfortable silence. The spirit had urged Houdini to try his own hand at automatic writing. Why not attempt it now? Aimlessly, Houdini picked up a pencil and wrote the first thing that came to his mind—the name *Powell*. Doyle was thunderstruck. To him, the name could mean only Ellis Powell, an ardent spiritualist and the editor of the *London Financial News*. "Dr. Ellis Powell," Doyle later wrote, "my dear fighting partner in spiritualism, had just died in England . . . here was his name coming through the hand of Houdini!" It was proof positive, Doyle surmised, that the magician was a medium. But Houdini,

although he did not say so, knew otherwise. His close friend Frederick Eugene Powell, an American magician, had suffered a series of setbacks recently. The Houdinis had been discussing the situation that very day. It was he, not Doyle's friend, who was on the conjurer's mind.

Houdini and Doyle parted warmly after the séance, but the seeds of a rift had been sown. The magician waited a decent interval, not wanting to embarrass his friend while he was still in America. But about six months after the séance, he released a statement to the effect that the experiment had been a failure. Houdini had tried to retain his respect for the Doyles' convictions, but he believed the proceedings had travestied his painful longing to communicate with his mother. For his part, Doyle felt he had given Houdini ironclad proof of spiritualism's validity. It was, he thought, both obstinate and ungrateful for the magician to resist.

For a time the two men made halfhearted attempts to confine their correspondence to other topics, but in truth their friendship was over. In later years, the gentlemanly Doyle would comment that the incident with Houdini "made some alteration in my feelings toward him," while Houdini said of Doyle, "He is good-natured, very bright, but a monomaniac on the subject of spiritualism." The obsession that had drawn them together now forced them apart. There could be no pretending with a matter that both felt so deeply. When next the two met, it would be to cross swords over the most controversial physical medium of the twentieth century—Mina Crandon, known to her public as the Amazing Margery.

Events began in a stately four-story brick home at 10 Lime Street in the fashionable Beacon Hill neighborhood of Boston. In the spring of 1923, Dr. Le Roi Goddard Crandon, a wealthy, middle-aged physician, spent a sleepless night poring over a book. It told the strange story of Kathleen Goligher, a young woman apparently able to lift a heavy table into the air using a mysterious pseudopod that extruded from her body. Crandon was a former instructor of surgery

Sir Arthur Conan Doyle and Harry Houdini stand companionably together in 1922 on an Atlantic City beach. While conducting a séance that summer at the New Jersey resort, Lady Doyle, a practitioner of automatic writing, scribbled a florid message purportedly from the magician's cherished mother. Houdini was unconvinced—in part because he knew his Jewish mother would not have begun a communication by drawing a Christian cross at the top of the first page, reproduced above.

Mechanisms for Mystical Messages

Still popular with would-be communers with spirits, the Ouija board, in one form or another, dates back to ancient times.

An early predecessor was the wheeled Mystic Table used in the sixth century BC by the Greek mathematician Pythagoras. The table rolled over a stone slab inscribed with esoteric signs, and Pythagoras interpreted for his followers the mystical import of its starts and stops. Some scholars believe he adapted the table from similar Oriental devices.

With the nineteenth-century craze for spiritualism came the planchette, an automatic-writing apparatus consisting of a pencil and a pair of casters mounted on a heart-shaped wooden wafer. Under the hands of one or more operators, the planchette moved over a sheet of paper, inscribing presumed spirit messages. A major drawback was its tendency to produce an indecipherable scrawl. Since the pencil never left the page, a script of any length involved so much criss-crossing that words were unreadable.

This problem did not exist with devices such as the Ouija board, which pointed to letters rather than writing them. A contemporary of the planchette, the Ouija board was probably invented in Europe. It was popularized by American businessman William Fuld, who began marketing it as a game in 1899. It was a huge commercial success during World War I, when thousands of families bought it, not as a toy, but in hopes of contacting their fallen loved ones. Parker Brothers, a

A girl experiments with a planchette. Operators of automatic-writing devices were sometimes blindfolded in an effort to tune out any extraneous influences on its movement. The planchette enjoyed a brief mania as a parlor game after toy manufacturers introduced it to Britain and the U.S. in 1868.

Massachusetts-based game maker, acquired rights to it in 1966.

Some users of Ouija boards have gotten startlingly long, fluent scripts. A nonspiritual explanation is that the messages' true source is submerged thoughts and desires, translated into involuntary muscular contractions that move the mechanism in response to its operator's unconscious wishes.

An advertisement published in the 1890s in a British spiritualist quarterly shows how a device called the Pytho worked. Two persons each held a handle connected to a pointer that pivoted to spell words and indicate numbers.

The pointer of a Ouija board glides to yield messages in letters and numbers. It can also answer questions with a yes or no. The name Ouija combines the French and German words for yes.

at Harvard Medical School and by no means a fanciful man. Yet he found himself intrigued by the story. Was such a thing possible?

A few weeks later, Crandon ordered a table built to the exact specifications of the one that had been used in the Goligher case. The wood was unvarnished and untainted by nails that might inhibit spirit activity. On May 27 Crandon, his wife, and four friends climbed the stairs to the top floor of the house, where the table had been placed at the center of a darkened chamber. Following Crandon's terse instructions, the sitters joined hands and waited for a sign of a spirit presence.

For several moments nothing happened. Crandon's wife and several of the guests grew restless and began to feel silly. Uneasy laughter broke the stillness. Then, abruptly, the séance table began to move—only slightly at first, but then more violently, tilting up on two legs before crashing to the floor. Crandon was beside himself. He demanded to know which of his guests was the medium producing the manifestation. Then he ordered his guests to leave the room one by one. The table stopped rocking only when the last sitter departed. Crandon had his answer. The medium was his own wife, Mina.

The daughter of a Canadian farmer, Mina Stinson had moved to Boston as a teenager to play piano, cornet, and cello in various local dance bands and orchestras. Having also worked as a secretary, an actress, and an ambulance driver, Mina settled down in 1910 to marry the owner of a small grocery. She divorced him eight years later to marry Crandon, who had himself been twice divorced. Mina was then thirty years old. Crandon was forty-four.

A spirited, vivacious woman, Mina seemed to cast a spell on every man that she met. Her saucy blue eyes, bobbed blond hair, and trim figure combined to make her, in the words of one bedazzled admirer, "too attractive for her own good."

For Mina Crandon, discovery of her mediumship was a great lark—all the more so, perhaps, because it seemed to please her somber and demanding husband. She delighted

Dr. Le Roi Crandon, husband of Margery the Medium, stands with his wife during a trip to England in the 1920s. Crandon, a prominent Boston physician, eagerly participated in Margery's séances.

as he rushed to furnish their séance room with the proper trappings—an open-front cabinet, a Victrola, and various other props. All through the summer of 1923 the Crandons conducted séances, and at each Mina appeared to manifest some strange new power. Early on, she produced mysterious rappings and flashes of light. Later, phantom instruments were heard to play. On one occasion, she apported a live pigeon into the séance chamber. The table, too, grew ever more active. At one especially lively sitting, it chased a sitter from the room and knocked him off his feet. This range of manifestations was to become Mina's hallmark. It seemed that Crandon had only to read of a new psychical marvel for Mina to duplicate it.

She conducted her first few séances while fully conscious. But after a month or so, on Crandon's orders, Mina switched to trance performances. Crandon hoped she would summon a spirit guide while entranced, and here, too, Mina scored a remarkable success. One evening a disembodied male voice broke the silence of the room. "I said I could put this through," it said. The speaker, it seemed, was Walter Stinson, Mina's beloved older brother. He had been crushed to death a dozen years earlier when a railroad boxcar overturned on him. Walter would serve as Mina's spirit control for eighteen years, guiding her through the world beyond in much the same way he might once have led her down an unfamiliar street.

Walter's personality proved just as engaging as his sister's. He had a ready wit, an impatient manner, and a penchant for rough language. In fact, many visitors to the Crandon's séance room were converted simply because such coarse and irreverent monologues surely could never have issued from the lips of demure Mina, the doctor's wife. "Hell is now completely up to date," Walter once quipped to a roomful of clergymen. "We burn oil!"

Medium and spirit seemed separated by more than slang and syntax. Indeed, Walter's voice did not appear to come from Mina at all, but from a different part of the room. Moreover, it could continue unabated even while Mina snored her way through a trance, or held her mouth full of

109

water. The effect was so remarkable that one skeptic, searching for a trick, wondered aloud if perhaps the lady could speak through her ears.

Crandon was so thrilled with his wife's mediumship that he sent a detailed account of it to Arthur Conan Doyle. Doyle responded with characteristic enthusiasm, wholeheartedly endorsing Mrs. Crandon as genuine before he had even met her. When the meeting did come, at a private séance in England, Doyle found his faith entirely justified and reported as much to J. Malcolm Bird, an associate editor of *Scientific American* magazine. At Sir Arthur's urging, Bird would later write a series of articles extolling Mina's gifts. To protect the lady's privacy, Bird bestowed on her the name Margery the Medium. The name's renown grew steadily.

Researcher J. Malcolm Bird stands behind Mina Crandon, alias Margery the Medium. Bird backed Margery for years, despite critics who branded her a fraud.

ry Houdini, king of the medium bashers.

The Crandons did not share Sir Arthur's apprehension; on the contrary, they seemed to welcome the chance to test their mettle against Houdini. *Scientific American*'s $2,500 prize meant little to the wealthy couple, but the opportunity to win over such a prestigious body—especially the super-skeptic Houdini—had great allure. Crandon wrote to Sir Arthur of his plan to "crucify" the magician and thereby cement Mina's fame.

Houdini was on tour with his illusion show in the spring of 1924 when the investigation began, so the committee began work without him. In fact, it was three months before the escape artist learned that an investigation was even under way. By that time, some of the other committee members had become so enthralled by the Lime Street medium that they were on the brink of declaring her genuine and awarding the prize. Bird, in particular, was eager to endorse Margery, and he allowed word of favorable findings to trickle into the press. "Boston Medium Baffles Experts," announced one headline. "Houdini the Magician Stumped," declared another.

In bringing Mrs. Crandon to the attention of *Scientific American,* Doyle inadvertently exposed her to her greatest challenge. At the time, the magazine was offering a prize of $2,500 to any medium who could produce conclusive proof of psychic phenomena. A special investigating committee had been formed to examine all mediums applying for the prize. This was not to Doyle's liking. He was much impressed by what he regarded as Bird's open-mindedness, but he had grave reservations about the rest of the committee. It included Walter Franklin Prince, chief research officer of the American Society for Psychical Research, and psychical researcher Hereward Carrington, both of whom had shown themselves in the past to be skeptics. Also participating were William McDougall, dean of psychology at Harvard, who had investigated Margery before and had grave doubts about her; and Daniel F. Comstock, inventor and former physics professor at Massachusetts Institute of Technology. Comstock, too, was a skeptic. Worst of all, rounding out the committee was none other than Har-

Houdini—who had yet to so much as meet Margery, much less be stumped by her—was outraged. Canceling his bookings, he rushed to Boston, where his anger grew as he began reviewing the findings of his peers. To his way of thinking, the investigation had been bungled from the start. Two of the committee members, Bird and Carrington, had availed themselves of the Crandons' lavish hospitality dur-

J. Malcolm Bird grasps the hand of a clearly amused Margery after being knocked to the floor by a panel from her medium's cabinet. The cabinet was supposedly wrenched apart by Walter, the medium's dead brother and rambunctious spirit control. Such dramatic scenes were a factor in Bird's declaring Margery genuine—but skeptics felt he had been taken in by her wiles and was probably in love with her.

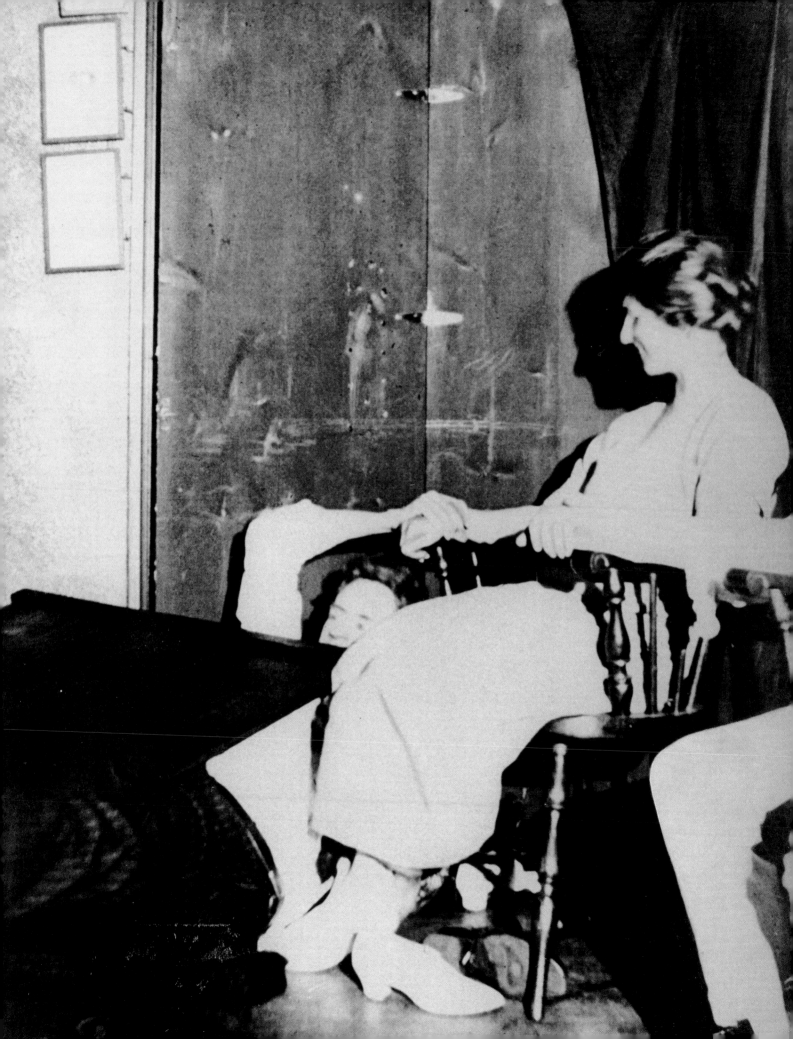

ing the course of the proceedings—living in their home, eating their food, and enjoying their company. This, Houdini believed, had fatally compromised the committee's objectivity. And it would be revealed that room and board were the least of the blandishments offered to the committee. Carrington had actually borrowed money from Crandon and was trying to win his backing for a research foundation. Worse yet, the attractions of Mrs. Crandon—who conducted her séances wearing only a filmy dressing gown and silk stockings—were not lost on some members of the distin-

guished panel. Bird was obviously enchanted by her, and Carrington, by his own account—and hers—later in life, was sleeping with her.

On July 23, 1924, Houdini made his way to the Crandon home for his first meeting with Margery. He was steeled against her wiles; still, he could not help being fascinated. His own wife once fled in panic when Houdini, using an arcane trick involving the selective subsurface rupturing of tiny blood vessels, caused the name of her dead father to appear in blood letters on his arm. Margery, how-

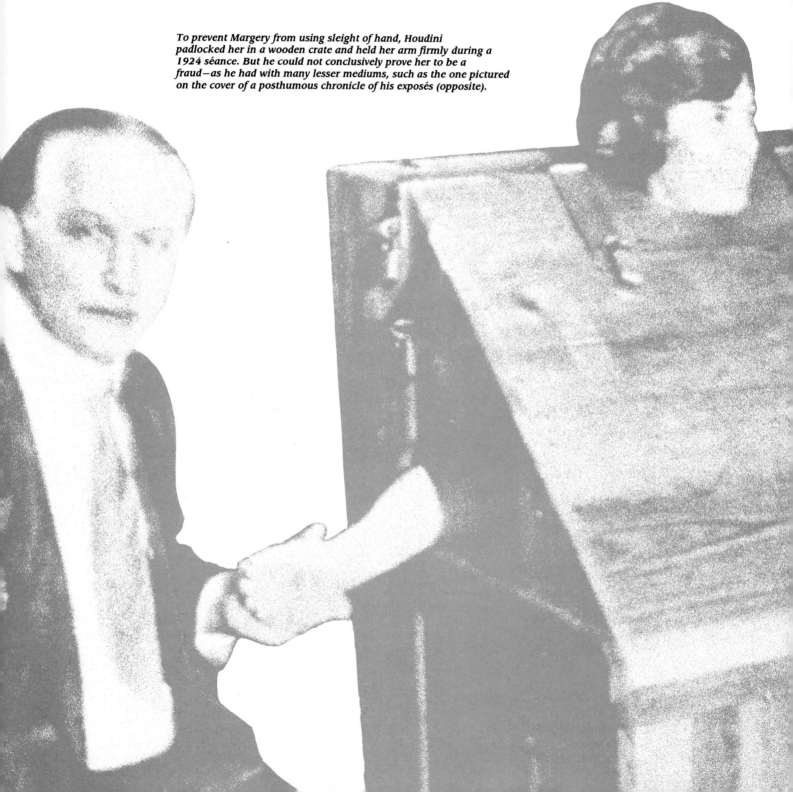

To prevent Margery from using sleight of hand, Houdini padlocked her in a wooden crate and held her arm firmly during a 1924 séance. But he could not conclusively prove her to be a fraud—as he had with many lesser mediums, such as the one pictured on the cover of a posthumous chronicle of his exposés (opposite).

ever, did not seem at all inclined to such vaporings. In her, Houdini found a woman unlike any he had ever known. Quite apart from her physical allure, she was something of a trickster, as he was, with an insouciant arrogance to match his own. He had no doubt that she was just as much a fraud as every other medium he had debunked. Nevertheless, this pert minx, known to many as the Witch of Lime Street, was a worthy adversary.

One of the feats that had baffled many of Margery's sitters was the ringing of a "spirit bell box," a small wooden box that, when pressed from the top, sounded an electric bell. In earlier séances for the *Scientific American* committee, the box was placed on the floor between Margery's feet. The bell rang even while her hands and feet supposedly were held. They were held on the left by an investigator, and they were *presumably* held on the right by Crandon or a close friend. With Margery assumed to be incapacitated, the ringing of the bell was ascribed to Walter. In the medium's debut performance for Houdini, he in-

sisted on a different arrangement. The bell box was placed on the floor between his feet, not hers. Despite the precaution, the bell rang as merrily as ever.

Soon Walter's voice echoed through the room, informing the sitters that a megaphone, one of Margery's props, was floating in the darkness above their heads. "Have Houdini tell me where to throw it," the alleged spirit commanded. "Toward me," answered Houdini, whereupon the megaphone instantly crashed down in front of him. The magician, seated to Margery's left, tightened his grip on her hand. After a few more rings of the bell box, Walter's voice bade the assembled sitters good night.

Houdini left the Crandon home mildly impressed by the famous Margery—but he was not, he hastened to tell his colleagues, converted. Back at his hotel, he explained why his conclusions differed from theirs. All that day, the magician revealed, he had worn a tight elastic surgical bandage around the calf of his right leg. By evening, the skin there was swollen and unusually sensitive. In the darkness of the

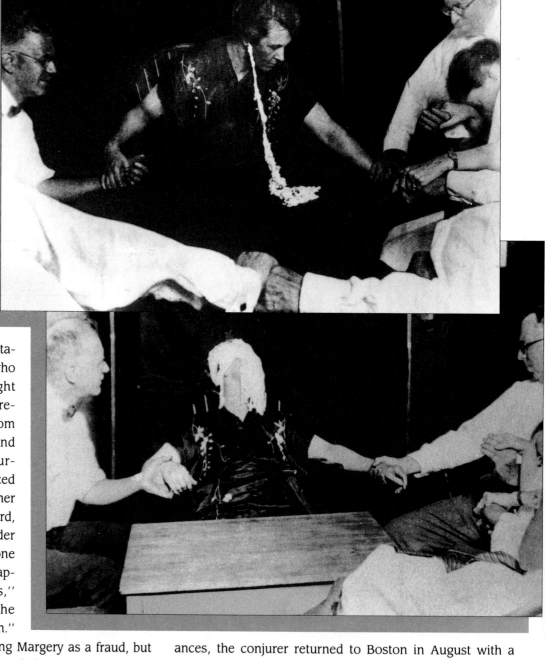

séance, he had rolled up the right leg of his trousers to expose the sensitized skin. He was therefore able to detect the slightest movements of Margery's leg as her foot inched forward. That agile foot, Houdini assured his fellows, had manipulated the bell box. The floating megaphone, too, was easily explained. Just prior to the manifestation, Walter had asked Bird—who was controlling Margery's right hand—to leave the table and retrieve a piece of apparatus from across the room. With her hand momentarily free, Houdini surmised, Margery must have seized the megaphone and put it on her head, like a dunce cap. Afterward, with both her hands again under control, she made the megaphone sail through the air simply by snapping her head forward. "This," Houdini acknowledged, "is the slickest ruse I have ever seen."

Houdini was all for exposing Margery as a fraud, but other committee members counseled restraint. Malcolm Bird, in particular, still believed Mrs. Crandon was at least half genuine. He wanted to continue the investigation the following month in the hope of producing more satisfactory phenomena. Later, Houdini would learn that Bird had apprised the Crandons of the magician's discoveries. In addition, the ostensibly impartial investigator continued to print flattering accounts of the medium's feats.

Bird's behavior only strengthened Houdini's resolve to expose Margery. To ensure proper control in future sé-

ances, the conjurer returned to Boston in August with a special cabinet he considered fraud-proof. It was a slant-topped wooden crate with semicircular openings for the medium's head and arms. Margery reluctantly agreed to conduct a séance using the cabinet, but not before Crandon and Houdini exchanged harsh words.

The first séance with the cabinet was held in the Boston apartment of committee member Comstock. It was a failure. Acting on a tip purportedly from Walter, Comstock discovered a small pencil eraser wedged into the bell box to prevent it from ringing. Outraged, the physician accused

A stream of what she claimed was ectoplasm flows from Margery's right
ear and covers her face in a 1925 session. Some investigators believed these grotesque
manifestations were not spirit essence, but animal tissue.

Houdini of trying to sabotage the proceedings, a charge the magician repeatedly denied.

A séance with the cabinet the following night proved even more dismal. Matters started badly when Malcolm Bird burst into the séance demanding to know why he had been excluded from it. Houdini accused him of compromising the investigation through collusion with the Crandons and with his premature accounts in print. Furious, Bird resigned from the committee and stormed out of the room. The sitting went from bad to worse when Walter's voice spoke up to defend his sister's honor. Someone, the spirit intoned, was trying to incriminate Margery. A collapsible carpenter's ruler—which might have been used to manipulate the bell box and other apparatus from within the cabinet—had been concealed inside the structure. According to Walter, Houdini had instructed his assistant to put the ruler there solely to discredit Margery. "Houdini, you God-damned son of a bitch," railed Walter, "get the hell out of here and never come back." A search of the cabinet proved Walter correct; there was a collapsible ruler concealed inside. The question remained whether Houdini had put it there, as Walter claimed, or whether Margery had smuggled it in and then staged the dramatic exposure in order to protect herself and discredit Houdini. The point is still argued today.

Margery failed to win the *Scientific American* prize, but she emerged from the Houdini episode essentially unscathed. She had succeeded in dividing the investigating committee, and though serious doubt had been cast on her authenticity, she continued to prosper. To no one's surprise, her most vocal support in the wake of the investigation came from Doyle, who was only too pleased to enter the fray and confront Houdini once more. Sir Arthur was amazed, he wrote, that a gathering of "honourable gentlemen" should permit an attack on the reputation of a lady. In a barb aimed straight at Houdini, Doyle deplored the committee's having allowed a man "with entirely different standards to make this outrageous attack."

Meanwhile, Margery herself had gone on to better things. By the end of 1924 she was producing ectoplasm similar to that of Eusapia Palladino. Sitters were treated to the sight of long, flexible rods of the stuff issuing from her nose, mouth, ears, and other body cavities. These emanations formed themselves into crude hands. The ectoplasmic hands, the medium claimed, were responsible for ringing the bell box, throwing the megaphone, and other spirit caperings. The extrusions could not have been more shocking—indeed, more ghastly—resembling nothing so much as human waste oozing from the medium's body and forming what one observer called a "heaped, knobby mass."

SPR research officer Eric J. Dingwall, an amateur magician, was one of the first to investigate Margery's latest phenomenon. Having evidently won Walter's confidence, Dingwall was permitted to view the ectoplasm—but only by the light of a red lamp that Crandon flashed on and off at the presumed behest of Walter. Too much light, Crandon explained, would inhibit the ectoplasmic flow. Nevertheless, Dingwall saw enough to be impressed. "The materialized hands are connected by an umbilical cord to the medium," he wrote to a friend. "They seize upon objects and displace them." Later, when Dingwall was allowed to clasp one of the hands, he described it as feeling like "a piece of cold raw beef or possibly a piece of soft, wet rubber."

Midway through his investigations, however, Dingwall began to entertain doubts. Crandon's flashing light never allowed him to see the ectoplasm actually extrude from Margery's body; he had seen it only after the fact, partially or fully formed. Odder still, photographs showed that many of the emanations seemed to be hanging from slender, almost invisible threads. Others who examined the photographs thought the ectoplasm looked suspiciously like animal lung tissue, a substance Crandon might have obtained through his work at Boston hospitals. Dingwall, a judicious investigator, could not be sure that Margery actually faked the manifestations, and in his final report on the matter, he did not come to any firm conclusions. He speculated, however, that Margery was concealing fake "ectoplasm" inside her vagina and then extruding it by muscular contractions.

Margery was characteristically unperturbed by investigators and their findings. She noted that had she lived 150 years earlier, she probably would have been executed as a witch. "But now they send committees of professors from Harvard to study me," she joked. "That represents some progress, doesn't it?" Walter, too, kept his sense of humor. "I never saw such a bunch of stiffs in my life," he exclaimed to one group of investigators. "Talk about dead people, my God!"

Despite Walter's raffishness, sitters continued to flock to Lime Street. One investigation after another raised the possibility of fraud, but none appeared to be able to make the charge stick. Even Joseph Banks Rhine, later a driving force of parapsychology, studied Margery. When Rhine came away unimpressed with her abilities, Arthur Conan Doyle rushed gallantly to the medium's defense. Rhine published an unflattering account of his experience with Margery, whereupon Sir Arthur bought space in several Boston newspapers to run a reply. The black-bordered message read simply: "J. B. Rhine is an ass."

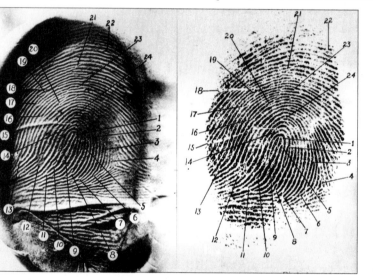

In 1926 Margery added yet another effect to her repertoire—one too many, as things turned out. The spectral fingerprint phenomenon began with Walter's hints that, since his ethereal body was an exact duplicate of his earthly one, he might be able to leave a fingerprint signaling his presence. Such evidence would be compelling, since few mediums had managed to produce so tangible an artifact. The idea prompted Margery to visit her dentist, Dr. Frederick Caldwell, and ask if the hot wax used to take dental impressions might also be used to obtain the fingerprint. After some experimentation, the two determined that dental wax would serve admirably. Caldwell, a frequenter of the Crandon séances, gladly provided some.

That very night, the dental wax was placed in a bowl on the séance table out of Margery's reach. Before the lights went out in the room, the wax was a featureless blob. When they came on again, there were two thumbprints in it—Walter's prints, the Crandons claimed. The performance was repeated on numerous subsequent occasions. In fact, spectral prints—usually from Walter, it was said, but sometimes from other dead people—became a new staple of the Margery séances. An alleged fingerprint expert, a shadowy figure who was most probably a fraud, attested that the presumed Walter prints matched prints he had lifted from one of Walter's old razors. A delighted Crandon hired a Margery partisan named E. E. Dudley to sort and classify the various prints that were continually turning up in the séances.

There were, however, detractors who contended the "Walter" prints were really those of some living member of the Crandon circle. The conscientious Dudley set out to prove them wrong. He painstakingly collected the fingerprints of everyone who had ever attended a Margery séance. After six years of gathering and filing, he made a disheartening discovery: The thumbprints allegedly belonging to Walter were identical to those of Dr. Caldwell, the obliging dentist. Someone, almost certainly not Walter, had apparently used Caldwell's wax sample to make a die, which in turn was used to make the "spirit" prints. Dudley could only conclude that the prints were a hoax.

Margery might have weathered even this blow had it

not been for Dr. Walter F. Prince, who had been dubious about her since his days as a member of the *Scientific American* investigating committee. The ASPR, having tied its own credibility to Margery's, declined to publish Dudley's results. This was too much for Prince, who had long since despaired of the ASPR and its Margery contingent and had left to found his own organization, the Boston Society for Psychic Research. The BSPR published Dudley's fingerprint findings after the ASPR blocked them. The disclosure spread quickly, with devastating results. "Find 'Ghost' Prints on Living Hands," read a headline in the *New York Times*.

The ax had finally fallen. Margery's support had already been eroding. Two years earlier, J. Malcolm Bird, long the medium's most devoted adherent, had backed away from her. In a confidential report to the ASPR's board of trustees, he admitted that he had, at times, told half-truths for Margery's benefit. Some of Margery's ASPR supporters were shaken by Bird's confession; but, predictably, the organization tried to keep his report quiet in order to salvage what remained of the ASPR's credibility. After the fingerprint revelation, however, there was no holding back the tide that had turned against Margery.

Wholesale desertion by her admirers touched off a decline in her that was both rapid and tragic. Although the séances continued, the medium was little more than a shell. The Margery alter ego had failed her, and now Mina Crandon turned increasingly to alcohol for the consolation that no longer came from adoring supporters. Depressions were frequent and deep. During one séance, the distraught Mina climbed to the roof of the Lime Street house and threatened to jump to her death. Only a few years earlier, Margery had dazzled all comers with her sprightly spirit and striking looks. Now she grew heavy and sour. And with Le Roi Crandon's death in 1939, her dissipation accelerated. The following year a sitter described her as "an overdressed, dumpy little woman."

In November of 1941, eighteen years after that first séance on the top floor, Margery lay dying in the house on Lime Street. She was a chronic alcoholic. Only fifty-four years old, she had the wizened look of an old woman—worse, a forgotten one. One last psychical investigator, Nandor Fodor, sat alone with her, close to the bedside. The end was near, he told her. Now was the time to make a clean breast of it, to confess whatever deceptions helped propel her to glory and now brought her so low. Mina listened quietly, then muttered something inaudible. Fodor asked her to repeat it.

"Sure," she said. "I said you could go to hell. All you 'psychic researchers' can go to hell."

Fodor watched as a smile spread across her pale features, and some remnant of the old sauciness lit her eyes. She laughed softly. "Why don't you guess?" she whispered. "You'll all be guessing . . . for the rest of your lives."

The passing of the Margery era all but sounded the death knell for psychic research in the United States. The case had destroyed the reputations of more than a dozen learned men and fractured the ASPR. Margery had become the standard by which spiritualism was judged; the entire movement stood or fell with her. Had the exposure of her deceit come earlier, debate over the spirits might have turned to other mediums and gone on much as before. But by 1941, the crusade had lost not only its lady fair, but its standard-bearers pro and con. Houdini and Doyle were both dead.

Perhaps the most serious consequence of the Margery affair lay in the fact that it precluded research that might have proved more fruitful. While Margery lived, she was the focus of nearly every major investigation undertaken in Britain and the United States. A result was that other, even more extraordinary cases went largely undocumented.

Prime among them was the case of Carlos Mirabelli. Born in Brazil in 1889, Mirabelli first attracted notice as a teenager by displaying an affinity for poltergeist-like phenomena. The youth was working as a shoe clerk in São Paulo when a swarm of shoeboxes flew off the store shelves and chased him into the street. Before long, he was locked up in a local lunatic asylum, where he became the subject of a makeshift

A series of three photographs shows Brazilian medium Carlos Mirabelli orchestrating the appearance of a robed human form. A master of spirit materializations, Mirabelli often worked in broad daylight or in brightly lighted rooms, allegedly summoning figures so substantial they cast shadows—and so lifelike they could be examined by doctors.

psychic investigation. His doctors quickly realized Mirabelli was not crazy; on the other hand, a young man who caused inanimate objects to sail through the air could hardly be regarded as normal. Whatever his peculiarities, the doctors failed to diagnose them, and after nineteen days Mirabelli was released.

Soon, stories of his amazing feats were spreading across Brazil. Mirabelli, it was said, transported himself a distance of fifty-six miles in two minutes on one occasion. On another, he reportedly levitated several feet into the air. Physicians attested that he produced full-figure manifestations, human in every detail, which dissolved into nothingness once the doctors had examined them. Mirabelli often materialized spirits of the famous dead, and in short order he became a wildly popular celebrity himself. As many as

5,000 people gathered to witness outdoor manifestations that occurred in broad daylight.

In 1919, the newly formed Cesare Lombroso Academy of Psychical Studies began a long investigation of Mirabelli. Although the academy lacked the credibility and experience of the larger British and American societies, no one could fault its thoroughness. More than 500 sitters participated in a total of 392 séances with the medium, all held in daylight or in brightly illuminated rooms. Not all the séances produced results, but those that did covered an astonishing range of phenomena. A prolific automatic writer, Mirabelli reportedly produced samples in twenty-eight different languages, all quite beyond the range of his rudimentary education. Many of the writings seemed to be inspired by history's great scholars. The scripts ranged from a treatise on inhabited planets, written in French, to a summary of the Russian-Japanese war, delivered in Japanese. Moreover, it was said that Mirabelli even produced three pages of untranslatable hieroglyphics.

Mirabelli had an unmatched talent for spirit materializations. While he sank into a trance one day, sitters from the Lombroso Academy heard the voice of a young girl. For one participant, a Dr. de Souza, the voice evoked a painful memory; he thought it belonged to his daughter, who had recently died of influenza. Straining to master his emotions, the doctor spoke a few words to the little girl. As he did, the child's figure, wearing burial clothes, appeared beside the entranced Mirabelli. De Souza was overwhelmed. Rising from his place, he took a few hesitant steps toward the specter and threw his arms around it. With Mirabelli motionless beside them, witnesses said, father and daughter spoke and comforted one another for more than half an hour. Another materialization account holds that the medium produced the double of a bishop who had drowned in a shipwreck. The figure was scrutinized by a doctor, whose minute examination supposedly turned up saliva in the spirit's mouth and noted rumblings in its stomach.

Not all Mirabelli's manifestations were so well fleshed out. During one séance, a skull belonging to the Lombroso

Academy was seen to float through the air, grinding its teeth as the rest of a purported spirit skeleton formed below. Sitters avowed that they handled and examined the skeleton for twenty-two minutes before all the bones but the skull faded into nothingness.

Writing of Mirabelli in 1930, Eric Dingwall admitted that reports of him seemed "frankly staggering to the intellect," but he cautioned against a hasty dismissal of the case. "It would be easy to condemn the man as a monstrous fraud and the sitters as equally monstrous fools," Dingwall wrote. "But I do not think that such a supposition will help even him who makes it." One could not overlook the sheer volume of Mirabelli's feats, Dingwall asserted, nor the fact that the medium performed before hundreds of observers in good light—not in covering darkness or the "feeble glimmer of ruby light" favored by certain American mediums. "The chaos in which psychical research finds itself at present prevents any really valuable systematic work being done," the investigator lamented. "Jealousy, spite, self-advertisement,

incompetence and even downright lying are now so common that research is delegated to a back place. . . . Such is the state of psychical research in the year of Grace 1930." Dingwall's bitter comments underscored an alarming paradox posed by the Margery exposure. Because Margery cheated, was Mirabelli to be branded a fraud? Regrettably, with Mirabelli's death in 1951 the question became merely an academic one.

Just as he might have wished, Harry Houdini drove yet another nail into mediumship's coffin—and he managed the feat a full three years after his death.

The king of escape had always believed that if anyone could break free of the spirit world's constraints, he was the man. At the height of his antispiritualist vendetta, he had

Houdini's widow, Bess, stands beside her husband's Long Island grave with magician and radio mentalist Joseph Dunninger, who carried on the antispiritualist crusade after the illusionist died in 1926.

A Bishop's Tale

Almost forty years after making headlines by claiming to receive a coded spirit message from the dead Harry Houdini, medium Arthur Ford found himself embroiled in another controversy. On September 3, 1967, the aging spiritualist sat blindfolded in a Toronto television studio with former Episcopal Bishop James Pike *(right),* conducting a two-hour séance in which he relayed supposed spirit communiqués from Pike's dead son.

The session created a sensation. Pike claimed that the messages Ford had conveyed were genuine. "Everything matched up," he asserted. Pike was a controversial figure himself, an ecclesiastical maverick who resigned as bishop of California in 1965 amid moves to oust him for heresy. He dabbled increasingly in spiritualism after the 1966 suicide of his twenty-two-year-old son. Still, he was a prominent figure, and his endorsement brought Ford a flurry of requests for private sittings and public appearances.

Ford's death in 1971 did not, it seemed, end his revitalized career. The medium began sending "eyewitness accounts of the hereafter" to writer and fellow medium Ruth Montgomery, who published a collection of his dispatches. In the great beyond, Ford cheerfully reported, he had chatted with Arthur Conan Doyle and observed Franklin Roosevelt conversing with Winston Churchill. The eminent statesmen's spirits, he added, cold-shouldered the ranting ghost of Adolf Hitler. Alas for Ford's renewed place in the spotlight, a biography published two years later revealed that Ford boned up for séances by using *Who's Who* and old newspaper files. When Ford "read a little poetry" to get into the mood for a session, he was actually taking a last peek at his notes. The authors suggested rather lamely that chicanery merely supplemented Ford's genuine powers and that indeed he was, in the words of their title, "The Man Who Talked with the Dead." Still, the revelations seemed to bear out an observation made by the greatest of all medium exposers. "Anyone can talk to the dead," said Harry Houdini, "but the dead do not answer."

devised a code with his wife, Bess. If he died before her, he vowed, he would do all in his power to deliver a message from the other side. She was to accept no message, he warned, that did not use the code.

On Halloween of 1926, Houdini died of peritonitis. Predictably, Mrs. Houdini was soon besieged by dozens of mediums, all claiming contact with her dead husband. None, however, could produce a properly coded message. On New Year's Day of 1929, Bess, weakened by a prolonged illness, fell down a flight of stairs in her New York home. Before losing consciousness, she cried out, "Harry, dear, why don't you come back to me from the other side?"

One week later, her plea appeared to have an answer. The Reverend Arthur Ford, a pastor of the First Spiritualist Church of New York, had earlier delivered a message to Mrs. Houdini purporting to be from her dead mother-in-law, one containing the word *forgive*. Bess was struck by the word, which was the one Houdini himself had vainly sought from his mother ever since her death. She arranged a séance with Ford.

On January 8, her head still bandaged from her fall, she and several trusted friends received him in the Houdini living room. While Bess rested on a sofa, the medium drew the blinds, then slumped into a chair and appeared to fall instantly into a trance. After a time, a voice calling itself Fletcher, Ford's spirit guide, issued from the reverend's lips. Fletcher soon gave way to another speaker, who identified himself as the spirit of Houdini. It seemed the magician retained in death the impatience that marked his life, for he wasted no time in getting to the point. His message consisted of only ten words: "Rosabelle, answer, tell, pray, answer, look, tell, answer, answer, tell."

The message seemed inscrutable, but it had a profound effect on Bess. Her face paled, as with some effort she propped herself up on the sofa. With trembling fingers, the widow removed her gold wedding band. Inside was an engraved portrait of her husband, along with the first lines of a song. It was one that Bess, Houdini's stage assistant in his early days, had sung in their very first performance togeth-er. In a voice thin with emotion, she sang it once more in the darkened living room: "Rosabelle, sweet Rosabelle / I love you more than I can tell. / Over me you cast a spell / I love you my sweet Rosabelle." With that, Bess Houdini fainted dead away.

While her companions revived her, Fletcher broke in to explain the significance of the message. It, too, dated back to the earliest days of the Houdini act, when the couple had used a numbered word code in a mind-reading act. When decoded, the spirit message consisted of just one word: *Believe.*

News of the remarkable message spawned a furor. Quoted in a Boston newspaper, Margery the Medium was quick to point out the irony. "Harry Houdini in death has furnished the world with evidence which conclusively refutes the theories which he so vigorously defended in life," she said. Bess herself confirmed that Ford had come up with the right code, known only to herself and her late husband. For a time, it appeared that the cause of physical mediumship had found vindication from the most unlikely postmortem source. But this was not to be.

Joseph Dunninger, the master radio mentalist, appeared on Mrs. Houdini's doorstep to contend that the Ford message was very likely a fraud. Houdini, Dunninger reminded her, had never specified the content of his message, only its coded form. Yes, Bess answered, but the message *had been* in the code. Dunninger cut her short, pointing out that the secret code, on which the validity of Arthur Ford's message depended, had been printed in a Houdini biography for the whole world to see just one year after the magician's death.

Bess instantly retracted her sponsorship of the Ford communication. Nevertheless, for many years the woman continued to hold séances on the anniversary of Houdini's death, hoping against hope that a true message would come. It never did. As she neared the end of her own life, Bess wearied of mediums and all they represented. "When I go," she told a friend, "I'll be gone for good. I won't even try to come back."

Secrets of the Spirit Mediums

If I can only get your attention intently," a magician once confided to a friend, "an elephant can pass behind me and you will not see it." The same principle, according to many magicians, could have easily been applied to the so-called spirit manifestations of most practicing mediums. There was nothing otherworldly in the mysterious rappings and janglings of the séance room, they asserted. Rather, the secret was to be found in clever stagecraft.

Almost from the dawn of spiritualism, magicians and other skeptics came forward to discredit professional mediums by duplicating—and then exposing—their effects. Both Harry Houdini and Joseph Dunninger spent a good part of their careers laying bare the methods of fraudulent séance artists, who they felt were cruelly bilking a credulous public. Mediums, for their part, were quick to argue that mere imitation did not prove fraud, just as a good copy of a famous painting did not render the original a fake.

Through the early years of the twentieth century, the challenges of magicians had only a limited impact on the flourishing spiritualism industry. Although some mediums were driven out of business, most simply devised new and better wizardry. Ultimately, the success of spirit mediumship owed more to the public's eagerness to believe and marvel than to the skill of individual practitioners.

On the following pages, magicians and investigators turn a harsh light on the darkness of the séance room, revealing some all-too-earthly secrets of mediums and their alleged spirits.

Ringing Bells, Rising Tables

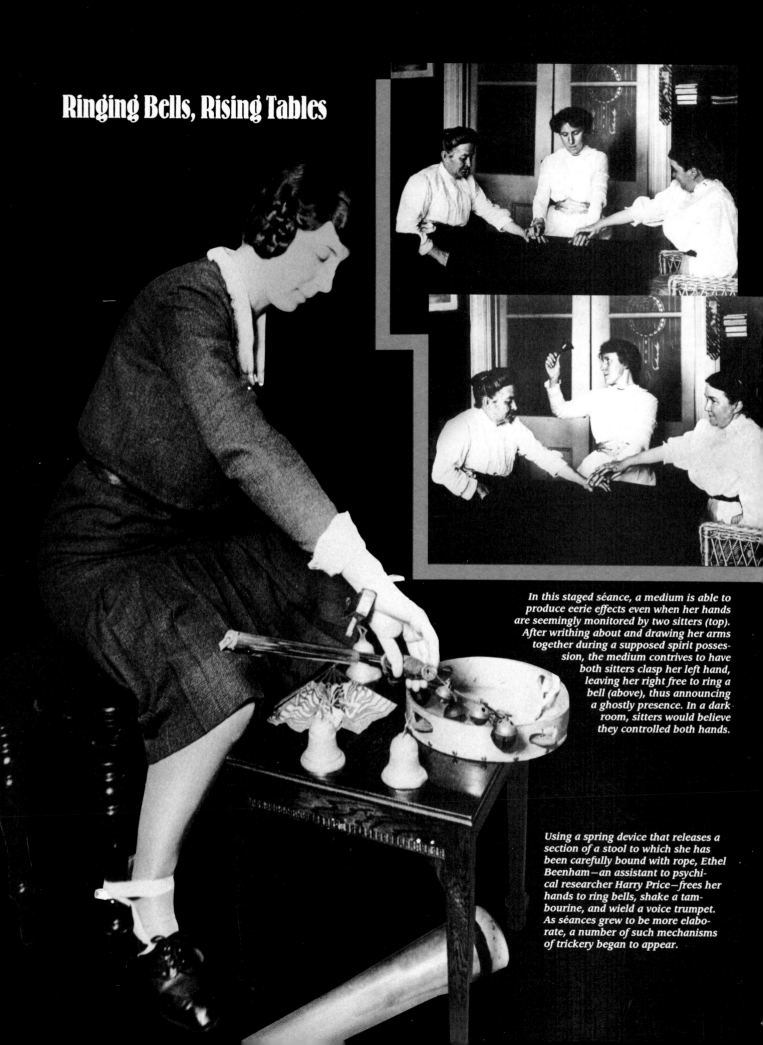

In this staged séance, a medium is able to produce eerie effects even when her hands are seemingly monitored by two sitters (top). After writhing about and drawing her arms together during a supposed spirit possession, the medium contrives to have both sitters clasp her left hand, leaving her right free to ring a bell (above), thus announcing a ghostly presence. In a dark room, sitters would believe they controlled both hands.

Using a spring device that releases a section of a stool to which she has been carefully bound with rope, Ethel Beenham—an assistant to psychical researcher Harry Price—frees her hands to ring bells, shake a tambourine, and wield a voice trumpet. As séances grew to be more elaborate, a number of such mechanisms of trickery began to appear.

After extricating his hands from a simple rope tie, a medium uses a telescoping rod to hoist a tambourine high in the air so the sound is heard from well above the heads of his sitters. Sometimes the tambourine would be treated with glowing phosphorus for an even more dramatic effect.

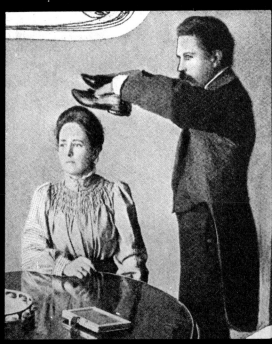

Having announced from within his curtained spirit cabinet that he is levitating, a medium steps from the enclosure to brush his shoes across a sitter's hair, leaving her believing that he is floating overhead (right). Once the suggestion had been planted in the mind of the sitters, such deceptions proved surprisingly effective.

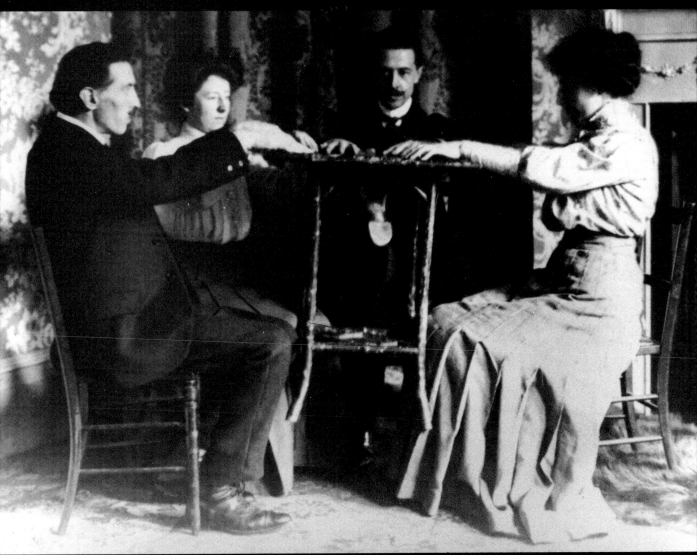

With his foot, magician William Marriott (second from right) shows that a floating table does not necessarily indicate spirits.

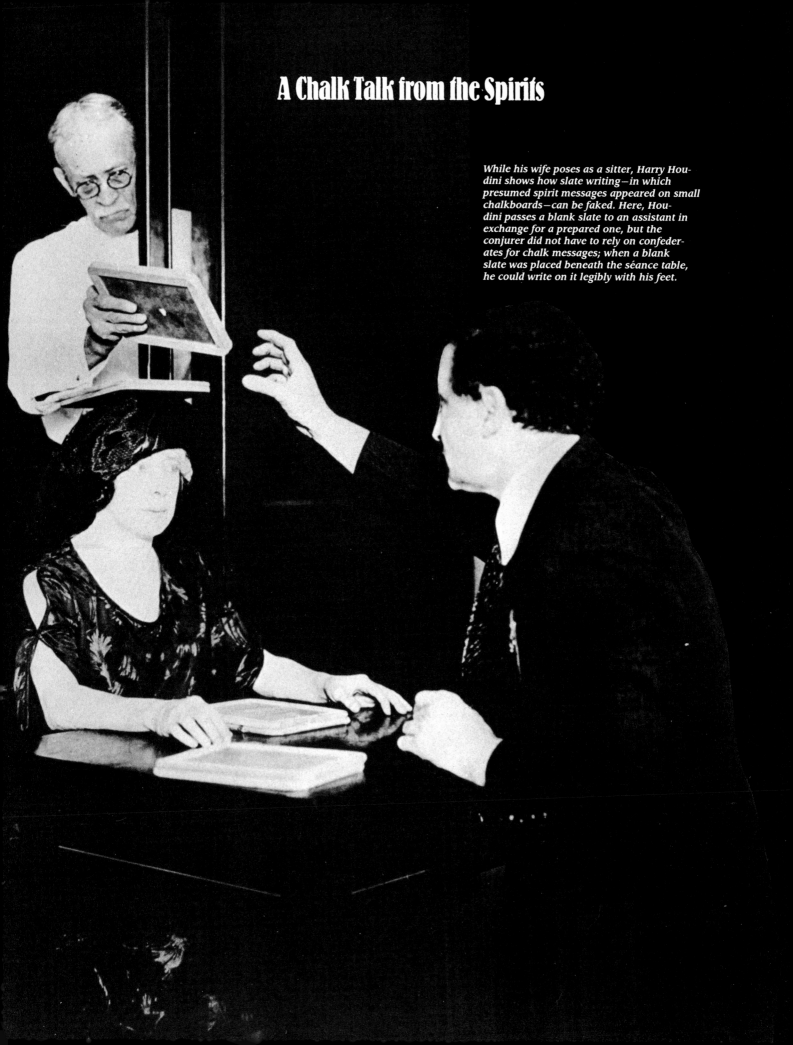

A Chalk Talk from the Spirits

While his wife poses as a sitter, Harry Houdini shows how slate writing—in which presumed spirit messages appeared on small chalkboards—can be faked. Here, Houdini passes a blank slate to an assistant in exchange for a prepared one, but the conjurer did not have to rely on confederates for chalk messages; when a blank slate was placed beneath the séance table, he could write on it legibly with his feet.

With both hands tightly held by a sitter, mentalist Joseph Dunninger grips a piece of chalk in his teeth to produce a sample of slate writing. With practice, an adept medium could not only write in the dark but also backward and upside down.

Psychical investigator Harry Price (left) exhibits a pair of hinged chalkboards rigged with a trick slate flap. When the two blank surfaces were pressed together, a hidden spring triggered the flap. Pulling the slates apart revealed a drawing and a written message, supposedly inscribed just instants before by spirit hands.

Miracles By Mail

As the nineteenth century drew to a close, demand for newer and more baffling séance effects grew so great that an enterprising Chicago firm began offering such items as telescoping rods and spirit padlocks through the mail. "Gambols With the Ghosts," the catalog of the Ralph E. Sylvestre Company, promised to supply the working medium's every conceivable want, from slates, bells, and trumpets to luminous false hands and faces.

Together with those basic supplies, the company offered its customers detailed instruction in such practices as table lifting, hypnotism, divination, and silent transmission of thought. Perhaps most important, all of the company's services were rendered and maintained in strictest confidence. "Our effects are being used by nearly all prominent mediums, entertainers and others of the entire world," the proprietor stated with obvious pride. "You can, therefore, be assured of receiving fraternal and honest treatment in all transactions."

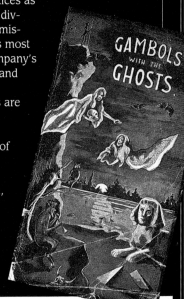

107. Spirit Messages on Paper Between Slates.

This is a manner of producing a message or writing on a blank sheet of paper, placed between two slates, that is very striking and effective. Any ordinary writing paper used, and slates bear examination. Requires only moderate skill or practice. Price, complete, delivery charges prepaid throughout United States, Canada and Mexico $2.50

109. Slate Writing on Marked Slates.

Two slates are used, thoroughly cleaned in presence of sitter, who puts his marks or initials on one. Slates are placed together and held by sitter or medium. When opened a message is found on the marked slate. Very original. Price, including slates, complete, delivery charges prepaid throughout United States, Canada and Mexico $3.00

110. New and Mysterious Slate Writing.

With this you can write on any slate at any time and place, and even while the end of slate is being held by investigator. Requires some skill; most suitable for male mediums. Price, complete, delivery charges prepaid throughout United States, Canada and Mexico. $5.00

111. Our Unexcelled Spirit Slate Writing.

This excellent manner of producing a message on an ordinary slate that can be thoroughly examined and cleaned, is one of the very best in existence. Slates are closely inspected and then held underneath any ordinary table by both operator and the sitter, or the sitter alone, and upon replacing them on table a message is found thereon, as full and complete as the operator desires. It can be easily produced in any room, at any time, by either lady or gentleman, and even in the presence

—8—

of several sitters. Slate or slates can be taken away and kept by the sitter if desired. Price, complete $10.00

112. Dark Seance Slate Writing.

For canopy or cabinet work only, under test conditions. Two slates are examined, any question is written on paper by "sitter," sealed and sewed in an envelope, which is placed between the slates; these are then tied and sealed together. In a short time when reopened an answer to the question is found written on inside of slates and envelope is undisturbed. Price $10.00

113. Non Plus Ultra Slate Writing Test.

In this remarkably fine test, a finely finished small box is used, this box is of a size to hold the slate, and is securely closed with

—9—

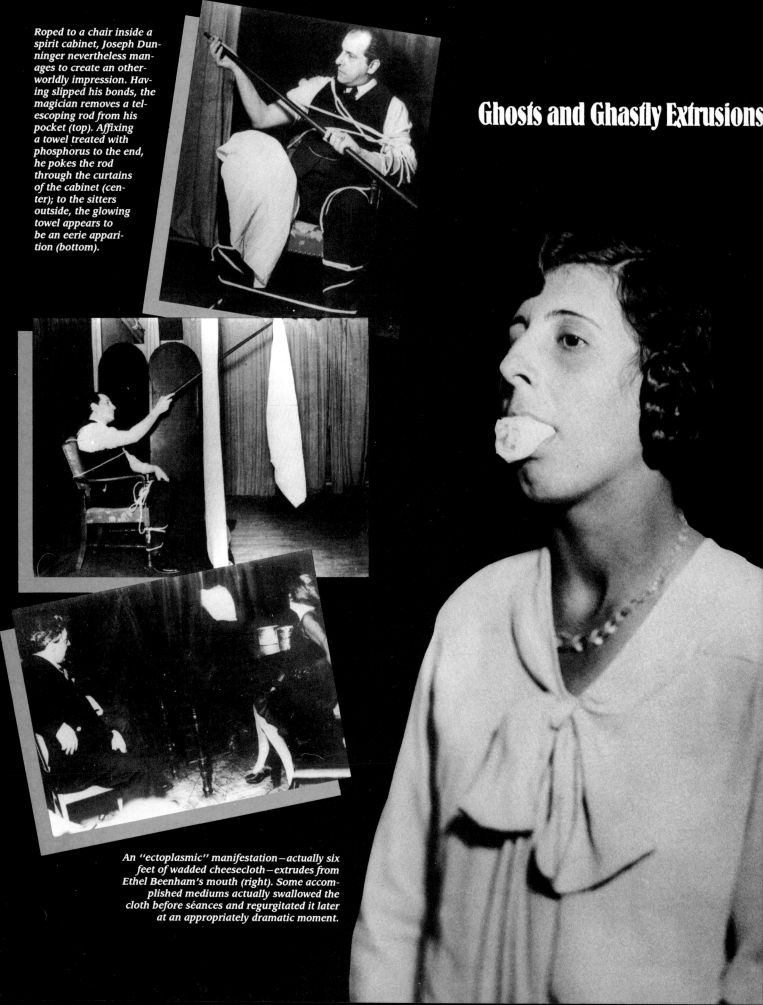

Roped to a chair inside a spirit cabinet, Joseph Dunninger nevertheless manages to create an otherworldly impression. Having slipped his bonds, the magician removes a telescoping rod from his pocket (top). Affixing a towel treated with phosphorus to the end, he pokes the rod through the curtains of the cabinet (center); to the sitters outside, the glowing towel appears to be an eerie apparition (bottom).

An "ectoplasmic" manifestation—actually six feet of wadded cheesecloth—extrudes from Ethel Beenham's mouth (right). Some accomplished mediums actually swallowed the cloth before séances and regurgitated it later at an appropriately dramatic moment.

Magician William Marriott exhibits a collection of ghost forms—actually sheets and masks—used to produce plausible spirit materializations. Although the figures appear crude to the camera, darkness and the raised expectations of séance sitters made them convincing.

CHAPTER 5

Pipelines to the Beyond

he channeler is fortunate—it is a good night for medieval saints. Thomas Aquinas has departed, but one of his old teachers has now presumably taken control of the channeler's body. The newcomer is Albertus Magnus, a German theologian and alchemist who was canonized in 1931. He died in 1280.

Albertus is talking about gems and crystals. Crystals are all the rage among New Age mystics, who believe they harbor mysterious energies that facilitate healing, meditation, and the expansion of psychic powers.

Rubies, Albertus says, are good for the blood. "Those of you who are so inclined, if there is a bit of a circulatory problem, grind up a ruby and put it in a little wine and drink it," he advises, adding with a chuckle, "It's a rather expensive remedy these days."

It seems the dead saint may be joking, but most of his audience appears to think otherwise. The listeners are rapt: Presumed enlightenment from beyond the grave is a serious business. It is not, however, a particularly unusual one—at least, not for this audience and for tens of thousands of like-minded devotees of channeling.

Supposed communications with the disembodied occur daily, even simultaneously, at thousands of locations throughout the United States and abroad as a growing network of channelers purport to provide a link between earth and ether. In California alone, for example, seekers after the great beyond can choose from more than 1,000 professional channelers, who charge anywhere from $10 to $1,500 per session to act as conduits for alleged astral messages. Not that a shortage of cash precludes a session with the spirits: In a field that recognizes few barriers, material or otherwise, there are channeling schools for metaphysical do-it-yourselfers who choose not to hire a professional. The pervasiveness of channeling, along with its democratic accessibility to anyone wanting to give it a try, brings to mind the rambunctious early days of spiritualism.

Indeed, channeling is easily recognizable as mediumship's offspring, despite the difference in labels. No one seems to know exactly when and how the term *channeler* arrived to supplant *medium*, but both cases involve practitioners claiming to be human pipelines for the transmission of messages from discarnate sources. Moreover, channeling and spiritualism each can be seen as unique products of their times. Just as spiritualism was fueled by the Victorian ferment of industrialism, scientism, and religious doubt, channeling arose in another time of doubt and turmoil, amid fear of the nuclear age, the social upheaval and iconoclastic fervor of the 1960s, and the inward-gazing self-realization movements of the 1970s and 1980s.

Victorian spiritualists thought that mediums heralded a new age. Similarly, to their adherents, channelers are harbingers of a new age—the New Age, in fact, with its promise of unprecedented social and spiritual harmony. But, as mediumship had in its day, channeling has detractors who see it as only the most recent in a long line of attempts to deceive the public. James Randi, author and debunker of the paranormal, calls channeling "the latest supernatural fad," replete with "the imaginative babblings of self-appointed 'gurus' supported by the need-to-believe of a certain segment of the population."

Be that as it may, the segment that needs to believe has shown itself to be quite large. New Age pursuits ranging from holistic health to astral travel may once have been the province of counterculture outposts. But by the mid-1980s they had become comfortably mainstream—so much so that a study conducted by the University of Chicago's National Opinion Research Center revealed that nearly one-third of all Americans believed in reincarnation or claimed to have had a psychic experience, and almost one-half claimed to have been in contact with someone dead. Such statistics

were disquieting for the movement's detractors. Literary critic George Steiner, for instance, gloomily concluded that "ours is the psychological and the social climate most infected by superstition, by irrationalism, of any since the decline of the Middle Ages and, perhaps, even since the time of the crisis in the Hellenistic world." Others surveyed what they deemed to be a bleak cultural landscape, a moral wasteland where the twin totems of materialism and narcissism rose above the wreckage of orthodox belief. For them, channeling was a fatuous, shallow quasi faith. Marcello Truzzi, professor of sociology at Eastern Michigan University, called channeling "the perfect yuppie religion." Such jaundiced attitudes differed little from the scorn once heaped on spiritualism by many nineteenth-century religious and cultural leaders.

Despite its similarities to spiritualism, however, channeling remains a distinctly twentieth-century phenomenon. In this more mechanized age, channelers variously describe themselves as human telephones or radio receivers, or as antennas picking up blips and bleeps of cosmic thought. And there are differences of substance as well as style. While channelers, like mediums, purport to span the void between living and dead, mediums limited their contacts almost exclusively to the dead. Channelers, on the other hand, reportedly plug into spirits in a variety of forms—not only dead souls, but also discarnate entities that never lived on earth. Some also claim to commune with angels, extraterrestrials, elves, dolphins, or their own so-called higher selves. Others avow contact with a universal mind, which they interpret as the aggregate of all minds in the cosmos, or the shared memory of the human race, or even the mind of God.

Mediums' messages were usually of a personal nature and therefore potentially verifiable. But channelers often relay only generalities that, intentionally or not, defy verification. Partly for that reason—and partly for lack of cooperation from channelers themselves—channeling does not attract much attention from science. Here again, channelers differ from Victorian mediums, many of whom were objects of intense scientific scrutiny.

Still, mediumship and channeling have more similarities than differences. For one thing, both had their prophets. For the spiritualists, it was Andrew Jackson Davis; for the channelers, it was the early-twentieth-century Kentucky seer Edgar Cayce.

Like Davis, Cayce was young when he had his first encounter with the Other Side. It took place in 1890, when the vision of a lovely woman supposedly appeared to the teenage Cayce and granted him a single wish. Taking her up on the offer, Cayce asked to be able to help others.

Soon thereafter, Cayce began to display a seeming gift for clairvoyance, just like Davis had. Also like Davis, the Sleeping Prophet, as Cayce came to be called, went on as an adult to use his alleged powers to heal the sick. Supposedly he could peer telepathically into a diseased body, no matter how many miles separated him from his "patient." His unorthodox diagnoses were generally followed by equally bizarre treatments, often involving rare herbs and strange dietary regimens. Cayce's followers compiled some 30,000 case histories spanning a career of four and a half decades; many of the cases ended with apparent cures. These, along with a plethora of books about the seer's healing talents and supposed ability to foresee the future, helped inspire the New Age.

As a prognosticator, Cayce claimed access to the so-called akashic records, the "cosmic memory bank" of the thoughts and actions of all souls. Nonetheless, Cayce never professed to be a medium. On a conscious level, he said, he was completely unaware of his powers, since they came to him only when he was in a trance. He therefore considered himself ill-equipped to analyze or pigeonhole his abilities. Hugh Lynn Cayce, his son and bearer of the Cayce torch, was equally wary of labels. He wrote of his father: "In the usual sense Edgar Cayce was not a medium. His voice was always his own. No guide or controls came forward to identify themselves and take over his physical body. In communicating with the minds of people either living or dead, the flow of information always seemed to come through his own unconscious."

Not a channeler himself, Cayce nevertheless blazed a trail for channeling, primarily because of his well-publicized talent for tapping into some power far greater than his own. His example was all the more inspiring because Edgar Cayce, in his conscious state, was such a thoroughly ordinary and unassuming man. His speech was plain, and his education was scant. He lived simply, enjoyed few luxuries, and was often discomfited by the publicity that always seemed to seek him out.

Many of the channelers who follow in Cayce's path are similarly nondescript, although some of the more successful ones court fame and money as Cayce never did. There is no comprehensive profile delineating the characteristics of the breed. They seem to be average people, representing many diverse walks of life and different ethnic, religious, and cultural backgrounds. Nevertheless, some generalizations can be made.

Channelers, like mediums before them, are more often than not women, although some of the leading exponents of both groups have been men. Also, some researchers detect a link between a predisposition to channeling and a lonely or unhappy childhood—a condition that often applied to mediums as well. Like many other children, young channelers-to-be often have imaginary friends. But unlike most children, who outgrow such companions by the age of six or seven, channelers sometimes continue to rely on

their imaginations for company as adults. One critic of channeling, Stephan Schwartz, director of the Mobius Society—a research foundation for the study of consciousness—hints at imagination's role in the phenomenon. "Channelers could be making all this up," he says, "or they could be self-deluded or confusing a telepathic experience with contact with a spirit guide." On the other hand, Schwartz concedes, "no reputable scientist has any handle whatever on what is going on."

One researcher who has at least tried to understand the phenomenon is Los Angeles psychologist Margo Chandley, who did a four-year study of channeling. Among her conclusions, Chandley believes that the making of a channeler is a progressive process of amalgamating a human host and a disembodied visitor. Beginning with the host's initial awareness of the presence of some entity apart from his or her own personality, Chandley says, there are subse-

quent phases of increasing closeness, culminating in the merger of the two into what Chandley describes as "one being, one unit, one aware personality."

This sort of sequential integration seems traceable in the career of Jane Roberts, one of the earliest and most renowned channelers. Roberts, a would-be poet and novelist and former Avon lady from Elmira, New York, channeled an entity that eventually became famous and widely published. His name was Seth.

According to her own account, Jane Roberts had never had a psychic experience before September 9, 1963—a day that, for the most part, ran a routine course. The evening, too, was unexceptional: supper followed by a short walk to the living room and the old table where Roberts worked at her poetry. Meanwhile, as was his custom, her artist husband, Robert Butts, was painting in another room, while the couple's cat contentedly slept off its dinner.

Bolstered by her ninth or tenth cup of coffee for the day and further fortified by the cigarette she held, Roberts made her way to the living room and sat down at the table. She sat quietly for a moment, scanning for the frequency of her poetic voice. Suddenly, her brain erupted into almost volcanic activity. It was, she wrote later, as though "someone had slipped me an LSD cube on the sly."

"A fantastic avalanche of radical, new ideas burst into my head with tremendous force, as if my skull were some sort of receiving station turned up to unbearable volume," Roberts later wrote in *The Seth Material*. "It was as if the physical world were really tissue-paper thin, hiding infinite dimensions of reality, and I was suddenly flung through the tissue paper with a huge ripping sound. My body sat at the table, my hands furiously scribbling down the words and ideas that flashed through my head."

In all, some one hundred pages flowed onto paper—words and ideas that immediately and forever upended Roberts's conceptions of reality. "We are individualized portions of energy," the unseen entity announced, "materialized within physical existence, to learn to form ideas from energy and make them physical." And what was this portion of energy? "The basic self," came the reply, "immortal, nonphysical. It communicates on an energy level with other entities, and has an almost inexhaustible supply of energy at its command."

Roberts thought of this first encounter—and of the manuscript it engendered—as extensions of her creative subconscious, her "normal creativity suddenly 'turned on' or stepped up to an almost incredible degree." She had just taken the first step toward channeling: becoming aware of a nonphysical entity. Though unclear as to exactly who or what this force was, she did recognize the importance of its advent. "I'm certain that the affair set off the emergence of my own unsuspected 'psychic' abilities and acted as a trigger for the production of *The Seth Material*," Roberts asserted. "Apparently, I'd reached a point where these abilities were ready to show themselves, so they did." "These abilities" allegedly included telepathy and clairvoyance.

Over the next few weeks, Roberts wrote later, she quickly attuned herself to the visiting entity. Her supposed psychic powers expanded to include dream recall and precognitive dreams, and she and her husband developed an interest in the workings of the Ouija board. At first, Roberts was skeptical, even embarrassed, at the thought of two rational adults watching a pointer drift across a board while they hung on its every move. But after a few sessions, they ostensibly contacted a spirit that called itself Frank Withers. Withers claimed to be a former resident of Elmira who had died in 1942—apparent facts that Roberts and her husband maintained they later verified.

But Withers's stint as an entity was far shorter-lived than his stay on earth. After a few sessions—during which he described his alleged past life experiences—Withers suddenly announced through the Ouija board: "I prefer not to be called Frank Withers. That personality was rather colorless." Roberts and her husband were surprised by this abrupt development and even more so by what followed. "What would you prefer to be called?" Rob Butts asked.

The Ouija board's pointer sped from letter to letter.

"To God all names are His name," came the answer. "You may call me whatever you choose. I call myself Seth. It fits the me of me, the personality more clearly approximating the whole self I am or am trying to be."

Frank Withers, it seemed, was only part of a larger entity, just as Jane Roberts and Robert Butts themselves, in Seth's estimation, were parts of greater wholes. In fact, Seth took the liberty of renaming Jane "Rubert" and her husband "Joseph" in order to capture "the sum of your various personalities in the past and future."

Subsequent sessions with Seth were just as perplexing and unsettling—all the more so when Jane suddenly began to anticipate the board's replies. By the fourth session, in fact, she claimed to be hearing entire sentences and paragraphs before the Ouija board spelled them out. Soon she felt compelled to speak the words she was hearing in her mind. "I felt as if I were standing, shivering, on the top of a high diving board," Roberts wrote of that time, "trying to make myself jump while all kinds of people were waiting impatiently behind me." But instead of people, "it was the words that pushed at me. They seemed to rush through my mind. In some crazy fashion, I felt as if they'd back up, piles of nouns and verbs in my head, until they closed everything else off if I didn't speak them." She was edging closer to becoming a vocal conduit for the presumed entity that was courting closer contact.

Roberts hesitated, unsure whether to surrender to the increasing pressure she felt. Then, "without really knowing how or why," she opened her mouth—and broke the logjam of words. "For the first time I began to speak for Seth, continuing the sentences the board had spelled out only a moment before," she wrote later. Within a month, Roberts was entering trances and, it seemed, speaking for Seth, without benefit of the Ouija board.

The symbiotic relationship continued for twenty-one years, until Roberts's death in 1984 at the age of fifty-five. It produced hundreds of sessions and thousands of pages of channeled material. Among other works, Roberts published

This portrait of an enlightened entity called Seth is the work of artist Robert Butts, whose wife, Jane Roberts, purportedly channeled the transcendent being. Both Roberts and Butts (inset) claimed a special awareness of Seth. Butts said the spirit visitor appeared to him in visions and, from time to time, in a nearly materialized form that inspired several paintings. During Roberts's channeling sessions with Seth in the 1960s, Butts took copious notes that later became best-selling books, helping to trigger the channeling mania.

five entire books allegedly channeled by Seth, as well as two more detailing her relationship with him. Throughout Seth's tenure, Roberts continued to grapple with his nature. Was Seth a separate personality, or was he merely some unearthed facet of her own psyche?

Seth described himself as "an energy personality essence no longer focused in physical reality." He was, he said, composed of several personality fragments, including that of Frank Withers. Moreover, since his own definition of death was being "completely unfocused in physical reality," one might infer that Seth, or part of him, was a spirit of the dead. He explained that he, like all other group entities, was in turn only a piece of even greater conglomerate entities and ultimately a part of what he called All That Is. He defined All That Is as the multidimensional spirit that animates the universe and is called God by most Westerners. Underscoring the notion that Seth was a sort of group personality subsumed in an infinitude of larger groups, Roberts eventually began channeling an entity she called Seth Two. This new energy force seemed to contain the original Seth.

The first Seth was adamant in insisting that he was a separate entity, not merely a part of Jane Roberts's mind. The information he relayed through her only passed through her subconscious, he said, "as a fish swims through water." But just as the fish "is not the water, I am not Rubert's subconscious." Whatever he was, self or other, Roberts was certain that Seth was her "channel to revelational knowledge."

Thanks to the efforts of later channelers, who seldom stray far afield from it, Seth's basic message has become rather familiar: People create their own realities. Each person is part of a larger entity and ultimately a part of God, or All That Is. The physical world as humans know it is only "camouflage" concealing a more profound reality. People are not dependent on the physical world but only take physical form temporarily in various incarnations as they evolve toward eventual reunion with All That Is. According to Seth, "physical existence is one way in which the soul chooses to experience its own actuality. The soul, in other words, has

created a world for you to inhabit, to change—a complete sphere of activity in which new developments and indeed new forms of consciousness can emerge."

Seth defined the soul variously as "an electromagnetic energy field," a "powerhouse of probabilities or probable actions," and "a grouping of nonphysical consciousness that nevertheless knows itself as an identity." Death, he said, was only a transition from one realm of consciousness to another, a part of the "process of becoming." After death, the entity declared, the discorporate spirit has a form that seems physical but is invisible to living humans and is endowed with superhuman powers. "It can do anything that you can do now in your dreams," Seth explained. "Therefore it flies, goes through solid objects, and is moved directly by your will, taking you, say, from one location to another as you may think of these locations. . . . If you wonder what Aunt Sally is doing in, say, Poughkeepsie, New York, then you will find yourself there."

Through Roberts, Seth also proposed the existence of a number of "Speakers"—keepers of esoteric secrets who spoke to humankind through the ages. According to Seth, there were millions of Speakers in all, but fewer than thirty great ones, among them Jesus Christ, the Buddha, and American essayist and poet Ralph Waldo Emerson.

Like most channelers, Roberts was more receptive to her source while in a trance. However, unlike many of her colleagues, who are almost inanimate during their altered states, Roberts was often quite active while in a trance. She moved about and even smoked or enjoyed a beer, wine, or coffee. As Seth, she usually spoke in a deep, accented voice very unlike her own. The accent was difficult to place. Those who heard it described it as Irish, or German, or Dutch, or Russian, or Italian. Seth himself chalked up the confusion to his many reincarnations. They had given him, he said, a "cosmopolitan background."

Seth and Seth Two were not the only entities that Roberts supposedly channeled. She also claimed to have "translated" American philosopher and psychologist William James, as well as the French impressionist painter Paul Cézanne—both long dead by the time she caught up to them. Those sessions resulted in two more books, *The World View of Paul Cézanne: A Psychic Interpretation* and *The Afterlife Journal of an American Philosopher: The World View of William James.* But, as she was with Seth, Roberts was vague about the true nature of her sources. Of the supposed Cézanne, she said: "I didn't ask if this was really Cézanne." She knew only that the presumed entity's sentences "were not natural for me; they had an unaccustomed feel to them." As for James, Roberts eventually concluded that his persona was a fabrication of her own mind. He was, she said, "unconsciously formed as an automatic process when my consciousness tunes in to his reality—and it stands for or represents whatever James's reality 'really is' now."

Roberts's vagueness was a legacy to the legions of channelers who followed her—one that rankles with critics, who note how carefully channeling sticks to high-flown metaphysical generalities and avoids material that is amenable to scientific probing. But such criticism encounters a stone wall in the form of New Agers' contempt for traditional science, which they generally dismiss as narrow-minded, dead-end rationalism. To their followers, channelers' etheric verbiage marks them as enlightened prophets. To their detractors, this same trait brands them as frauds or lunatics. To the charge of dementia, channelers sometimes make their very numbers a defense. As a Berkeley, California, channeler says, "The fact that I'm not the only one doing it gives me some indication that there is *something* going on. Unless we are *all* going crazy."

There is diversity as well as safety in channelers' numbers. In the vanguard are some whose sources make Seth seem almost pedestrian—channelers of space aliens, for instance. By and large, however, the information coming through channelers—whatever its source—takes a rather predictable form. It usually purports to be nuggets of age-less wisdom, generally propounding Seth-like notions of a self-conceived reality, an immortal soul, and an all-encompassing God, or All That Is. In this metaphysical construct, individuals are seen as godlets, divine bits of the cosmic divinity.

Sometimes channeled material assumes a personalized cast, offering guidance for daily living—advice involving love affairs, career moves, family, or health problems. Other channeled material purports to allow glimpses of the past or future, to describe life after death, or to inspire an individual's creative expression. In certain quarters it has become fashionable to have a spiritual master in the form of a personal channeler. Some clients look to their spiritual masters for advice before investing in the stock market, for example, or asking their bosses for raises. Frustrated New Yorkers have been known to seek channelers' aid in divining a suitable apartment or an open parking place. One channeler charges fifty dollars per half hour to help her clients find lost car keys.

While many channelers enjoy small but lucrative operations, not all are equal in the channeling pantheon. Some are more famous and materially successful than others. Rising to the apex of the elite in the 1980s was J. Z. Knight, a one-time homemaker and cable-television executive from Yelm, Washington, who claims to be the conduit for Ramtha, the Enlightened One. Ramtha identifies himself as a 35,000-year-old warrior spirit who, in his corporeal days on the legendary lost continent of Lemuria, helped conquer the equally legendary lost continent of Atlantis. The darling of celebrities, Knight has become a media star, commanding fees that have propelled her income into millions of dollars. Moreover, her personal appeal is so magnetic that hundreds of followers have moved to the Pacific Northwest, in order to be near her and to avoid the series of natural disasters Ramtha predicts are on the way. Her fame has rubbed off on her source, and Ramtha is so well known that the name is trademarked.

Fame—and Ramtha—were not always J. Z. Knight's companions. Like many other channelers, she had a difficult childhood. She was abandoned by her alcoholic natural father and molested by her uncle. Nevertheless, by Knight's

Entities at the Easel

By his own account, Brazilian psychotherapist Luiz Antonio Gasparetto cannot paint a stroke. Nevertheless, he has been known to turn out canvases at a staggering rate and in an impressive variety of styles. These he attributes not to his own talent, but to the spirits of dead artists who have chosen him as the vehicle to carry on their postmortem work.

Born in São Paulo in 1949, Gasparetto first discovered his peculiar channeling function when he was seven years old. His mother is a medium, and during one of her séances, young Luiz began to do automatic painting, his hand seemingly guided by spirits. After a six-year hiatus, he took up the practice again and has subsequently produced paintings in the styles of Goya, Picasso, van Gogh, and some four dozen other great masters.

On a visit to England in 1978, Gasparetto rapidly produced twenty-one pictures while appearing on a television program. Some were done simultaneously, with one hand drawing normally and the other creating an upside-down painting. In the spring of 1988, Gasparetto gave a series of demonstrations of psychic painting in California. In a single fifteen-minute tour de force, he produced six paintings. They more or less resembled the works of Renoir, Manet, Toulouse-Lautrec, and Modigliani.

Gasparetto's dexterity is beyond question, even if its spirit origins are not. But if, in fact, the dead masters are painting through him, there remains the question of what they might have lost in moving on to the Other Side. Art critics generally say the artists' talents seem to have diminished considerably.

Certainly, Gasparetto's methods would have confounded the geniuses he allegedly channels. He works in the dark or with his eyes closed, his face contorted as he furiously assaults the canvas with bare hands or feet. He uses no brushes or other implements. He says he is fully conscious as he paints but feels removed from the creative effort. Still, he says, he can chat with the dead masters during the collaboration, both telepathically and verbally.

Odd though it might seem to others, the channeler does not regard his presumed talent for psychic contact as all that unusual. It seems to run in the family. His mother claims to channel best-selling writers, while one of his brothers tunes in dead pop musicians.

Gasparetto does not charge admission to his frequent demonstrations, although he does sell the paintings, which bring about $200 to $300 each. Proceeds from the psychic art reportedly go to help meet expenses at a center he operates in São Paulo, whose mission is to provide food, medical care, counseling, and job training for the poor. Gasparetto's personal income, he says, comes from his psychotherapy practice at his own clinic in São Paulo. In addition, he hosts a popular television show about metaphysics.

Though perhaps the most prolific of current psychic artists, Gasparetto is not the only toiler in the field. British psychic Matthew Manning says he contacted the spirit of Pablo Picasso shortly after the Spanish master's death in 1973. Still a teenager at the time, Manning purportedly channeled several dead artists. He would sit quietly, he says, pen in hand, and concentrate on selected departed painters. Almost immediately, the pen would begin to draw in a style reminiscent of the artist, be it Arthur Rackham, Paul Klee, Leonardo da Vinci, Aubrey Beardsley, or others.

Like Gasparetto, Manning was conscious during his channeling episodes. But while Gasparetto calls his activity as an art conduit "pure joy," Manning found it tiring and has done little automatic art since adolescence, choosing instead to focus on psychic healing.

Apparently, discarnate genius is not confined to the visual arts. London homemaker Rosemary Brown says that since 1964 she has channeled for some of the the world's great deceased composers, including Beethoven, Brahms, Chopin, Schubert, Stravinsky, and Franz Liszt. It was Liszt, Brown claims, who contacted her as a child and foretold her coming collaboration with the tuneful dead. Critics have called her work less than masterful.

Psychic artist Luiz Antonio Gaspa-retto says the spirit of Vincent van Gogh guided the creation of this still life.

own account, her poor but devoted mother managed to give her a Christian upbringing in this dismal environment.

Knight was, she asserts, always psychic. Moreover, she believed herself to be the reincarnation of her drowned older sister. Her lifelong mystic bent notwithstanding, it seems doubtful she could have expected the events that reportedly transpired in her kitchen one winter day in 1977.

Horsing around with her husband that afternoon, Knight playfully donned a paper pyramid as a hat. When the makeshift headgear slipped down over her face, both she and her husband broke out laughing and kept on laughing until they were in tears. But lifting the pyramid from her eyes, Knight was amazed to see not just her husband, but a decidedly strange visitor. "Through my tears I saw what looked like a handful of gold and silver glitter sprinkled in a ray of sunshine," she once told an interviewer. "A very large entity was standing there. . . . He looked at me with a beautiful smile and said, 'I am Ramtha, the Enlightened One. I have come to help you over the ditch.' "

Crossing the ditch proved at first to be a lonely task: Knight and Ram-

tha labored virtually unknown for the next eight years. It was not until 1985, when actress Shirley MacLaine spotlighted Knight in her book *Dancing in the Light,* that fame caught up to the erstwhile homemaker and her Lemurian mentor. Once it did, however, Knight nurtured her long-awaited celebrity through a combination of books, semi-monthly seminars, and more than 900 hours of video- and audiotapes that carried Ramtha's message to thousands of fans throughout the world.

The message's touchstone is the same self-reliant,

While two enthusiasts follow her lead (above), J. Z. Knight (the initials stand for Judy Zebra) points the way as Ramtha during a San Diego channeling session in 1985. At right, she leads devotees at a desert retreat in Yucca Valley, California. The white-clad Knight is perched on a rock at the picture's far left.

New Age philosophy that fuels so much channeled material. "You are masters of your destiny. . . . You will receive what you want. . . . God the Father lives within each of us," forms the gist of Ramtha's wisdom. Expanding on those themes, Ramtha sometimes exhorts his audiences, "Love what you are. Love the god that you are. Embrace the wind, and the willow, and the water, for it is the creation of your importance, and be at peace." The familiarity of the message has proved no barrier to its acceptance. Hundreds of admirers happily shell out hundreds of dollars each to experience Ramtha firsthand at Knight's intensive weekend seminars.

At those sessions, Knight appears to succumb to a deep trance, and after shaking all over and then going limp, she resurfaces as the gruff-voiced Ramtha. "It's like a death process," Knight says of the transformation. "I go through a tunnel and there's a whistling sound and a light at the end. As soon as I hit the light I come back."

Like Jane Roberts, J. Z. Knight is not given to sedentary trances. As Ramtha, she stomps from one end of the stage to the other—bellowing wisdom, gesturing broadly, pausing

occasionally to dispense a hug or study a disciple. Question-and-answer sessions are usually a part of the seminars. In them, Ramtha tackles inquiries ranging from the cosmic ("Is there anything I can do in my lifestyle at this time that will bring me closer to the grand Father and the Creative One?") to the ridiculous ("How can I learn to become a tree?"). All are handled with equal ease.

Ramtha's answers to most queries are, in the tradition of channeling, often vague. Asked to depict his spiritual home, the Enlightened One begs the question by saying that words cannot describe it because "words themselves are a limitation." To a question regarding his true nature, Ramtha rattles on cryptically: "I am Ramtha, the Enlightened One, indeed, that which is termed servant unto that which is called Source, to that which is termed the Principal Cause, indeed, unto that which is termed Life, unto that which is termed Christus—God experiencing that which is termed Man, man experiencing that which is termed God—am I servant unto also."

Knight herself can be equally nebulous when questioned about her role in Ramtha's reappearance after a 35,000-year hiatus. When asked why Ramtha chose her to channel his message, for example, Knight answers, "Why not?" (Perhaps the choice makes sense in light of Ramtha's conjecture that Knight was one of his ten children in a former life.)

As Knight/Ramtha's following grew, the questions began centering more and more on Ramtha's authenticity. Rumors arose that one staff member quit after overhearing Knight practicing Ramtha's voice. Another protégé left the fold after allegedly seeing Knight slip into her Ramtha role without benefit of trance. "We thought she did a better job of doing Ramtha than Ramtha," recalls the former follower.

There were problems with the message as well as the messenger. Disciples who found little to question when Ramtha spoke of an advanced civilization thriving at the earth's core were nevertheless troubled when the dead guru's dicta on love and peace turned into sermons of gloom and doom. Predictions that Mother Nature would "get rid of" homosexuals caused some to doubt Ramtha's wisdom. So did forecasts that, among other calamities, earthquakes would topple California into the sea, and Florida would become a vast sinkhole. "Many people now speculate that whatever energy came through J. Z. Knight has either shifted, departed, or been replaced by a less benign entity," a critic declared in the mid-1980s. Another interested party, the director of a counseling service that specializes in helping former cult members over the hump of withdrawal, is not surprised by Knight's partial slip from grace. "It's the same pattern I've seen with other gurus," explains Susan Rothbaum. "The guru starts with a simple message of openness and love, then it becomes complicated, baroque, paranoid, and fearful."

Such detractions aside, most of Ramtha's followers remain steadfast. Some credit him with teaching them to love themselves or with helping them make needed alterations in their lives. "I credit me for making changes," one young follower says. "But I credit Ramtha for showing me that I can." Even Knight's snowballing wealth does not shake the faith of her admirers. They do not doubt her essential spirituality, even while she ensconces herself in a multimillion-dollar mansion, rides in Rolls-Royce comfort, and shelters her purebred Arabian horses in barns lit by chandeliers. Knight herself downplays her material windfall and the palatial estate it has paid for. "It isn't nearly as nice as the Pope's house," she says of the house that Ramtha built.

The popularity that makes channeling a New Age centerpiece—and a highly profitable business—has stimulated considerable competition in the field. One of the best-known of Ramtha's rivals is Mafu, purportedly an "ascended master who has gone beyond the Seventh Dimension." Mafu supposedly last walked the earth as a leper in first-century Pompeii. He was channeled by Penny Torres, wife of a Los Angeles policeman (she later remarried and used the name Penny Torres Rubin). Her first encounter with her source occurred one dark night in February of

1986, when a disembodied voice announced, "It is I, Mafu, and I come to tell you that you are loved."

The experience would have been eerie at any hour, let alone four in the morning. Reaching for a protective talisman, an amethyst crystal, she found herself "physically guided" by some unseen agent toward the bedroom of her infant son, Andrew. The boy, suffering from pneumonia, lay in an unquiet sleep. Yielding to some inner urge, she held the crystal over Andrew's bed, then watched in amazement as the crystal's tip shattered into a fine powder that floated down over her ailing son. The next morning, she later recalled, the boy was cured.

As she told the story in a 1987 interview, Mafu's second visit came shortly after the first, when he materialized in her bedroom—all seven feet of him. He was wrapped in a belted toga, from which jutted the largest hands she had ever seen. His mission, the apparition declared, was to "bring the message of love to the human plane." To accomplish this, he said, he needed to borrow her body for seven years. He offered in exchange whatever she desired, including "a kingdom of gold." She agreed to an indefinite loan in return for "enlightenment." Thus the bargain was struck, according to the channeler.

Penny Torres Rubin's subsequent fortunes might be regarded as a testament to Mafu's good faith. Although she exacted no kingdom of gold, the entity apparently chose to throw in at least a modest stipend. Rubin, who has a sizeable following, charges $125 a head for day-long sessions with Mafu and $250 for two-day retreats.

Like J. Z. Knight, Rubin is a former homemaker. And the resemblance between Knight and Rubin—and Ramtha and Mafu—does not end there. Mafu's heavily accented voice, his philosophy, and his odd syntax are remarkably similar to Ramtha's. "Be-

loved woman, how be you?" is how Mafu sometimes greets a guest. In a similar situation, Ramtha is wont to say, "Woman, beautiful entity, what say you?" In fact, Mafu's speech is liberally laced throughout with such Ramtha-isms as "indeed," "so be it," and "that which is termed." Like Ramtha, Mafu tells of a race inhabiting "the inner earth," albeit with the added details that the subterraneans travel through secret polar tunnels and have the mission of guiding earthlings to a better way of life.

Not surprisingly, Ramtha supporters accuse Rubin/Mafu of trying to cash in on Ramtha's popularity. They point to the fact that Mafu made his debut only in the wake of Ramtha's wide acclaim. Rubin simply denies the charges. With Mafu supposedly expropriating her body some forty-five hours each week, she appears to have little time for invidious comparisons.

Another threat to Ramtha's channeling supremacy is Lazaris, the self-styled "consummate friend" and self-proclaimed group entity from another dimension. According to his channeler, the very human Jach Pursel, Lazaris "is not now and never has been physical or human."

Pursel himself is a former Florida insurance supervisor who supplements his generous income from channeling by working as an art dealer. A company he formed to oversee

"I'm not really into learning about metaphysics and whatnot," says Penny Torres Rubin, who claims to channel a being she calls Mafu. "I'm into more the message that this entity brings." The message, she says, is to love yourself, do your best, and "have a great time."

Tuning In to the Departed

Retired West German fire equipment inspector Klaus Schreiber channels in a very literal way. Mostly, he does it with his television set.

Schreiber was quaffing a few beers with friends one spring day in 1982 when talk turned to a radio program about messages from other dimensions. Half in jest, Schreiber suggested trying to contact a recently departed friend, Peter, with a tape recorder.

"Hello Peter, where are you?" Schreiber asked into his machine. "Come on over and have a drink." After about ten minutes of silence, Schreiber switched off the recorder, rewound the tape, and hit the replay button. He and his friends heard his invitation, then nothing but a long, low hum. He was about to turn the machine off, when suddenly a voice said, "Hello, friends." All present identified the voice as Peter's. Shortly thereafter, Schreiber's cronies left his house. Shaken by the experience, most never returned.

Schreiber, meanwhile, got busy turning his basement into a small-scale laboratory for further experiments in electronic contact with the dead. He worked first with tape recorders, then, supposedly at the behest of spirit voices on the tapes, he moved on to video recorders and his television set. The result was a collection of videocassettes of what Schreiber calls his "new friends." The friends' faces are fuzzy and washed out when first captured on the channeler's video camera. But by transferring individual frames back and forth between video recorders, then superimposing the images and fine-tuning them with a special amplifier, Schreiber often brings the hazy shapes into focus as faces.

Many of the faces belong to Schreiber's dead relatives or to deceased celebrities. The latter group includes King Ludwig II of Bavaria and film star Romy Schneider.

Schreiber was neither the first nor most famous person to try contacting the dead with electronics. The best known experimenter was American inventor Thomas Edison, who reportedly spent his later years attempting to build an instrument to receive spirit messages. He failed. More recently, several experimenters, most of them in Europe, have allegedly made video contact with the dead.

There are several theories about tuning in the spirits electronically. One is that taped "spirit" voices and images are merely what vivid imaginations read into static, dead air, blank screens, or stray broadcasts. An alternate view, held by some researchers of the paranormal, is that spectral speech and faces come from the experimenters' unconscious minds and are imprinted in some mysterious way on the audio- and videotapes.

One spirit Klaus Schreiber claims to have captured on television belongs to his deceased daughter, Karin. The living Karin is shown in a photo (above), and her spirit, it seems, appears on the television screen (right).

Lazaris's metaphysical labors, Concept: Synergy, collects more than $1 million a year in Lazaris-related income. Nonetheless, Pursel prefers not to think of channeling as a business, but as "a labor of love." It is only the "loony tunes out there," he says, who focus more on dollar signs than cosmic signs.

The amiable, bearded Pursel claims he had no interest in channeling before his first encounter with his discarnate source. His New Age pursuits centered mainly on attempts to meditate, and those left him so relaxed that he usually dropped off to sleep. But in October of 1974, after nodding off during meditation, Pursel allegedly found himself subsumed by the entity he would later dub Lazaris. Moreover, his wife, Peny, found herself talking to the entity and taking notes on the impromptu session. At the end of that first session, Lazaris warned Pursel not to plumb his own consciousness for further interaction. "When it's time, I'll contact you again," Pursel was told. "Don't try to contact us."

That session was the first of several thousand channeled hours in which Lazaris expanded on themes already propounded by Seth and soon to be further explored by Ramtha: that the universe is essentially spiritual; that souls are immortal; that every person has the power to create reality, and that, in Lazaris's words, "the only way to get to God/Goddess/All That Is, is over the bridge of belief."

Those and other subjects form the basis of a collection of Lazaris videotapes bearing such titles as "Awakening the Love," "Forgiving Yourself," and "Developing a Relationship with Your Higher Self." For adherents unable to attend a Lazaris session—or unwilling to add their names to the two-year waiting list to speak to Lazaris in person or on the telephone—the tapes provide an opportunity to come face to face with him in the person of Jach Pursel.

As Pursel describes it, the process of attuning to Lazaris's wavelength is relatively simple: He merely takes his seat, closes his eyes, and draws a few deep breaths, and within moments he is in a trance, his body commandeered by the ever-ready Lazaris. For the spirit entity, however, the process is apparently much more complicated. "Basically how it works," Lazaris explains, "is that we create the thoughts as a mumbo jumbo, and we then project those thoughts through the planes of reality. We project the conglomeration of all the thoughts and all the bleeps and blips we want to work with, and we project them down into a denser level and a denser level, and these enter in through the star system Sirius, to be quite specific with you, into the physical world."

On their way to the physical world, Lazaris's thoughts reportedly pass through the so-called Mental Plane, Causal Plane, and Astral Plane—three of the levels of reality that supposedly separate the earthly plane from All That Is. Ultimately, the Lazaris thoughts reach the channel, or "antenna," in the form of signals that can then be decoded and articulated as words.

Like most fellow entities, Lazaris is vague about his origins and general in his advice. "How old are you?" he was once asked. "In our reality, we have no time," was the answer. "Why are you making your presence known to man?" came the follow-up question. "Because you are ready now." "Is the world about to end?" "No. In a word, no," said the always optimistic Lazaris. "This is not the ending. This is the beginning."

Many channelers—Knight, Rubin, and Pursel among them—feature only one entity. California's Kevin Ryerson, on the other hand, is notable for the number and variety of sources he claims to host.

Ryerson's presumed enlightenment began in the early 1970s, when he joined a meditation group whose soul-searching focused on the teachings of Edgar Cayce. A year later, Ryerson was able to induce channeling at will, tapping into what he called the universal mind.

He describes his version of channeling as "rather like falling backwards into sleep." Like Jach Pursel, Jane Roberts, and others, Ryerson reenters reality with no apparent recall of the dialogue he has just finished channeling. He thus describes himself as a "human telephone or radio receiver"—an observation echoed by actress Shirley Mac-

Laine, who calls him "one of the telephones in my life."

Ryerson claims to commune with discarnate entities who lived in other times. Among them is the Apostle John, a follower of Christ; Obadiah, a Haitian who speaks in a West Indian dialect, and Tom McPherson, a loud and good-natured Celt whose brogue bespeaks his last incarnation in Elizabethan Ireland. A verbal globetrotter, Ryerson also channels sages from ancient Egypt and Japan.

Given the range of his entities, Ryerson seems to run the risk of tripping over his own tongue and confusing the characters. Indeed, critics watch for any sign of unintentional ethnic crossover. But over the years, the entities have continued to come through clearly and distinctly, each consistent with its cultural background.

Ryerson has become one of the most prominent channelers on the New Age scene, making frequent appearances on radio and television and even playing himself—while entities Tom and John "played" themselves—in a television movie version of Shirley MacLaine's popular metaphysical

autobiography *Out on a Limb.* His popularity affords him a substantial income. For his clients, it means a months-long wait to schedule private sessions.

In scope and content, his channeled information is fairly standard fare. Ryerson's entities expound, for example, on the reality of reincarnation and the need to look to the higher self for guidance.

A channeled message with a decidedly Eastern slant comes from a purported entity named Michael through a San Francisco Bay area woman with the pseudonym Jessica Lansing. The material, which holds out the promise of "access to eternity," has resulted in two best-selling books by the writer Chelsea Quinn Yarbro, entitled *Messages from Michael* and *More Messages from Michael.* According to Michael, eve-

Jach Pursel channels his "consummate friend," Lazaris. Apparently, Jach's entrée to the entity hinged on his marriage: Lazaris wanted to communicate with Peny Pursel, who, the entity said, had interesting destinies he hoped to help guide. Lazaris has stuck with his channeler, however, even though Jach and Peny have been divorced.

ry person is the essence of the Tao, the ancient Chinese principle of cosmic unity. Humans, he propounds, are fragments of an entity slowly evolving back to Tao. In order to achieve the perfection of cosmic oneness, however, not only must all the fragments recombine as a single entity, but the entity

Channeling is sometimes done in intimate, private sessions. Here, Verna Yater (right) channels a spirit for New Age writer Kit Tremaine.

must then transcend seven planes of existence. Indeed, the number seven has a central role in Michael's teachings. There are, for example, seven basic soul stages, ranging from infant to infinite, each of which has to be experienced in a minimum of seven reincarnations. There are also seven "roles"—slave, artisan, warrior, scholar, sage, priest, and king—that remain constant throughout the many reincarnations of each soul.

The complexity of this multilayered message has led some to question whether it is worth the effort to follow Michael's lead. That concern becomes even more understandable in light of Michael's claim that, like humans, whales and dolphins also have souls. In fact, he says, there are more than ten million ensouled species in the Milky Way alone, all capable of reincarnation and growth.

"Why should we bother with this stuff?" an interrogator once asked.

"Because you choose to do so," Michael shot back. "To learn. To know. To satisfy your curiosity. To be free."

"Is that enough?" he was asked.

"It is all there is," Michael proclaimed.

Michael represents himself as a "recombined entity," a spirit comprising more than a thousand "old soul" fragments. Age, however, does not seem to guarantee patience in the entity's component parts. He often bristles at questions he evidently considers trivial—the sort of questions supposed entities often attract. "We are not the Ann Landers of the cosmos," Michael once snapped at an advice seeker. In an epilogue to *Messages from Michael,* he ex-

pounded in a similar vein. "We are not the way," he said. "We do not promise a paradise, or, for that matter, a hell, either, only progressive evolution, the ultimate state of which is bliss."

One of Michael's more unusual characteristics is his apparent ability to drop in from time to time on more than one host. Along with Lansing, several other San Francisco area residents have supposedly made contact with the entity, as though to confirm his avowal that he "comes to all who ask." Ubiquitous as he seems to be, Michael claims to be merely a conveyor of information, without desire to proselytize or convert. "Belief or faith is definitely not required, or even desired," he informs his followers, "for evolution will happen to you whether or not you believe." Perhaps such reassurance is a comfort to Lansing herself, who has her own moments of doubt, even after nearly two decades of channeling Michael. "Do I believe it?" she asks herself. "The only answer I can give is: sometimes."

Equally noncommittal about his source's identity and reality is channeler Tam Mossman of Charlottesville, Virginia, who hosts a discarnate visitor called James. "When you channel," Mossman wonders, "are you getting Leonard Bernstein conducting the symphony orchestra live, or are you getting the *recording* of it?"

Mossman was for fourteen years the editor of Jane Roberts's Seth books. But in 1975, midway through that editorial stint, he began channeling, an experience he describes as being "like a hose with air in it" through which ideas flow evenly. Unlike most of his channeling colleagues, Mossman remains more or less conscious during his sessions with James, succumbing only to a light trance. Still, the channeler says, after each session whatever dialogue he recalls soon fades like a dream.

Mossman is generally considered to be one of the more serious and thoughtful of the phenomenon's practitioners. So, too, is Pat Rodegast, a former executive secretary from Connecticut whose road to enlightenment began, like Jach Pursel's, with meditation. Rodegast channeled an "area of consciousness" that she called Emmanuel, whose last earthly tenure was in the sixteenth century. According to the channeler, she first saw Emmanuel clairvoyantly as "a being of golden light." Although she was unsure whether her visitor was truly what he seemed or only some unconscious fragment of her own personality, Rodegast felt that Emmanuel produced concepts that "I couldn't *possibly* have conceived of."

Even so, Emmanuel's message sounds quite similar to that of most other channeled entities, especially when describing how all humans are one with God, how everything in the human plane exists in spirit, and how the power to reshape reality resides within. "There is divinity in all things," Emmanuel proclaims, "and in order to find that divinity one must work with the material at hand." Pat Rodegast sums up her source's message this way: "Don't be afraid. All there *is* is love. The only reality is love. All the rest is an illusion."

Its critics often contend that all of channeling is an illusion—at best. More commonly, the explanation they offer for the phenomenon is fraud, pure and simple. For example, journalist Philip Haldeman of Northwest Skeptics, a Seattle, Washington, group concerned with the proliferation of superstition in modern society, describes most channelers as charlatans in pursuit of fame and money. Their disciples, he believes, have "a deep need to feel better—and all this pseudoscientific nonsense about creating your own reality and loving yourself above all and never really dying is a lot more pleasant to deal with than reality."

Arguably, reality is not a close acquaintance of some of the more avant-garde channelers—most of them somewhat less famous than J. Z. Knight, for example, or Penny Torres Rubin. To skeptics, both the methods and the sources of these cutting-edge conduits seem outlandish. "I feel like I'm going through a paper-towel tube," says David Swetland, a channeler whose source is a 35,000-year-old,

six-foot-eight-inch black female spice trader named Matea. "It's like w-h-o-o-s-h and then pop," is how Swetland elucidates his channeling mode. He made the remark at a seminar held by Taryn Krivé of Los Angeles, a former legal secretary who channels a bevy of otherworldly visitors, including Bell Bell, a giggly voiced six-year-old from fabled Atlantis; Aeffra, a deep-voiced Eastern European; and Barking Tree, a Hopi Indian woman.

Eschewing anthropomorphic spirits altogether is Neville Rowe, a one-time electrical engineer from New Zealand who channels dolphins. Dressed completely in aqua, right down to his socks, Rowe begins his sessions with a piercing, dolphinlike squeal, followed by a spiritual tête-à-tête in which a half dozen or so dolphins "talk" through him. The sea mammals' inability to speak English is no impediment, since they allegedly rely on Rowe to translate their "vibrations."

Extraterrestrials are the specialty of Ruth Norman, who, in her late eighties, is the *grande dame* of channeling. Norman claims to have undergone no fewer than fifty-five incarnations—including tours as Socrates, Mary Magdalene, the Buddha, Charlemagne, King Arthur, and Russian czar Peter the Great. In addition, she says, as far back as the 1950s she began channeling "space brothers" from distant worlds. Some, she contends, helped cowrite her books—more than 100 of them at last count. Not to be outdone, Norman's husband, Ernest, who died in 1971, claimed to have been Jesus Christ in a former life. Both Ruth Norman and her husband at various times also professed to be archangels.

As befits an archangel, Norman wears her worldliness lightly. "I am not indigenous to this earth," she insists. She looks forward to the year 2001, when, she predicts, thirty-three spaceships will arrive on earth, each bearing a full complement of 1,000 "other planetary dwellers." The event is to usher in the age of UNARIUS—for Universal Articulate Interdimensional Understanding of Science—in Norman's estimation, a "new golden age of logic and reason."

Norman gained preeminence among alleged conduits

The Spirits in Print

The public appetite for channeling has spawned some new periodicals that put the term "ghostwriting" in an entirely whole new light.

One such magazine is *Spirit Speaks,* published in Los Angeles by Glenn and Molli Nickell, who were self-described "happy, overachieving, agnostic yuppies" before channeling changed their lives. What makes *Spirit Speaks* unusual is that most of its supposed contributing authors are dead—departed masters who channel their way into print for the bimonthly magazine. Cast generally in the self-help, or self-realization, mode, the channeled wisdom resolves itself into articles with titles such as "Spiritual Psychology," "What is Truth?" "Unconditional Love," and "Attitudes We Get Stuck On."

According to publicity releases, Glenn Nickell was a corporate executive and his wife a freelance writer and "car pool queen of Orange County" in their prepublishing days. They were tennis-playing, Mercedes-owning, designer-dressed Republicans, active in the ultraconservative John Birch Society.

All that changed when business reverses left the Nickells broke, and about the same time, they discovered channeling. On the advice of their teenaged daughter Penny, Glenn Nickell read one of the "Seth" books. Soon thereafter, both Nickells were delving into New Age literature. The next step was attending a channeling session, at which Molli learned that her future lay in publishing. A few months later, the name *Spirit Speaks* came to her in dreams. The Nickells and a few friends pooled $1,200, and in 1984, the enterprise was launched. None of the group had any publishing experience—"in this life, anyway," Molli notes—but she claims they had spirit advice from such talents as journalists Ernie Pyle and Edward R. Murrow, writer Pearl S. Buck, and psychic visionary Edgar Cayce.

Editor-publisher Molli *(shown below with art director Gary Lund)* has also launched a book series written by spirit teachers—among them Seth and J. Z. Knight's Ramtha—and has plans to begin a line of children's books, magazines on tape, videos, and "who knows what else?" The upheaval in her family's life, she reports, has left all its members happier and spiritually healthier. When the stress of her new publishing ventures begins to tell, she says, she recalls some early advice from a spirit entity: "If you seek enlightenment, simply lighten up and don't take it all so seriously."

of interplanetary communiqués, but others rivaled her in strangeness. One of the earliest extraterrestrial messages was beamed to a man named George Van Tassel in 1952. "Hail to you being of Shan [earth]," it began. "I greet you in love and peace. My identity is Ashtar, commandant quadrant sector, patrol station Schare, all projections, all waves." Only slightly less cryptic was a purported message from a being named Orlon, received clairaudiently by an Oregon woman in the 1950s. It warned of the approach of "the midnight hour" and of "changes, changes vast and tremendous on the face of the planet earth: changes in frequency, of density, of consciousness of being."

Ashtar, Orlon, and their fellow "space brothers" allegedly belonged to such astral realms as the Saturn Tribunal, the Confederation of Planets, and the Intergalactic Confederation. They were said to live in the same physical plane as earth or else in that etheric level between the physical and astral planes that was supposedly home to spirits of the human dead.

No less bizarre than channelers who tune in to the cosmos are those who claim to be cosmic amplifiers for spirits of dead rock stars. They supposedly have succeeded in bringing in the voices of Otis Redding, Janis Joplin, and John Lennon, among other fallen idols. William Tenuto, the "voice" of John Lennon, is a California channeler who also claims to commune so often with the spirit of Jesus Christ that he chummily refers to the Christian Messiah as "a good friend." Lennon, as channeled by Tenuto, appears philosophical about his 1980 death. "It was the end of my time in that incarnation," the late Beatle allegedly says. "Now I don't have to talk to reporters."

Clearly, there is virtually no limit to the variety of discarnate sources available for channeling, nor to the virtuosity of the humans who claim to contact them. In much shorter supply, however, are scientific theories—and theorists—to explain the phenomenon. Few scientists have any interest in it. No modern-day William Crookes or Oliver Lodge has emerged to give so much as a passing thought to the matter, which physical science generally regards, if at all, as irrational and irrelevant. Even parapsychology, with its concern for paranormal phenomena, has taken little interest. By the time channeling made its advent, parapsychologists had long since confined themselves mainly to their laboratories, where they concentrated on trying to detect or quantify such supposed extrasensory powers as telepathy and clairvoyance. For most of these scientists, alleged appearances of nonterrestrial entities are well off the beaten path.

What little notice channeling has attracted comes mostly from psychology and the social sciences. This indicates, perhaps, that the phenomenon is more a product of mental peculiarities or social need—or both—than of any intervention in this world by denizens of other realms.

There is some speculation, for example, that channeling is the product of hypnosis. This view is shared by Carl Raschke, a professor of religion at the University of Denver. Raschke posits that channeling may involve self-hypnosis of the channeler, perhaps in combination with hypnosis of an audience prepared, even anxious, to believe. In regard to J. Z. Knight in particular, Raschke theorizes that she "puts herself in a self-induced hypnotic state that mesmerizes an audience already predisposed to accept that 'God is everywhere.'" Stanford University professor and hypnosis authority David Spiegel agrees with the self-hypnosis theory and describes channeling as little more than "a fantasy acted out in a very intense way."

Some investigators see channeling as a form not of mental manipulation, but of mental disorder. The favored pathology posited by this school of thought is multiple-personality disorder—the same aberration cited by some earlier researchers to explain mediumship (pages 84-85). The idea of two or more distinct personalities, each with its own memory, behavior pattern, and beliefs, does seem pertinent to channeling. Perhaps a channeler can misinterpret a secondary personality as an entity exterior to his or her self. This possibility seems bolstered by evidence that 97 percent of all multiple-personality disorder subjects suffer traumatic childhoods, a statistic that calls to mind investi-

Ruth Norman, a channeler of space aliens, views earth as a sort of cosmic dumping ground whose inhabitants lack the spiritual development to live somewhere better. More enlightened beings, she says, live on other planets.

gator Margo Chandley's finding that most channelers were abused or neglected as children.

Of course, the clinical question of whether channelers are mad involves a time-honored philosophical question: What is madness? Visions of unseen entities are strange, to be sure. But are they pathological? The question greatly absorbed Wilson Van Dusen of California, a clinical psychologist whose years of practice brought him into contact with thousands of mental patients. Van Dusen, who wrote a book in 1964 about the Swedish mystic Emanuel Swedenborg, devoted extensive study to psychotic hallucinations. He sees some startling similarities—even "an almost perfect fit"—between Swedenborg's visions of nonphysical realms and the psychotic hallucinations of his patients. Was Swedenborg mad—a possibility Van Dusen discounts, or were his patients not so mad as believed? Van Dusen is elusive on the latter count, concluding only that, like Swedenborg, his patients appeared to have plugged into some inner world "more consistent than the outer natural world."

Were mediums simply attuned to a different—but valid—reality? Are channelers? The question of sanity's borders and how they might relate to those who claim to host unseen beings arises again in the ongoing theory that a normal, healthy personality can harbor disparate and disconnected parts. The idea of "coconsciousness" was first articulated by psychic researcher Walter Franklin Prince in the first half of the twentieth century. Prince was a veteran investigator of mediums. Later, the notion was resurrected by Dr. John Beahrs, an Oregon psychiatrist. Beahrs has no special interest in mediums or channelers. Nevertheless, some point to his coconsciousness theory as a possible explanation for how a normal person might misconstrue some splinter of his own psyche as a wholly separate being.

Beahrs defines coconsciousness as "the existence within a single human organism of more than one consciously experiencing psychological entity, each with its own identity and selfhood, relatively separate and distinct from other entities." As explained by Prince, coconsciousness very much resembles multiple-personality disorder.

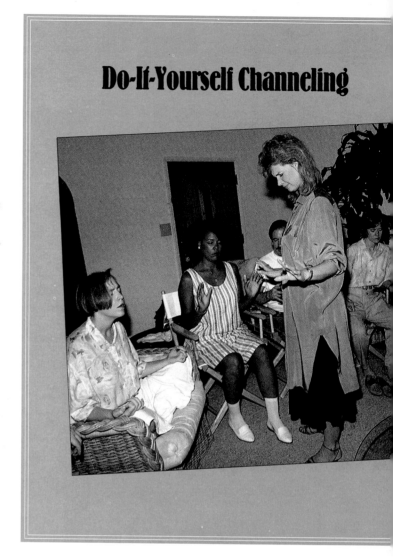

Do-It-Yourself Channeling

Significantly, however, Beahrs believes coconsciousness is a natural state and not a mental aberration. If so, the ability to tap another, perhaps higher, self might be less a gift than a given, and channeling a universal faculty, available to all.

Psychotherapist Adam Crabtree also wrestles with the question of what is normal and what is aberrant in his 1985 book *Multiple Man*. Crabtree outlines a theory that multiple-personality disorder is not really a disorder, but an unusual form of normal multiple consciousness.

Crabtree's research builds on the earlier studies of Ernest Hilgard, professor emeritus at Stanford University and a leading hypnosis investigator. Hilgard theorized the presence of a "hidden observer"—an ever-vigilant source of awareness and knowledge—tucked within the shadows of the subconscious mind. Crabtree takes Hilgard's theory a step further, postulating that "there is more and more evidence that even 'normal' people are multiple" and that "hypnotic research on 'hidden observers' indicates that there is reason to posit any number of individual hidden

For people who want ready access to a spirit guide without having to consult human intermediaries, learning how to channel has become a popular alternative to visiting professional channelers. In the beginning, however, most do-it-yourselfers need instruction on how to open their own pipelines.

One teacher is Shawn Randall of Los Angeles (left, standing with a group of students). A writer suffering from writer's block, Randall tried channeling in the early 1980s in hopes of breaking the logjam. Soon, she says, she established close contact with Torah, an "interdimensional consciousness." The channeler and her entity now offer twelve-week courses on how to channel. Anyone dedicated to learning the process can do it, says Randall, who calls channeling "an intuitive skill" that merely needs developing.

The Randall/Torah instruction involves nine basic steps. The channeler describes the highlights this way:

1. Classes begin with "sensitizing exercises" aimed at helping students mobilize their intuition. Students practice telepathy and learn techniques for relaxation, meditation, and visualization.

2. Torah helps participants get in touch with their unconscious minds, guiding them toward discovering destructive beliefs. Randall calls these beliefs the "negative ego—the part of the self that does not want to grow spiritually." The negative ego, she says, "can pollute channeling communications."

3. Students work at "putting the self aside" and "learning to let go." This involves "listening interdimensionally" for energies outside oneself. Gentle falling exercises that supposedly help the mind fall into altered states are part of the process.

4. Torah helps individuals get in touch with their higher selves and inner personalities, which include, according to Randall, such interior fragments as the "inner child and inner adolescent." The contact purportedly sets a "high resonance" that encourages communion between channeler and spirit.

5. Students try to connect with a discarnate consciousness through a process that includes relaxing, affirming oneness with "Light, Love, and God/Goddess/All That Is," asking for a guide to communi-

cate, asking the guide a question and listening for an answer, and writing down or speaking the answer.

6. Students solidify mental rapport with their guides by regularly speaking and writing the guide's messages. This establishes mutual trust, Randall believes, and teaches both channeler and entity how better to reach each other.

7. Students share and examine their channeled writing with an eye toward evaluating its usefulness, sense, and ability to uplift and enlighten.

8. Torah invites the entities to blend their energies with those of the channelers so messages can be appropriately expressed. The idea, Randall says, is to help the channelers toward "an act of love" in which they are "joined in consciousness and vibration in a sharing of time and space in order to bridge the physical and nonphysical realities for the highest good of all concerned."

9. In ongoing classes, Torah continues to help the new channelers and their entities clarify and affirm their connections.

---

personalities within the ordinary human subconscious." In this regard, Crabtree seems to corroborate the coconsciousness research of John Beahrs, who states that there are "an unlimited, potentially infinite number of hidden observers or 'personalities' within a single human individual." To Beahrs—and to Crabtree—"people function like an orchestra—made up of multiple selves—rather than like solo instruments." It follows, then, that perhaps channelers were only making better use of their string sections.

Like Beahrs, Crabtree does not link his conclusions and channeling. Still, his ideas seem to provide a framework within which—theoretically, at least—the phenomenon might be understood.

There are few theories about channeling—and no proof. But in the end, as with all things mystical, the issue is not proof, but faith. This was the lesson that, in spiritualism's day, often confounded the brilliant men and women who spent lifetimes trying to prove the unprovable. For the skeptic,

hardly any proof is sufficient; for the believer, hardly any proof is necessary. The unknowable is a chasm, unbridgeable to some, a beguiling challenge to those who would make the leap. As for those balancing on the edge, the dying words of Margery the Medium have a prophetic ring: "You'll all be guessing . . . for the rest of your lives."

The gap between reason and faith calls to mind an incident involving the late British philosopher and inveterate atheist Bertrand Russell. A student asked Russell what he would say if, after his death, he suddenly found himself face to face with St. Peter—and with the reality of Christianity. Russell matter-of-factly replied, "I would say to him: 'You didn't give us enough evidence.' "

But in matters of faith, perhaps a rationalist should not have the last word. Maybe that should go to Lazaris, that supposedly ageless, supposedly formless group entity who peers out at life through the eyes of Jach Pursel and states with the conviction of one who has seen it all, "The bridge from this world to that is belief."

ACKNOWLEDGMENTS

The editors wish to thank these individuals and organizations: Ascentia, Munich, West Germany; Dr. Hans Bender, Institut für Grenzgebiete der Psychologie und Psychohygiene, Freiburg, West Germany; Nicholas Clarke-Lowes, Society for Psychical Research, London; Abd el-Halim Nour el-Din, Egyptian Antiquities Organization, Cairo, Egypt; Sarah Estep, American Association Electronic Voice Phenomena, Severna Park, Maryland; Hilary Evans, London; Leif Geiges, Staufen, West Germany; Paola Giovetti, Modena, Italy; Dr. Arthur Hastings, Institute of Transpersonal Psychology, Mountain View, California; Diana Hoerig, Violet Flame Network, Westlake Village, California; Rainer Holbe, Cologne, West Germany; Jim Hughson, Lily Dale Assembly, Lily Dale, New York; Manfred Kage, Weissenstein, West Germany; Fidelio Köbele, Düsseldorf, West Germany; Hans-Otto König, Mönchengladbach, West Germany; Taryn Krivé, Sherman Oaks, California; Dr. Hubert Larcher, Institut Métapsychique International, Paris; Milbourne Christopher Collection, New York; Mohammed Mohsen, Egyptian Museum of Cairo, Cairo, Egypt; Tam Mossman, *Metapsychology*, Charlottesville, Virginia; Molli Nickell, *Spirit Speaks*, Los Angeles; Eleanor O'Keeffe, London; Shawn Randall, Studio City, California; W. G. Roll, Psychical Research Foundation, Carrollton, Georgia; Rev. Neville Rowe, West Hollywood, California; Lyssa Royal, Los Angeles; Penny Torres Rubin, Vacaville, California; Klaus Schreiber, Aachen, West Germany; Dr. Ernst Senkowski, Mainz, West Germany; Prof. Giorgio di Simone, Naples, Italy; Society for Psychical Research, London; June Sprigg, Hancock Shaker Village, Pittsfield, Massachusetts; Dr. Rolf Streichardt, Institut für Grenzgebiete der Psychologie und Psychohygiene, Freiburg, West Germany; Alan Wesencraft, Harry Price Library, University of London, London.

BIBLIOGRAPHY

Abbott, David P., *Behind the Scenes with the Mediums*. Chicago: Open Court, 1908.

Abell, George O., and Barry Singer, eds., *Science and the Paranormal*. New York: Charles Scribner's Sons, 1981.

Almeder, Robert, *Beyond Death: Evidence for Life after Death*. Springfield, Ill.: Charles C. Thomas, 1987.

Anderson, Rodger I., review of *The Enigma of Daniel Home: Medium or Fraud?* by Trevor H. Hall. *Journal of the American Society for Psychical Research*, April 1985.

Andrews, Edward Deming, and Faith Andrews, *Visions of the Heavenly Sphere*. Charlottesville, Va.: University Press of Virginia, 1969.

Angoff, Allan, *Eileen Garrett and the World beyond the Senses*. New York: William Morrow, 1974.

Angoff, Allan, ed., *The Psychic Force*. New York: G. P. Putnam's Sons, 1970.

Angoff, Allan, and Betty Shapin, eds., *Parapsychology Today: A Geographic View*. New York: Parapsychology Foundation, 1973.

Apsler, Alfred, *Communes through the Ages: The Search for Utopia*. New York: Julian Messner, 1974.

Ascher, Barbara Lazear, "A Peek across the Psychic Edge." *New York Times*, November 27, 1986.

Ashby, Robert H., *The Guidebook for the Study of Psychical Research*. New York: Samuel Weiser, 1972.

Ashley, Nancy, *Create Your Own Reality: A Seth Workbook*. Englewood Cliffs, N.J.: Prentice-Hall, 1984.

Auerbach, Loyd M., "Psi and the Art of Magic." *Fate*, June 1988.

Baird, A. T., *One Hundred Cases for Survival after Death*. London: T. Werner Laurie, 1943.

Baker, Jean H., *Mary Todd Lincoln: A Biography*. New York: W. W. Norton, 1987.

Balfour, Jean, "The 'Palm Sunday' Case: New Light on an Old Love Story." *Proceedings of the Society for Psychical Research*, February 1960.

Bander, Peter, *Voices from the Tapes: Recordings from the Other World*. New York: Drake Publishers, 1973.

Beahrs, John O., "Co-Consciousness: A Common Denominator in Hypnosis, Multiple Personality, and Normalcy." *American Journal of Clinical Hypnosis*, October 1983.

Bletzer, June G., *The Donning International Encyclopedic Psychic Dictionary*. Norfolk, Va.: Donning, 1986.

Bordewich, Fergus M., "Colorado's Thriving Cults." *New York Times Magazine*, May 1, 1988.

Brandon, Ruth, *The Spiritualists*. New York: Alfred A. Knopf, 1983.

Braude, Stephen E.:
Review of *The Enigma of Daniel Home*, by Trevor H. Hall. *Journal of the Society for Psychical Research*, February 1985.
Review of *Multiple Man: Exploration in Possession and Multiple Personality*, by Adam Crabtree. *Journal of the Society for Psychical Research*, January 1987.

Brown, Rosemary, *Immortals by My Side*. Chicago: Henry Regnery, 1974.

Brown, Slater, *The Heyday of Spiritualism*. New York: Hawthorn Books, 1970.

Buckland, Raymond, and Hereward Carrington, *Amazing Secrets of the Psychic World*. West Nyack, N.Y.: Parker, 1975.

Burton, Jean, *Heyday of a Wizard: Daniel Home the Medium*. London: George G. Harrap, 1948.

Caddy, Eileen, *The Spirit of Findhorn*. Romford, Essex, England: L. N. Fowler, 1977.

Cannell, J. C., *The Secrets of Houdini*. New York: Dover Publications, 1973.

Carlisle, Dolly, "To Country Star Razzy Bailey, Nashville's More than 'Music City'—It's Twilight Zone South." *People*, July 25, 1982.

Carr, John Dickson, *The Life of Sir Arthur Conan Doyle*. New York: Harper & Brothers, 1949.

Carrington, Hereward, *The Physical Phenomena of Spiritualism*. New York: American Universities Publishing, 1920.

"Case of the Will of Mr. James L. Chaffin." *Proceedings of the Society for Psychical Research*, November 1927.

Cassirer, Manfred, " 'Spirit Hands': Fact or Fraud?" *Journal of the Society for Psychical Research*, September 1978.

Cayce, Edgar Evans, and Hugh Lynn Cayce, *The Outer Limits of Edgar Cayce's Power*. New York: Harper & Row, 1971.

Cerullo, John J., *The Secularization of the Soul*. Philadelphia: Institute for the Study of Human Issues, 1982.

Chandley, Margo, *The Channeling Process*. Beverly Hills, Calif.: Light & Sound Communications, 1987.

Christopher, Milbourne:
ESP, Seers & Psychics. New York: Thomas Y. Crowell, 1970.
Houdini: A Pictorial Life. New York: Thomas Y. Crowell, 1976.
Houdini: The Untold Story. New York: Thomas Y. Crowell, 1969.
Search for the Soul. New York: Thomas Y. Crowell, 1979.

Coates, James, *Photographing the Invisible*. Chicago: Advanced Thought Publishing, 1911.

Cook, Emily Williams, "The Survival Question: Impasse or Crux?" *Journal of the American Society for Psychical Research*, April 1987.

Cooper, Irving S., *Theosophy Simplified*. Wheaton, Ill.: Theosophical Publishing House, 1979.

Cox, W. E., "Magicians and Parapsychology." *Journal of the Society for Psychical Research*, October 1984.

Cummins, Geraldine, *Swan on a Black Sea: A Study in Automatic Writing*. Ed. by Signe Toksvig. London: Routledge and Kegan Paul, 1965.

Cunnington, C. Willett, and Phillis Cunnington, *Handbook of English Costume in the Nineteenth Century*. Philadelphia: DuFour Editions, 1959.

Davenport, Reuben Briggs, *The Death-Blow to Spiritualism*. New York: Arno Press, 1976.

Dean, Stanley R., ed., *Psychiatry and Mysticism*. Chicago: Nelson-Hall, 1975.

Dingwall, Eric John:
"The Mediumship of Carlos Mirabelli." *Psychic Research*, July 1930.
Some Human Oddities: Studies of the Queer, the Uncanny and the Fanatical. New Hyde Park, N.Y.: University Books, 1962.
Very Peculiar People: Portrait Studies in the Queer, the Abnormal and the Uncanny. New Hyde Park, N.Y.: University Books, 1962.

Douglas, Alfred, *Extra-Sensory Powers: A Century of Psychical Research*. Woodstock, N.Y.: Overlook Press, 1976.

Doyle, Sir Arthur Conan:
The Edge of the Unknown. New York: G. P. Putnam's Sons, 1930.
The History of Spiritualism. Vols. 1 and 2. New York: George H. Doran, 1926.
Memories and Adventures. Boston: Little, Brown, 1924.

Ducasse, C. J.:
A Critical Examination of the Belief in a Life after Death. Ed. by Marvin Farber. Springfield, Ill.: Charles C. Thomas, 1961.
"What Would Constitute Conclusive Evidence of Survival." *Journal of the Society for Psychical Research*, December 1962.

Dugdale, Blanche E. C., *Arthur James Balfour*. Vol. 1. Westport, Conn.: Greenwood Press, 1937.

Dunninger, Joseph, *Inside the Medium's Cabinet*. New York: David Kemp, 1935.

Ebon, Martin, *They Knew the Unknown*. New York: World Publishing, 1971.

Ebon, Martin, ed.:
Communicating with the Dead. New York: New American Library, 1968.
The Psychic Reader. New York: World Publishing, 1969.

Ehrenwald, Jan, *Anatomy of Genius: Split Brains and Global Minds*. New York: Human Sciences Press, 1984.

Feilding, Everard, *Sittings with Eusapia Palladino & Other*

Studies. New Hyde Park, N.Y.: University Books, 1963.

Fiore, Edith, *The Unquiet Dead: A Psychologist Treats Spirit Possession*. Garden City, N.Y.: Doubleday, 1987.

Fodor, Nandor:

    Between Two Worlds. West Nyack, N.Y.: Parker, 1964.

    Encyclopaedia of Psychic Science. New Hyde Park, N.Y.: University Books, 1966.

Ford, Arthur, *Unknown but Known*. New York: Harper & Row, 1968.

Ford, Arthur, as told to Jerome Ellison, *The Life beyond Death*. New York: G. P. Putnam's Sons, 1971.

Foster, Lawrence, *Religion and Sexuality: Three American Communal Experiments of the Nineteenth Century*. New York: Oxford University Press, 1981.

Frazier, Kendrick, ed., *Science Confronts the Paranormal*. Buffalo, N.Y.: Prometheus Books, 1986.

Freedland, Nat, *The Occult Explosion*. New York: G. P. Putnam's Sons, 1972.

Friedman, Philip H., "The Magic, Mystery, and Muses of Love." *New Realities*, July-August 1987.

Fuller, John G., *The Great Soul Trial*. New York: Macmillan, 1969.

Gardner, Martin, *Science: Good, Bad and Bogus*. Buffalo, N.Y.: Prometheus Books, 1981.

Garrett, Eileen J., *My Life as a Search for the Meaning of Mediumship*. New York: Arno Press, 1975.

Gauld, Alan:

    The Founders of Psychical Research. New York: Schocken Books, 1968.

    Mediumship and Survival. London: Paladin Books, 1983.

Geist, William E., "Spiritual Chic: Gaining Success with Channeling." *New York Times*, May 30, 1987.

Gettings, Fred, *Ghosts in Photographs*. New York: Harmony Books, 1978.

Gibson, Walter B., and Morris N. Young, eds., *Houdini on Magic*. New York: Dover, 1953.

Ginsburg, Madeleine, *Victorian Dress in Photographs*. New York: Holmes & Meier, 1982.

Goldfarb, Russell M., and Clare R. Goldfarb, *Spiritualism and Nineteenth-Century Letters*. Cranbury, N.J.: Associated University Presses, 1978.

Goran, Morris, *Fact, Fraud, and Fantasy*. Cranbury, N.J.: A. S. Barnes, 1979.

Grattan-Guinnes, Ivor, ed., *Psychical Research*. Wellingborough, Northamptonshire, England: Aquarian Press, 1982.

Green, Celia, and Charles McCreery, *Apparitions*. New York: St. Martin's Press, 1975.

Gregory, Anita, *The Strange Case of Rudi Schneider*. Metuchen, N.J.: Scarecrow Press, 1985.

Grosso, Michael, *The Final Choice: Playing the Survival Game*. Walpole, N.H.: Stillpoint, 1985.

Haining, Peter, ed., *The Sherlock Holmes Scrapbook*. London: New English Library, 1973.

Hall, Trevor H.:

    The Enigma of Daniel Home: Medium or Fraud? Buffalo, N.Y.: Prometheus Books, 1984

    The Medium and the Scientist. Buffalo, N.Y.: Prometheus Books, 1984.

    New Light on Old Ghosts. London: Gerald Duckworth, 1965.

    The Strange Case of Edmund Gurney. London: Gerald Duckworth, 1964.

Haraldsson, Erlendur, and Ian Stevenson, "A Communicator of the 'Drop-In' Type in Iceland: The Case of Runolfur Runolfsson." *Journal of the American Society for Psychical Research*, January 1975.

Hardinge, Emma, *Modern American Spiritualism*. New Hyde Park, N.Y.: University Books, 1970.

Harris, Marlys, "Shirley's Best Performance." *Money*, September 1987.

Harrison, Barbara Grizzuti, "Spiritual Glitz." *Ms.*, July-August 1987.

Haynes, Renée, *The Society for Psychical Research 1882-1982: A History*. London: Macdonald, 1982.

Healy, Joan, "The Happy Princess: Psychological Profile of a Psychic." *Journal of the Society for Psychical Research*, June 1984.

Heywood, Rosalind, "Notes on Rosemary Brown." *Journal of the Society for Psychical Research*, December 1971.

Higham, Charles, *The Adventures of Conan Doyle*. New York: W. W. Norton, 1976.

Holzer, Hans, *Life after Death: The Challenge and the Evidence*. Indianapolis: Bobbs-Merrill, 1969.

Home, Mme. Dunglas, *D. D. Home: His Life and Mission*. Ed. by Sir Arthur Conan Doyle. London: Kegan Paul, Trench, Trubner, 1921.

Houdini, Harry:

    Houdini: A Magician among the Spirits. New York: Arno Press, 1972.

    Miracle Mongers and Their Methods. Buffalo, N.Y.: Prometheus Books, 1981.

Inglis, Brian:

    The Hidden Power. London: Jonathan Cape, 1986.

    Natural and Supernatural. London: Hodder and Stoughton, 1977.

    Science and Parascience: A History of the Paranormal, 1914-1939. London: Hodder and Stoughton, 1984.

Irwin, H. J., "Charles Bailey: A Biographical Study of the Australian Apport Medium." *Journal of the Society for Psychical Research*, April 1987.

Jackson, Herbert G., Jr., *The Spirit Rappers*. Garden City, N.Y.: Doubleday, 1972.

Jacobson, Nils O., *Life without Death?: On Parapsychology, Mysticism, and the Question of Survival*. Transl. by Sheila La Farge. New York: Dell, 1973.

Jastrow, Joseph, *Wish and Wisdom*. New York: D. Appleton-Century, 1935.

Jaynes, Julian, *The Origin of Consciousness in the Breakdown of the Bicameral Mind*. Boston: Houghton Mifflin, 1976.

Jenkins, Elizabeth, *The Shadow and the Light: A Defence of Daniel Dunglas Home, the Medium*. London: Hamish Hamilton, 1982.

Johnson, Alice, "A Reconstruction of Some Concordant Automatisms." *Proceedings of the Society for Psychical Research*, January 1914.

Judah, J. Stillson, *The History and Philosophy of the Metaphysical Movements in America*. Philadelphia, Westminster Press, 1967.

Kastenbaum, Robert, *Is There Life after Death?* New York: Prentice Hall Press, 1984.

Kautz, William H., and Melanie Branon, *Channeling: The Intuitive Connection*. San Francisco: Harper & Row, 1987.

Keene, M. Lamar, as told to Allen Spraggett, *The Psychic Mafia*. New York: St. Martin's Press, 1976.

Kendall, Lace, *Houdini: Master of Escape*. Philadelphia: MacRae Smith, 1960.

Kerr, Howard, *Mediums, and Spirit-Rappers, and Roaring Radicals: Spiritualism in American Literature, 1850-1900*. Urbana, Ill.: University of Illinois Press, 1972.

Kerr, Howard, and Charles L. Crow, eds., *The Occult in America: New Historical Perspectives*. Urbana, Ill.: University of Illinois Press, 1983.

Klimo, Jon, *Channeling: Investigations on Receiving Information from Paranormal Sources*. Los Angeles: Jeremy P. Tarcher, 1987.

Krippner, Stanley, ed., *Advances in Parapsychological Research*. New York: Plenum Press, 1987.

Kurtz, Paul, ed., *A Skeptic's Handbook of Parapsychology*. Buffalo, N.Y.: Prometheus Books, 1985.

Lambert, Angela, *Unquiet Souls: A Social History of the Illustrious, Irreverent, Intimate Group of British Aristocrats Known as "the Souls."* New York: Harper & Row, 1984.

Lellenberg, Jon L., ed., *The Quest for Sir Arthur Conan Doyle: Thirteen Biographers in Search of a Life*. Carbondale, Ill.: Southern Illinois University Press, 1987.

LeShan, Lawrence, *Alternate Realities: The Search for the Full Human Being*. New York: M. Evans, 1976.

Lindsey, Robert:

    "Spiritual Concepts Drawing a Different Breed of Adherent." *The New York Times*, September 29, 1986.

    "Spiritual Go-Betweens: New Channel for Advice." *New York Times*, May 12, 1987.

Lipman, Jean, and Tom Armstrong, eds., *American Folk Painters of Three Centuries*. New York: Hudson Hills Press, 1980.

Litvag, Irving, *Singer in the Shadows: The Strange Story of Patience Worth*. New York: Macmillan, 1972.

Longford, Elizabeth, *Queen Victoria: Born to Succeed*. New York: Harper & Row, 1964.

McHargue, Georgess, *Facts, Frauds, and Phantasms: A Survey of the Spiritualist Movement*. Garden City, N.Y.: Doubleday, 1972.

MacKenzie, Andrew, *The Unexplained: Some Strange Cases in Psychical Research*. London: Arthur Barker, 1966.

McLaughlin, Corrine, "Tuning In to the Best Channel: Some Tools for Discrimination." *New Realities*, July-August 1987.

Marks, David, and Richard Kammann, *The Psychology of the Psychic*. Buffalo, N.Y.: Prometheus Books, 1980.

Marryat, Florence, *There Is No Death*. New York: Causeway Books, 1973.

Martin, Katherine, "The Voice of Lazaris." *New Realities*, July-August 1987.

Matlock, James G., "Cat's Paw: Margery and the Rhines, 1926." Unpublished ms. *American Society for Psychical Research*.

"The Medium Medium." *Newsweek*, April 8, 1974.

Meyer, Bernard C., *Houdini: A Mind in Chains, a Psychoanalytic Portrait*. New York: E. P. Dutton, 1976.

Montgomery, Ruth, *The World Before*. New York: Fawcett Crest, 1976.

Moore, R. Laurence, *In Search of White Crows: Spiritualism, Parapsychology, and American Culture*. New York: Oxford University Press, 1977.

Morris, Kate, "The Medium and the Message." *Blitz* (London), December 1986.

Mulholland, John, *Beware Familiar Spirits*. New York: Charles Scribner's Sons, 1938.

Murphy, Gardner, and Robert O. Ballou, comps. and eds., *William James on Psychical Research*. New York: Viking Press, 1960.

Myers, F. W. H., *Human Personality and Its Survival of Bodily Death*. Ed. by Susy Smith. New Hyde Park, N.Y.: University Books, 1961.

"Mystics on Main Street." *U.S. News & World Report*, February 9, 1987.

Naylor, Gloria, "Spiritualism Has a Place in the Age of Disbelief." *New York Times,* February 13, 1986.

Nelson, Geoffrey K., *Spiritualism and Society.* London: Routledge & Kegan Paul, 1969.

Oppenheim, Janet, *The Other World: Spiritualism and Psychical Research in England, 1850-1914.* Cambridge: Cambridge University Press, 1985.

Pearsall, Ronald, *The Table-Rappers.* New York: St. Martin's Press, 1972.

Permutt, Cyril, *Beyond the Spectrum: A Survey of Supernormal Photography.* Cambridge, England: Patrick Stephens, 1983.

Phylos the Thibetan, *A Dweller on Two Planets or the Dividing of the Way.* Alhambra, Calif: Borden, no date.

Pike, James A., with Diane Kennedy, *The Other Side: An Account of My Experiences with Psychic Phenomena.* Garden City, N.Y.: Doubleday, 1968.

Playfair, Guy Leon:
The Indefinite Boundary: An Investigation into the Relationship between Matter and Spirit. New York: St. Martin's Press, 1976.
"This Perilous Medium." *The Unexplained* (London), vol. 13, issue 147.

Podmore, Frank:
Mediums of the 19th Century. Vol. 2. New Hyde Park, N.Y.: University Books, 1963.
The Newer Spiritualism. New York: Arno, 1975 (reprint of 1910 edition).

Porter, Katherine H., *Through a Glass Darkly: Spiritualism in the Browning Circle.* New York: Octagon Books, 1972.

Price, Harry, and Eric J. Dingwall, *Revelations of a Spirit Medium.* New York: Arno Press, 1975.

Prince, Walter Franklin:
The Case of Patience Worth. Boston: Boston Society for Psychic Research, 1927.
The Enchanted Boundary: Being a Survey of Negative Reactions to Claims of Psychic Phenomena 1820-1930. Boston: Boston Society for Psychic Research, 1930.
Noted Witnesses for Psychic Occurrences. New Hyde Park, N.Y.: University Books, 1963 (reprint of 1928 edition).
"The Riddle of Patience Worth." *Scientific American,* July 1926.

Progoff, Ira, *The Image of an Oracle.* New York: Garrett, 1964.

Proskauer, Julien J.:
The Dead Do Not Talk. New York: Harper & Brothers, 1946.
Spook Crooks! New York: A. L. Burt, 1932.

Ramtha, *I Am Ramtha.* Ed. by Cindy Black, Richard Cohn, Greg Simmons, and Wes Wait. Portland, Oreg.: Beyond Words Publishing, 1986.

Randi, James, *Flim-Flam!* Buffalo, N.Y.: Prometheus Books, 1982.

Rao, K. Ramakrishna, ed., *Case Studies in Parapsychology.* Jefferson, N.C.: McFarland, 1986.

Raudive, Konstantins, *Breakthrough: An Amazing Experiment in Electronic Communication with the Dead.* Ed. by Joyce Morton. Transl. by Nadia Fowler. Gerrards Cross, Buckinghamshire, England: Colin Smythe, 1971.

Rawcliffe, D. H., *Occult and Supernatural Phenomena.* New York: Dover, no date.

Rinn, Joseph F., *Sixty Years of Psychical Research: Houdini and I among the Spiritualists.* New York: Dodd, Mead, 1920.

Roberts, Jane:
The Afterdeath Journal of an American Philosopher: The World View of William James. Englewood Cliffs, N.J.: Prentice-Hall, 1978.
The Seth Material. Englewood Cliffs, N.J.: Prentice-Hall, 1970.
Seth Speaks: The Eternal Validity of the Soul. Toronto, Canada: Bantam Books, 1972.

Rogo, D. Scott, *Life after Death: The Case for Survival of Bodily Death.* Wellingborough, Northamptonshire, England: Aquarian Press, 1986.

Rogo, D. Scott, and Raymond Bayless, *Phone Calls from the Dead.* Englewood Cliffs, N.J.: Prentice-Hall, 1979.

Roll, W. G., "Poltergeist Phenomena and Interpersonal Relations." *Journal of the American Society for Psychical Research,* January 1970.

Roman, Sanaya, and Duane Packer, *Opening to Channel: How to Connect with Your Guide.* Tiburon, Calif.: H. J. Kramer, 1987.

Roraback, Dick, "An Artist's Brush with Immortality." *Los Angeles Times,* April 19, 1988.

Salter, W. H.:
"The Palm Sunday Case: A Note on Interpreting Automatic Writings." *Journal of the Society for Psychical Research,* June 1960.
Zoar. New York: Arno Press, 1975.

Saltmarsh, H. F., *Evidence of Personal Survival from Cross Correspondences.* New York: Arno Press, 1975.

Sandburg, Carl, *Abraham Lincoln: The War Years.* Vol. 3. New York: Harcourt, Brace, 1939.

Sears, Hal D., *The Sex Radicals: Free Love in High Victorian America.* Lawrence, Kan.: Regents Press of Kansas, 1977.

Shepard, Leslie, ed., *Encyclopedia of Occultism & Parapsychology.* 3 vols. Detroit: Gale Research, 1984.

Sidgwick, Arthur, and Eleanor Mildred Sidgwick, *Henry Sidgwick: A Memoir by A. S. and E. M. S.* London: Macmillan, 1906.

Sinclair, Upton, *Mental Radio.* Springfield, Ill.: Charles C. Thomas, 1930.

Smith, E. Lester, "The Raudive Voices—Objective or Subjective?" *Journal of the American Society for Psychical Research,* January 1974.

Smith, Susy, *The Mediumship of Mrs. Leonard.* New Hyde Park, N.Y.: University Books, 1964.

Spraggett, Allen, *The Case for Immortality.* New York: New American Library, 1974.

Sprigg, June, *Shaker Design.* Exhibition catalog of Whitney Museum of American Art. New York: W. W. Norton, 1986.

Sprigg, June, and David Larkin, *Shaker: Life, Work, and Art.* New York: Stewart, Tabori & Chang, 1987.

Stemman, Roy, *Spirits and Spirit Worlds.* London: Aldus Books, 1975.

Stevenson, Ian, "A Communicator Unknown to Medium and Sitters." *Journal of the American Society for Psychical Research,* January 1970.

Stevenson, Ian, and John Beloff, "An Analysis of Some Suspect Drop-in Communications." *Journal of the Society for Psychical Research,* September 1980.

Sun, Patricia, "Understanding Trance Channeling." *New Realities,* July-August 1987.

Symons, Julian, *Conan Doyle: Portrait of an Artist.* New York: Mysterious Press, 1979.

Tabori, Paul:
Companions of the Unseen. New Hyde Park, N.Y.: University Books, 1968.
Harry Price: The Biography of a Ghost-Hunter. London: Athenaeum Press, 1950.

Taplin, Gardner B., *The Life of Elizabeth Barrett Browning.* New Haven: Yale University Press, 1957.

Tietz, Thomas R.:
Margery. New York: Harper & Row, 1973.
"The 'Margery' Affair." *Journal of the American Society for Psychical Research,* July 1985.

Tisdall, E. E. P., *Queen Victoria's Private Life: 1837-1901.* New York: John Day, 1961.

Torrey, Joanna, "Play Mystic for Me." *New York Daily News Magazine,* May 10, 1987.

Toynbee, Arnold, et al., *Man's Concern with Death.* New York: McGraw-Hill, 1968.

Trachtenberg, Jeffrey A., ed., "Mainstream Metaphysics." *Forbes,* June 1, 1987.

Tremaine, Kit, *The Butterfly Rises.* Grass Valley, Calif.: Blue Dolphin, 1987.

Tyrrell, G. N. M., *Apparitions.* London: Gerald Duckworth, 1943.

Unger, Merrill F., *The Haunting of Bishop Pike.* Wheaton, Ill.: Tyndale House, 1971.

Van Dusen, Wilson, *The Presence of Other Worlds: The Psychological/Spiritual Findings of Emanuel Swedenborg.* New York: Swedenborg Foundation, 1974.

Watkins, Susan M., *Conversations with Seth.* Vol. 1. Englewood Cliffs, N.J.: Prentice-Hall, 1980.

Webb, James, ed., *The Mediums and the Conjurors.* New York: Arno Press, 1976.

Weinberg, Steven Lee, with Randall Weischedel, Sue Ann Fazio, and Carol Wright, eds., *Ramtha.* Eastsound, Wash.: Sovereignty, 1986.

Weintraub, Stanley, *Victoria: An Intimate Biography.* New York: Truman Talley Books, 1987.

Westen, Robin, *Channelers: A New Age Directory.* New York: Putnam, 1988.

White, John, and Stanley Krippner, eds., *Future Science: Life Energies and the Physics of Paranormal Phenomena.* Garden City, N.Y.: Doubleday, 1977.

Wickland, Carl A., *30 Years among the Dead.* No. Hollywood, Calif.: Newcastle, 1974.

Williams, Beryl, and Samuel Epstein, *The Great Houdini.* New York: Julian Messner, 1950.

Wilson, Colin, *Afterlife: An Investigation of the Evidence for Life after Death.* Garden City, N.Y.: Doubleday, 1987.

Winkler, Gail Caskey, and Roger W. Moss, *Victorian Interior Decoration: American Interiors 1830-1900.* New York: Henry Holt, 1986.

Wolman, Benjamin B., ed., *Handbook of Parapsychology.* New York: Van Nostrand, 1977.

Worden, Helen, "Exposing Tricks of the Fake Mediums." *Popular Science Monthly,* November 1944.

Yarbo, Chelsea Quinn, *Messages from Michael on the Nature of the Evolution of the Human Soul.* Chicago: Playboy Press, 1979.

Young, Stanley:
"Inside the New-Age Medicine Show." *Santa Monica Monthly,* August 1986.
"Same Channel, Next Week." *Whole Earth Review,* fall 1986.

Zaretsky, Irving I., and Mark P. Leone, eds., *Religious Movements in Contemporary America.* Princeton, N.J.: Princeton University Press, 1974.

Zolar, *Zolar's Book of the Spirits.* New York: Prentice Hall Press, 1987.

Zorab, G., "Were D. D. Home's 'Spirit Hands' Ever Fraudulently Produced?" *Journal of the Society for Psychical Research,* December 1971.

PICTURE CREDITS

INDEX

Maskelyne, John, 101-102
Materializations: of Florence Cook, 53; of Mrs. Samuel Guppy, 53-54; hoaxes, *129;* of Daniel Dunglas Home, 37, 38, 39, *40-41,* 53; of Elizabeth Hope, 55; of Carlos Mirabelli, 117, *118-119,* 120
Mediums, 7; cabinets of, *36,* 37; and channelers, 131-132; defined, 18, 130-131; hoaxes of, 101-102, *123-129;* and multiple-personality disorder, 84-85. *See also specific mediums*
Merlin, *12-13*
Mesmer, Franz Anton: quoted, 26; and spiritualism, 26-27
Michael (spirit guide): and Jessica Lansing, 146-147; quoted, 147
Mirabelli, Carlos, 117-120; materializations of, *118-119,* 120
"Mr. Sludge, the Medium" (Browning), 39, 50
Montgomery, Ruth, 121
Mossman, Tam, 147-148; quoted, 147
Multiple-personality disorder: and channeling, 150-152; characteristics of, 84; and coconsciousness, 152; and Adam Crabtree, 152-153; and mediums, 84, 85
Myers, Frederic W. H. *(Human Personality), 77;* and Alice Kipling Fleming, 93, 94, 96; and William James, 77; and Annie Marshall, 77; and Eusapia Palladino, 60, 61, 62; and Leonora Piper, 86, 87, 93-94; quoted, 71, 86, 92, 93, 94; and Henry Sidgwick, 73; and Society for Psychical Research, 71; as spirit guide, 81, 87, 92, 93-94, 96; and Helen Verrall, 94; and Margaret Verrall, 94, 96

N

Napoleon III, 22, 39
New Age, 7, 18
Nichol, Agnes. *See* Guppy, Mrs. Samuel
Nickell, Molli, *149;* quoted, 149
Noel, Madame, 66, 67
Norman, Ruth, 148-150, *151*

O

Ochorowicz, Julien, 61
Ouija board, *107;* and William Fuld, 107; and Jane Roberts, 134

P

Painting, automatic: of Luiz Antonio Gasparetto, 138-*139;* of Matthew Manning, 138
Palladino, Eusapia, *61, 62, 63;* apports of, 59; background of, 58-59; and Wortley Baggally, 64; and Hereward Carrington, 64; and Marie Curie, 63; and Pierre Curie, 63; death of, 64; and Eric J. Dingwall, 59; and ectoplasm, 61; and Everard Feilding, 64; and Camille Flammarion, 63; hoaxes of, 58, 60, 61, 62-63, 64; and Richard Hodgson, 62; and Oliver Lodge, 60, 61, 62; and Cesare Lombroso, 59; and Enrico Morselli, 63; and Frederic W. H.

60, 61, 62; and Julien Ochorowicz, 61; and poltergeists, 58; and Franco Porro, 63; pseudopods of, 61; psychokinesis of, 64; quoted, 58, 61, 64; and Charles Richet, 60, 61, 62, 64; and Albert von Schrenck-Notzing, 62, 63, 64; and Eleanor Sidgwick, 61-62; and Henry Sidgwick, 61-62; and Society for Psychical Research, 62, 63-64; table turning of, 59-60, *62, 63*
Palm Sunday case, 96-99. *See also* Cross-Correspondences
Pellew, George (GP), 87
Phinuit, Dr., 86-87; quoted, 86
Pike, James, *121;* quoted, 121
Piper, Leonora, *82-83;* automatic writing of, 87, 92; and Chlorine, 83-86; and Elizabeth Webb Gibbens, 83; and Richard Hodgson, 82, 86, 87; and William James, 81-82, 83; and Oliver Lodge, 86-87, *87-88;* and Frederic W. H. Myers, 86, 87, 93-94; and George Pellew, 87; and Dr. Phinuit, 86-87; and J. G. Piddington, 93-94; and William Piper, 82; and Society for Psychical Research, 86; trances of, 83, 86
Planchette, *106,* 107
Pogroff, Ira, 85
Price, Harry, and hoaxes of mediums, *127*
Prince, Walter Franklin: and coconsciousness, 152; and Mina Crandon, 110, 116-117; and Pearl Curran, 85
Proxy sittings, 90, 91
Pseudopods, 61, 104. *See also* Ectoplasm
Psychokinesis, 64
Pursel, Jach, *146;* and Lazaris, 143-145, 153; quoted, 143, 145

R

Ramtha (spirit guide). *See* Knight, J. Z.
Randall, Shawn, *152-153;* quoted, 153
Randi, James, quoted, 131
Raschke, Carl, quoted, 150
Rhine, Joseph Banks, 85, 116
Richet, Charles, *64;* and Eva C., 64-66, 68, 70; and Eusapia Palladino, 60, 61, 62, 64; quoted, 66, 67
Richmond, Cora L. V., *30-31*
Roberts, Jane *(The Afterlife Journal of an American Philosopher, The Seth Material, The World View of Paul Cézanne), 135;* and Paul Cézanne, 137; and William James, 136-137; and Ouija board, 134; quoted, 133, 134, 136, 137; and Seth, 133-136; and Seth Two, 136; trances of, 134, 136; and Frank Withers, 134
Rodegast, Pat, quoted, 148
Rossetti, Dante Gabriel, 39
Rothbaum, Susan, quoted, 142
Rowe, Neville, and dolphins, *16-17,* 148
Rubin, Penny Torres, 142-*143*
Russell, Bertrand, quoted, 153
Ryerson, Kevin, *10-11;* and Apostle John, 10, 146; and Shirley MacLaine, 10, 145-146; quoted, 10, 145
Rymer, John S., and Daniel Dunglas Home, 38, 39, 43, 44, 46

Rymer, Mrs., and Daniel Dunglas Home, 43, 44, *46-47*

S

Schreiber, Karin, 144
Schreiber, Klaus, *144;* quoted, 144
Schrenck-Notzing, Albert von *(Phenomena of Materialization),* 64; and Eva C., 64, 68-70; and Eusapia Palladino, *62,* 63, 64; photograph by, *65, 69*
Schwartz, Stephan, quoted, 133
Seth (spirit guide). *See* Roberts, Jane
Shakers, *24-25*
Sidgwick, Eleanor, *74;* and Francis Maitland Balfour, 74; and Cross-Correspondences, 92; and Gladys Osborne Leonard, 91; and Eusapia Palladino, 61-62; quoted, 74, 91; and Henry Sidgwick, 74; and Society for Psychical Research, 71
Sidgwick, Henry, *72-73,* 74, 78; as spirit guide, 81, 92
Smith, Hélène, 84-*85*
Society for Psychical Research (SPR): and William Barrett, 71; and Eva C., 64, 70; and Arthur Conan Doyle, 100, 101; founding of, 60-61, 71; and Edmund Gurney, 71; and Gladys Osborne Leonard, 90; and Frederic W. H. Myers, 71; and Eusapia Palladino, 62, 63-64; and Leonora Piper, 86; and Eleanor Sidgwick, 71; and Henry Sidgwick, 71, 73
Spiegel, David, quoted, 150
Spirit guides. *See specific spirit guides*
Spirit photographs: and William Crookes, 57; and Mrs. Samuel Guppy, *54;* of John King, *60*
Spirit Speaks (magazine), 149
Spiritualism: and Albert, 22, 23; and Alexander II, 22-23; and Susan B. Anthony, 31; and Elizabeth Barrett Browning, 39; in Burned-over District, 19-22; characteristics of, 26; and William Crookes, 56; and Andrew Jackson Davis, 26, 27-28, 132; and Charles Dickens, 27; and Arthur Conan Doyle, 100, 101, 102; and Thomas Edison, 144; and Ralph Waldo Emerson, 27; and Eugénie, 22; and Leah Fox Fish, 21; history of, 19-22, 26; and Harry Houdini, 102, 103, 104; and Abraham Lincoln, 22-23; and Franz Anton Mesmer, 26-27; and Napoleon III, 22; and James Pike, 121; and Shakers, *24-25;* and Elizabeth Cady Stanton, 31; and Harriet Beecher Stowe, 23; and Emanuel Swedenborg, 26, *27;* and Victoria, 22, 23; and Alfred Russel Wallace, 54; and women's rights, 31
SPR. *See* Society for Psychical Research
SPR Cross-Correspondences. *See* Cross-Correspondences
Steiner, George, quoted, 131
Stinson, Walter: and Mina Crandon, 109-110, 113, 114, 115, 116; fingerprint, alleged, 116; quoted, 116
Strutt, John William, quoted, 54

Swedenborg, Emanuel: and Andrew Jackson Davis, 27; and spiritualism, 26, *27;* and Wilson Van Dusen, 152; visions of, 152
Swetland, David, quoted, 148

T

Table turning, *19;* of Mina Crandon, 108, 109; defined, 22; and Michael Faraday, 33; of Leah Fox Fish, 32; of Kathleen Goligher, 104; hoaxes in, *125;* of Daniel Dunglas Home, 37, 38, 39, *44-45,* 50; of William Marriott, *125;* of Eusapia Palladino, 59-60, *62, 63*
Tennant, Edward Wyndham, *90-91*
Tenuto, William, 150
Thomas Aquinas, Saint, 18
Torres, Penny. *See* Rubin, Penny Torres
Trances: of channelers, 7; of Mina Crandon, 109; of Andrew Jackson Davis, 27; of J. Z. Knight, 141; of Leonora Piper, 83, 86; of Jane Roberts, 134, 136
Transits, 54
Tremaine, Kit, *147*
Truzzi, Marcello, quoted, 131
Turgenev, Ivan, 39

U

Underhill, Leah Fox Fish. *See* Fish, Leah Fox

V

Van Tassel, George, 150
Verrall, Helen, 95; automatic writing of, 92, 97; and Frederic W. H. Myers, 94
Verrall, Margaret, 95; automatic writing of, 92, 97; and Frederic W. H. Myers, 94, 96
Victoria (queen of Great Britain), 22, 23
Visions: of Leonora Piper, 82; of Emanuel Swedenborg, 152
Volckman, William, 55

W

Wallace, Alfred Russel, 53-54
Weiss, Cecilia, *102,* 104
Wells, David, 38
Williams, Charles, 54
Witch of Lime Street. *See* Crandon, Mina
Withers, Frank, quoted, 134
Women's rights, 31
Woodhull, Victoria Claflin, *30-31*
Worth, Patience, 85
Writing, automatic: of Winifred Coombe-Tennant, 92, 97; defined, 87; of Lady Doyle, 103-104, *105;* of Alice Kipling Fleming, 92, 97; of Carlos Mirabelli, 119; of Leonora Piper, 87, 92; of Hélène Smith, *85;* of Helen Verrall, 92, 97; of Margaret Verrall, 92, 97
Writing, slate, *126-127*
Wyndham-Quin, Windham Thomas, 41, 42
Wynne, Charles Bradstreet, 41

Y

Yater, Verna, *147*

Time-Life Books Inc.
is a wholly owned subsidiary of
TIME INCORPORATED

FOUNDER: Henry R. Luce 1898-1967

Editor-in-Chief: Jason McManus
Chairman and Chief Executive Officer: J. Richard Munro
President and Chief Operating Officer: N. J. Nicholas, Jr.
Editorial Director: Ray Cave
Executive Vice President, Books: Kelso F. Sutton
Vice President, Books: Paul V. McLaughlin

TIME-LIFE BOOKS INC.

EDITOR: George Constable
Executive Editor: Ellen Phillips
Director of Design: Louis Klein
Director of Editorial Resources: Phyllis K. Wise
Editorial Board: Russell B. Adams, Jr., Dale M. Brown,
Roberta Conlan, Thomas H. Flaherty, Lee Hassig, Donia
Ann Steele, Rosalind Stubenberg
Director of Photography and Research:
John Conrad Weiser
Assistant Director of Editorial Resources:
Elise Ritter Gibson

PRESIDENT: Christopher T. Linen
Chief Operating Officer: John M. Fahey, Jr.
Senior Vice Presidents: Robert M. DeSena, James L. Mercer,
Paul R. Stewart
Vice Presidents: Stephen L. Bair, Ralph J. Cuomo, Neal
Goff, Stephen L. Goldstein, Juanita T. James, Hallett
Johnson III, Carol Kaplan, Susan J. Maruyama, Robert H.
Smith, Joseph J. Ward
Director of Production Services: Robert J. Passantino
Supervisor of Quality Control: James King

Editorial Operations
Copy Chief: Diane Ullius
Production: Celia Beattie
Library: Louise D. Forstall

Library of Congress Cataloging in Publication Data
Spirit summonings / the editors of Time-Life Books.
    p.   cm. (Mysteries of the unknown)
    Bibliography: p.
    Includes index.
    ISBN 0-8094-6344-X.   ISBN 0-8094-6345-8 (lib. bdg.)
    1. Spiritualism—History. 2. Channeling (Spiritualism).
I. Time-Life Books.   II. Series.
BF1241.S7 1989
133.9—dc19   88-29485 CIP

MYSTERIES OF THE UNKNOWN

SERIES DIRECTOR: Russell B. Adams, Jr.
Series Administrator: Myrna Traylor-Herndon
Designer: Susan K. White

Editorial Staff for *Spirit Summonings*
Associate Editors: Scarlet Cheng (pictures);
Laura Foreman (text)
Assistant Designers: Susan Gibas, Lorraine D. Rivard
Copy Coordinators: Mary Beth Oelkers-Keegan,
Jarelle S. Stein
Picture Coordinator: Richard A. Karno
Researchers: Christian D. Kinney, Sharon Obermiller,
Elizabeth Ward
Editorial Assistant: Donna Fountain

Special Contributors: Christine Hinze (London, picture
research); Mary Ford Dreesen (lead research); Barbara
Cohn, David Mitchell, Susan Moses, Ruth Moss, Jacqueline
L. Shaffer (research); Sarah Brash, George Daniels, Dónal
Kevin Gordon, Lydia Preston Hicks, Linda Lee, William M.
Moore, Dirk Olin, Shirley Sealy, Daniel Stashower (text);
John Drummond (design); Jane B. Clark, Karen Siatras
(copyediting); Hazel Blumberg-McKee (index)

Correspondents: Elisabeth Kraemer-Singh (Bonn), Vanessa
Kramer (London), Maria Vincenza Aloisi (Paris), Ann
Natanson (Rome)
Valuable assistance was also provided by Mirka Gondicas
(Athens); Angelika Lemmer (Bonn); Judy Aspinall
(London); Elizabeth Brown, Christina Lieberman (New
York); Ann Wise (Rome).

The Consultant:
Marcello Truzzi, the general consultant for the series, is a
professor of sociology at Eastern Michigan University. He
is also director of the Center for Scientific Anomalies
Research (CSAR) and editor of its journal, the *Zetetic
Scholar.* Dr. Truzzi, who considers himself a ''constructive
skeptic'' with regard to claims of the paranormal, works
through the CSAR to produce dialogues between critics
and proponents of unusual scientific claims.

Other Publications:

AMERICAN COUNTRY
VOYAGE THROUGH THE UNIVERSE
THE THIRD REICH
THE TIME-LIFE GARDENER'S GUIDE
TIME FRAME
FIX IT YOURSELF
FITNESS, HEALTH & NUTRITION
SUCCESSFUL PARENTING
HEALTHY HOME COOKING
UNDERSTANDING COMPUTERS
LIBRARY OF NATIONS
THE ENCHANTED WORLD
THE KODAK LIBRARY OF CREATIVE PHOTOGRAPHY
GREAT MEALS IN MINUTES
THE CIVIL WAR
PLANET EARTH
COLLECTOR'S LIBRARY OF THE CIVIL WAR
THE EPIC OF FLIGHT
THE GOOD COOK
WORLD WAR II
HOME REPAIR AND IMPROVEMENT
THE OLD WEST

*For information on and a full description of any of the
Time-Life Books series listed above, please call 1-800-
621-7026 or write:*
    Reader Information
    Time-Life Customer Service
    P.O. Box C-32068
    Richmond, Virginia 23261-2068

This volume is one of a series that examines the history
and nature of seemingly paranormal phenomena. Other
books in the series include:

Mystic Places	*Visions and Prophecies*
Psychic Powers	*Mysterious Creatures*
The UFO Phenomenon	*Mind Over Matter*
Psychic Voyages	*Cosmic Connections*
Phantom Encounters	